Sustainability adapted to SMEs

Sustainability adapted to SMEs

Elisa Gomez Gonzalez

SOCIETY Publishing

www.societypublishing.com

Sustainability adapted to SMEs

Elisa Gomez Gonzalez

Society Publishing
224 Shoreacres Road
Burlington, ON L7L 2H2
Canada
www.societypublishing.com
Email: orders@arclereducation.com

ISBN: 978-1-77469-009-3 (Hardcover)

ABOUT THE AUTHOR

Born in the Canary Islands, **Elisa Gomez** has always been aware of the immense potential and limitations that resources provide to communities. Following her passion towards the environment and sustainable development mechanism, she completed the Madrid Environmental Sciences degree and later completed a Master's degree in International Sustainable Development and Corporate Sustainability.

She has worked for a wide range of industries and sectors as a sustainability consultant and analyst implementing international standards, achieving certifications, and ensuring the management processes were effective. The sectors englobe oil and gas, construction, telecommunications, and software design.

Moved by a great passion towards her work, she decided to quit the corporate environment and set up her own company, Better Together (www.bettertogether-sustainability.com) an online sustainability company that specializes in simple, effective, and understandable sustainability practices for all types of companies. They focus especially on Startups and SMEs, as these are growing; ensuring that they are sustainable right from the start without the burden of complicated, time-consuming, and expensive measures.

TABLE OF CONTENTS

LIST OF FIGURES

LIST OF TABLES

LIST OF ABBREVIATIONS

ACFCI	Association of French Chambers of Commerce and Industry
ACID	Association of Canadian Industrial Designers
ADB	Asian Development Bank
ADIQ	Association of Quebec Industrial Designers
ADM	Aéroports de Montréal
BCA	Building and Construction Authority
BP	British Petroleum
CCORP	Cirtronics Community Out-Reach Program
CSR	Corporate Social Responsibility
EAP	East Asia and the Pacific
EBRD	European Bank for Reconstruction and Development
EC	European Commission
ECA	Europe and Central Asia
ECAP	Environmental Compliance Assistance Program
EDTP	Enterprise Development and Training Program
EIA	Environmental Impact Assessment
EIB	European Investment Bank
EPD	Environment Product Declaration
ERP	Enterprise Resource Planning
ESOP	Employee Stock Ownership Plan
EU	European Union
EV	Electric Vehicles
FTEs	Full-Time Employees
GBRs	Green Building Ratings
GDP	Gross Domestic Product
GRI	Global Reporting Initiative
GVA	Gross Value-Added
GVCs	Global Value Chains

HIC	High Impact Companies
HIPs	High Impact Programs
ICT	Information and Communication Technology
IFC	International Finance Corporation
IFIs	International Financial Institutions
KfW	Kreditanstalt Für Wiederaufbau
MGI	McKinsey Global Institute
MSME	Micro, Small, and Medium-Sized Enterprises
NBA	National Bank of Arizona
NHBSR	New Hampshire Businesses for Social Responsibility
NIEA	Northern Ireland Environment Agency
NRM	Natural Resources Management
ODIMM	Organization for Small and Medium Enterprises Sector Development
PBE+	Performance Bretagne Environment Plus
PCW	Post-Consumer Waste
PMO	Project Management Office
SDBS	Structural and Demographic Business Statistics
SDGs	Sustainable Development Goals
SEARS	Scotland's Environmental and Rural Services
SEEDS	Startup Enterprise Development Scheme
SEPA	Scottish Environment Protection Agency
SMBA	Small and Medium Business Administration
SME DNC	SME Development National Center of Armenia
SMEs	Small and Medium-Sized Enterprises
SMPs	Small and Medium-Sized Practices
SSC	SPRING SEEDS Capital
STEM	Science, Technology, Engineering, and Mathematics
TCP	Technology Commercialization Platform
TEC	Trade by Enterprise Characteristics
TFP	Total Factor Productivity
UNFC	United Nations Framework Classification
UNRMS	United Nations Resource Management System
VIBES	Vision in Business for the Environment of Scotland
WED	Women Entrepreneurship Development

SYNOPSIS

This book will run you through the entire process of setting up a sustainability management system, that everybody feels accountable and responsible for, as well as highlighting how it can build resilient mechanisms towards enforcing small and medium enterprise performance.

The first chapters will set up the scene describing how sustainability is currently being implemented, what are the trends and challenges. These initial chapters are very important as they contemplate the main assumptions and characteristics of current practices, which will enable the reader to better understand the measures presented afterwards.

The last chapters focus mainly on how sustainability practices can be implemented effectively into small and medium enterprises providing different example of case studies.

EXECUTIVE SUMMARY

Sustainable business examples are progressively showing up on the radar of organizations around the globe because of current trends and communication efforts. An effective company or company is very much reliant on its investor's needs and expectation. Investors are interested in sustainability, impact, and added value.

A reasonable company meets the desires of diverse partners. A genuine feasible company is capable of bringing together monetary, social, and sustainable contemplations. Such businesses are effectively ready to meet the desires of both inward and outer partners, for example, investors, clients, government, employees, and groups to guarantee long-term success for all.

In any case, most businesses neglect to execute feasible objectives. Regularly, businesses neglect to execute sustainable business practices because of insufficient reconciliation with business methodology, absence of help from authority, constrained comprehension, and inclusion of workers at all levels, and additionally nonappearance of frameworks and procedures that enable a systematize support.

Sustainable can enable businesses to prevail with regards to current economic business trends. Albeit numerous businesses dedicate themselves to sustainability and frame a strategy, its implementation, and coordination depend upon effectively embracing the following:

- Empowering and driving economical business practices at all levels of the company.
- Creating effective frameworks and procedures.

PREFACE

Sustainability management systems have proven not only to benefit the company that applies them but also to the world as a whole. Sustainability is slowly but steadily being incorporated into public policies, governments, private sector companies, and even in freelancers. The world has begun to believe that we can actually operate and perform in a way that is respectful with the environment, society, and the economy enabling us to develop in a sustainable manner.

This is not merely a trend or the hot topic for the coming years, but it is a crucial aspect of we want to continue prospering a thriving. A great part of sustainable management practices relies on people. People that work with a purpose; feel engaged, accountable, and responsible for their actions. People that want to make a difference for good. These people together form teams that work with purpose, feel engaged, connected, accountable, and responsible for their actions. This group of people forms companies, businesses, organizations, and overall a community of people that have in mind to be sustainable and to provide the best for future generations.

The purpose is the main driver for millennials in choosing a workplace and a career, this shift from other generational trends implies that companies and the workplace industry globally need to face a transformation. Millennials which will shortly constitute the biggest generation in the workplace have a broader understanding of sustainability. Not only a broader understanding, but they go one step further and actually reject working for companies that do not create value and have a positive impact where they operate. Their understanding of sustainable development together with the immense technological capacity nowadays set the perfect scene for all types of companies and organizations to start implementing sustainability management systems.

With sustainability management systems, the renewable technology development goes hand-in-hand. Thus, along with an overview of what is happening around the world, this book covers the trends, future expectations, and forecasts.

Typically, sustainability management systems or sometimes referred to as corporate social responsibility (CSR) is very much dependent upon international standards, regulation, legislation, and certifications which are very much industry-related or country-related. This means that they are heavily influenced by the culture, the economic positioning in the market and the countries legal and political trends.

Moreover, globalization has enabled access to products and services where they were not available before. All of these changes and limitations have created a difficult scenario for companies, where implementing sustainability measures imply allocating a great part of the budget and result in very time consuming for employees.

The main aim of this book is to provide simple, effective, understandable, and applicable mechanisms for all readers. To enable and empower them to implement management systems that are adapted to the reality and expectations of their business.

In this book, you will find all of those mechanisms and resources needed to ensure that sustainability is well embedded into a company and specially SMEs.

This book is for all those that want to effectively implement sustainable management and culture into their current business practices. The book runs simply through all of the steps to design and create a strategy according to the needs and expectations of all the stakeholders, ensuring everyone involved feels accountable and responsible for their piece of the pie.

It is also intended for all those studying or professionals that work as sustainability consultants or analysts to broaden their perceptions of sustainability implementation in a millennial digital world.

INTRODUCTION

Sustainability emerged from the need to protect and ensure our environment, our society, and our economic system assumes responsibility and works to cause as little harm as possible. Sustainability as a concept stepped onto the world stage in 1992 at the World's first Earth Summit in Rio. Since then, awareness, and the application of sustainable practices have been on the rise.

This book will include the background information needed to understand sustainability management systems and their integration into businesses fully. The reader will be provided with the benefits, risks, and disadvantages of the different methods to assure comprehension and analytical thinking is stimulated.

Renewable technology development goes hand-in-hand with sustainability management systems. Thus, this book covers the trends, future expectations, and forecasts, as well as a thorough overview of what is happening around the world.

A simple methodology will be presented to effectively approach the integration of sustainability in all types of businesses. Case studies, practical examples, and templates will be provided in each phase of the methodology, enabling the reader to assess and implement sustainability as they read along. Relevant supporting information will be provided at the end of each chapter on specific topics to take into consideration.

Promoting and empowering people into incorporating sustainability are my personal mission. I strongly believe in the positive impact it provides and in the added value that it enables for all. Sustainability does not have to be complicated, expensive, or unrelated to the business activity. The numerous benefits its incorporation provides to all types of companies are always value the journey.

In the end, the main goal of sustainability, in my humble opinion, is to do and use business as a force for good.

Chapter 1

Sustainability Introduction

Everything starts with posing the rights questions. For sustainability we need to ask ourselves:

Who does what, when, and why? How does the company get the assets expected to endure and flourish? My emphasis here is on overseeing what I call the "physical measurements" of sustainable sustainability: the utilization of energy; the sources of energy, water, and materials; the decrease of waste and the environment impact of a company's creation; and the effect of the utilization of whatever the company produces. The key inquiry to be tended: How does a company figure out how to lessen its negative effect on nature?

Sustainability effectiveness lies within the fate of the board. Sustainability must be coordinated into the core of what companies do. In the 20th century, companies focused on including universal activities, supply chains, data innovation, refined advertising, implementing procedures, ensuring money flow, bookkeeping, and new types of gathering forms.

Today, companies all through the globe are endeavoring to decrease their carbon footprint, limit atmosphere pollution, and sustainable hazard, upgrade strength, and incorporate sustainability into their tasks. The issue is they do not have the foggiest idea how to do it.

Organizations, governments, and charities are remembering they have to take these activities, yet their ability lies in their very own center capacities, not in creating sustainability designs and evaluating operational hazard inside this specific circumstance. To have important change on sustainability, companies, not-for-profits, and governments must carry it into the customary texture of authoritative set-up.

Over the long haul, we ought not to require a "sustainability department;" each department should turn into a sustainability operating unit. Dealing with the physical components of sustainability should now be added to standard working methodology so all chiefs become sustainability supervisors. Huge thoughts, eager objectives, and delightful approaches do not convert into on-the-ground change until companies change.

The master plan issue we are trying to deliver at last comes down to the test of worldwide sustainability: how might we make a high throughput economy without decimating the planet? We are, actually, looking at sparing the planet for our kids.

The issues at the core of the sustainability issue are perplexing, worldwide, and fundamental, and cannot be effectively unraveled. These difficulties require activity by partners at all levels. Be that as it may, making an interpretation of these thoughts energetically requires far more prominent hierarchical limit than we right now have. We may realize how to construct a LEED-affirmed, energy productive structure, yet do we realize how to look after it? Frequently, we don't.

This hierarchical test is not generally recognized; it is not the flashiest issue that environment promoters are pointing out. In any case, companies are starting to comprehend that they cannot just make a sustainability department and anticipate that the issue should be unraveled. A significant number of our best heads realize they have to deal with the physical components of sustainability. There is ever more extensive acknowledgment of why sustainability is required, yet there is not yet a profound comprehension of how to do it. What we have to do is figure out how to fabricate that limit. As a scholastic, you will not be astounded to peruse that I accept the information we need must originate from scholastically thorough however applied research.

As an understudy of the board, I realize that every company and the authoritative condition is novel, yet there are examples and practices that can be distinguished and comprehended.

Under what conditions improve at lessening their utilization of energy and changing their wellspring of energy from high carbon to low? When do interests in shut frameworks building get made and when are they evaded? What sort of chiefs pays attention to environment components and what type believes it is a joke? In companies intensely subject to an all-inclusive production network, what techniques have succeeded and bombed when attempting to impact the conduct of providers?

As we gain more from the "bleeding edges" of sustainability the board, I additionally will be keen on the preparation and instruction needs that we distinguish. This will be added to our educational program in undergrad and graduate investigations in sustainability. Current courses should be adjusted and new courses should be created. I additionally anticipate that customary fields, for example, building, business, law, open organization, and general well-being, should add sustainability issues to their courses also.

There has been a propensity for some sustainable backers to concentrate on representative political fights, to some degree as a method for picking up consideration and instructing people in general. The appreciation for imagery goes back to the beginning of the advanced environment development.

The present unquestionably increasingly advanced variant of vehicle covering signals incorporate endeavors to strip benefits assets from petroleum derivative organizations and suing energy organizations for the environmental harm they have caused. It worked with the tobacco organizations; why not the oil organizations?

It may work in some sense, and it surely assumes a job in state-funded training. Be that as it may, the genuine work is persuading individuals to quit smoking and to utilize inexhaustible wellsprings of energy. Strolling in the city of New York or urban communities anyplace on the planet, I see a lot of individuals smoking. The tobacco organizations appear to do OK.

Driving down those equivalent lanes is a lot of vehicles controlled by petroleum derivatives. We are altogether dependent on petroleum derivatives, and non-renewable energy source-based energy is integral to our day-by-day lives. I concur that putting resources into petroleum product organizations is an impractical notion, yet regardless I fill my tank with gas. Those organizations get our cash one way or the other.

The genuine work is getting an electric vehicle framework fabricated, propelling battery, and sustainable power source innovation, and actualizing these new advancements. I am keen on figuring out how to energize and quicken genuine change. Representative signals have a task to carry out; however, we ought not to mistake emblematic motions for operational reality.

Companies and social orders can be exceptionally delayed to change, however, after some time they do advance. In the previous century, a great part of the change has been in light of the improvement of new advancements. We have to adapt considerably more about our planet's environments and significantly more about the effect of our innovation on our planet. I accept that with insight, care, and new innovation, we can achieve a type of financial advancement that accomplishes both development and environment quality. In any case, it will be troublesome work, and it will not be accomplished rapidly.

Chapter 2

Sustainable Development

CONTENTS

In 2019, we hoped to see preceded with political insecurity, progressively articulated atmosphere impacts and quickening paces of biodiversity misfortune. While the scale and multifaceted nature of the sustainability challenges we face is overwhelming, there is likewise an explanation behind good faith. We are seeing remarkable administration and advancement driven by urban areas, districts, and organizations, rising urban activism and promotion by Generation Z, and quickly developing mindfulness about issues, for example, plastic contamination. We anticipate that this developing force should drive truly necessary advancement on basic social and sustainable issues in 2019.

Just because, we are additionally sharing further investigation of five areas: nourishment and agribusiness, innovation, pharmaceuticals, and social insurance, energy, and utilities and budgetary administrations. In our part inclines, we investigate the key issues confronting these quickly evolving enterprises and talk about rising arrangements.

Current endeavors stay deficient to change our course towards risky atmosphere change. A quickly warming atmosphere and inability to enough diminish ozone-depleting substance discharges the pressing requirement for a more prominent spotlight on flexibility measures. Quick, enormous scale interest in successful arrangements is expected to keep an unsustainable weather change from coming to conceivably cataclysmic levels.

2.1. RISING GLOBAL EMISSIONS

Falling costs for both sustainable power source and flammable gas have brought about unobtrusive emanations decreases among top producers, for example, Europe and the United States.

In any case, none of the four biggest worldwide polluters (China, the United States, the European Union (EU), and India) are at present on track to do their part in worldwide endeavors to arrive at the Paris Agreement objectives.

Specialists report that worldwide ozone-depleting substance emanations rose by an expected 2.7% in 2018, arriving at a record-breaking high. This speaks to the second year of remarkable increments after a concise time of moderately stable emanations due to eased back monetary development.

Universal media center keeps on staying around outflows from power age, where the best progress is being made. Be that as it may, farming and transportation are additionally significant supporters, and just restricted consideration is being given to these areas and other littler producers.

The most recent IPCC report featured the seriousness of effects we are now encountering at 1°C warming and expressed that 2°C of warming is currently considered profoundly hazardous.

Nations have consented to provide details regarding their emanations like clockwork beginning in 2024, as per the new Paris Agreement rulebook concurred at COP24 in December 2018 in Poland.

China proceeds to intensely put resources into sustainable power source, electric vehicles (EV), and energy capacity, yet its absolute outflows are anticipated to keep moving until 2030. India's outflows are foreseen to top in 2033. Air contamination identified with utilization of non-renewable energy sources stays a significant worldwide issue. In excess of 3 billion individuals are breathing savage smoke in their homes from utilizing dirtying stoves and fills. The EU has attempted to keep up outflows decrease energy, in enormous part because of Germany neglecting to change away from coal. In the meantime, the US carbon dioxide outflows rose by 3.4% in 2018, the greatest increment in 8 a long time.

"To have a chance of limiting warming to 1.5°C, greenhouse gas emissions must be cut in half by 2030 and be net zero by 2050." Diana Liverman, University of Arizona, lead author for the IPCC 1.5°C report (Figure 2.1).

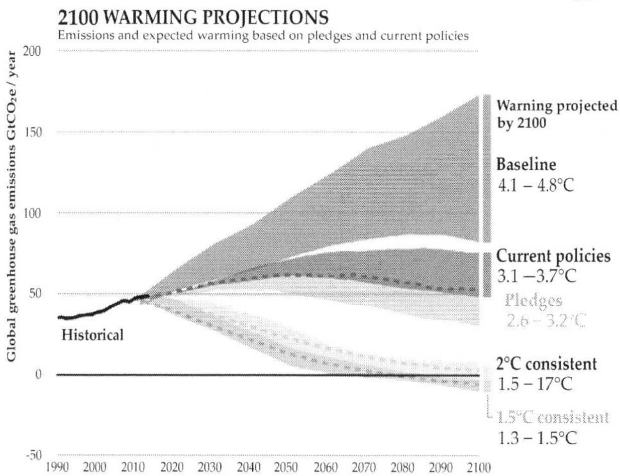

Figure 2.1. 2100 warming projections.

Source: Climate Action Tracker.

2.1.1. Adaptation Investment Is Urgent

The effects of 1°C warming are unmistakably more serious than anticipated. Extraordinary climate is causing billions in harm yearly, with flooding, storms, and dry season in Asia coupled with seething flames in the United States, Canada, Greece, and Sweden. While a few atmospheres relief and adjustment ventures are complimentary, as a rule, they are going after restricted government reserves.

Worldwide effects to urban situations are now evaluated at $314 billion every year and are anticipated to increment to more than $415 billion yearly by 2030.

Serious out-of-control fires in California caused billions of dollars in direct harm and protection payouts in 2018.

Warmth waves hit Europe in 2018, affecting financial execution and diminishing control age from wind turbines, featuring the dire requirement for additional interest in atmosphere flexible energy foundation and horticulture.

As per new gauges by FAO, dry seasons in Asia caused over $48 billion in lost harvests and domesticated animals somewhere in the range of 2005 and 2015.

A perilously warmed atmosphere is prompting recharged discourse among specialists about the upsides and downsides of geoengineering mediations. Geoengineering, for the most part, falls under two classifications: the expulsion and capacity of carbon from the climate and sunlight-based radiation the board, which is the impression of the sun's beams once again into space or on the other hand obstructing a little segment of daylight before it arrives at Earth. While there are numerous advocates of geoengineering arrangements, the science is still generally dependent on hypothetical models and has been reprimanded for being possibly risky and for exhibiting policymakers with the guarantee of a silver shot that may ease back endeavors to decrease emanations.

The New Carbon Economy Consortium is an activity of scholastic organizations, national research facilities, and NGOs hoping to utilize rising advancements to change the economy by emphatically using carbon. The United States and Norway are at the front line of the drive for carbon catch what is more, stockpiling (CCS), yet so far, the European Commission (EC) has been tepid about this innovation.

Y Combinator, the tech hatchery celebrated for kick-beginning organizations like Airbnb and Dropbox, is currently emptying a huge number of dollars into financing geoengineering arrangements.

Geoscientists, environmentalists, and urban organizers are attempting to improve soil to retain higher measures of carbon dioxide in both farming and urban situations. Other incipient innovations getting subsidizing incorporate hereditarily designed phytoplankton, direct air catch, marine cloud lighting up, and electrogeochemistry.

Regardless of expanding enthusiasm for geoengineering arrangements, a developing number of specialists are cautioning about potential risks related to the innovation, counting obscure and conceivably disastrous reactions, significant expenses, and the fracture of worldwide endeavors on ozone harming substance decrease.

"Geoengineering is the brave-new-world of climate mitigation. While the scientific jury is still out on risk and effectiveness, what's already becoming clear from our initial research is that any silver-bullet climate solution brings with it an additional "moral hazard" that it may desensitize the general public to climate risk and sap their motivation to support decisive mitigation." Victoria Campbell-Árvai, a Research Scientist at the University of Michigan's School for Environment and Sustainability (Figure 2.2).

GEOENGINEERING MEASURES UNDER DISCUSSION

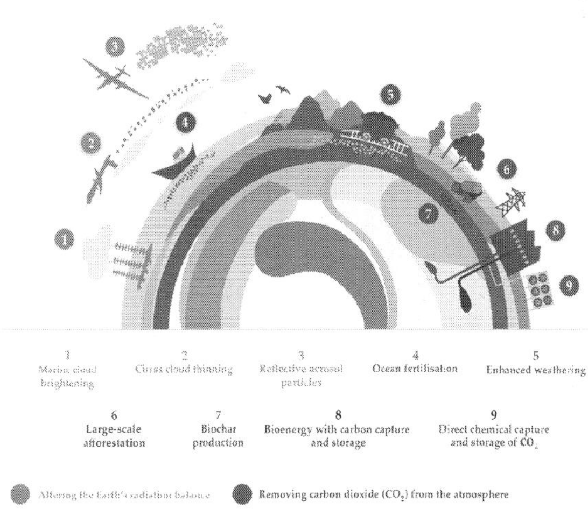

Figure 2.2. Geoengineering measures under discussion.

Source: IASS.

2.1.2. What to Expect in 2019

We hope to see billions of dollars of extra harm and a lot more lives lost because of extraordinary climate occasions. Versatility, adjustment, and obligation with respect to framework that is badly arranged for progressively outrageous climate will be front what is more, place for the two governments and business. Organizations will quicken activity to build atmosphere readiness in both direct tasks and their inventory chains. Geoengineering advancements could see more prominent speculation from the private area furthermore, restored exchange at the strategy level.

1. ***Organize Interest in Atmosphere Strength and Adjustment:*** Organizations need to build the versatility of their stockpile chains and direct tasks. This will require interest in atmosphere hazard evaluations and situation arranging.
2. ***Shape Strategy and Campaign Governments for More Atmosphere Activity:*** Organizations need to have a progressively dynamic influence in national and worldwide endeavors to execute the Paris Agreement and apply more noteworthy weight on governments to restrict a worldwide temperature alteration. This implies supporting for activities like a cost on carbon, forceful arrangement of renewables and EV, and atmosphere brilliant farming arrangements.
3. ***Increment Collaboration Efforts to Scale Low Carbon Economy Solutions:*** Quickly decreasing ozone harming substance outflows and expanding the versatility of framework may be accomplished through multi-area joint effort. Organizations need to work with corporate cohorts, governments, NGOs, and others to use the assorted aptitudes required scaling low carbon economy arrangements in all enterprises.

2.2. CITIZEN POWER

Citizens demand a more sustainable, equitable world from companies and institutions. Engaged citizens, joined by an increasing number of Gen Z teens, are taking to social media and the streets to demand action from governments and businesses on pressing social and environmental challenges.

Savvy companies are tapping into shifting consumer values and empowering people to act on important issues like climate change.

2.2.1. Power to the People

Around the world, a small but growing number of citizens are rising up to challenge institutions, companies, and governments to deliver a more equitable and sustainable society. They are increasingly using social media and other digital technologies to spread the message, elevate important issues, and mobilize people.

Civil disobedience movement Extinction Rebellion—a UK-born action group that calls for mass economic disruption using non-violent direct action and civil disobedience to prevent catastrophic climate change—has now spread to more than 35 countries around the world.

Americans took to the streets in 2018. Millions protested against gun violence, gender inequity and the separation of children from their migrant and asylum-seeking parents.

One in five Americans have protested in the streets or participated in political rallies over the last 2 years. Of those, 19% said they had never before joined a protest march or a political gathering.

In one of the biggest movements for women's rights in India, 5 million women lined up across the length of the southern state of Kerala to demand an end to outdated social norms that prevent women of childbearing age from entering places of worship.

In France, thousands of working-class protestors known as the gilets Jaunes (yellow vests) have taken to the streets to protest the newly-introduced green taxon diesel—highlighting the need for a more just energy transition—and call for an increase in the minimum wage.

Employees at multinational firms are increasingly making their voices heard, with Amazon employees protesting the sale of facial recognition software to law enforcement and unsafe work practices.

Meanwhile, over 1000 Google employees signed letters protesting the company's involvement with AI military development for the Pentagon, as well as its decision to aid China's online censorship. "Empowering Action at Home": A study of 30,000 people in 35 countries found that 62% of customers want companies to take a stand on issues such as sustainability, transparency, and fair employment practices."

"A majority of global consumers are concerned about climate change, but only a handful of these feel empowered to take action in their own lives.

Global companies, like IKEA, have an important role to play in inspiring and supporting more people to take action." Pia Heidenmark Cook, Chief Sustainability Officer, IKEA Group.

2.2.2. Gen Z Coming of Age

Conceived when the new century rolled over, Gen Z is as of now entering the workforce and will overwhelm recent college grads to turn into the biggest age of purchasers by 2020. While many are still too youthful to even consider voting, Gen Z is now significant influencers, locks in organizations and governments on a scope of social and environmental issues.

Youth turned marching through Main Street for COP24, the UN Climate Change Conference in Poland, and sent a record-breaking message calling for worldwide pioneers to meet the 1.5°C objective as 125,000 postcards spread out on Aletsch ice sheet in Switzerland.

In Australia, a large number of youngsters from in excess of 20 urban communities left their homerooms to fight the Australian government's inaction on environmental change as a major aspect of the Strike 4 Climate Action, roused by 15-year-old Swedish understudy Greta Thunberg.

The understudy drove March for Our Lives saw in excess of a million Americans take to the avenues supporting for more grounded weapon guidelines.

As acts of mass violence proceed over the US, American secondary school understudies are putting pressure on financial specialists, for example, Vanguard, and BlackRock to drop firearm producers from their speculation portfolios.

An ongoing report found that 68% of youngsters matured 14–18 in the UK have taken an interest in volunteering or different types of social activity.

A multi-year-old young lady reached Warriors basketballer Steph Curry on Twitter to inquire why his Under Armor shoes were accessible for young men, and Curry and Under Protective layer helped the issue in under 24 hours.

2.2.3. Empowering Action at Home

Individuals progressively need organizations to make significant move on environment and social issues. Driving organizations are discovering approaches to empower individuals to make simpler, sustainable, practical changes to their lives.

An investigation of 30,000 individuals in 35 nations found that 62% of clients need organizations to stand firm on issues, for example, sustainability, straightforwardness, and reasonable work rehearses.

Research by IKEA and GlobeScan found that a lion's share of shoppers needs to lessen their carbon outflows, however many are reluctant to pick less advantageous or, on the other hand, progressively costly choices.

Organizations including Patagonia and IKEA are implanting manageable advancement into their plans of action with the objective of engaging residents to lead more sustainable lives.

Unilever backup Ben and Jerry's is using blockchain to engage clients to carbon counterbalance each individual scoop of frozen yogurt.

Worldwide office-sharing organization WeWork has gone sans meat at its 502 areas—with meat never again served at staff occasions and WeWork workers not ready to cost meat dinners—in an offer to diminish carbon discharges.

2.2.4. What to Expect in 2019

Resident drove activism will keep the weight on governments and organizations to address squeezing social and environment issues. Desires for organizations to address issues, for example, environmental change, single-use plastics, and gender equality value will likewise keep on developing. Clients, particularly youth, will progressively move their loyalties to organizations they see to convey social and sustainable incentive to society.

1. ***Convey an Incentive to Society:*** In 2019, organizations need to reassess the sustainable and social effect of their center products and administrations and move their plans of action towards producing long haul an incentive for society on the off chance that they are to stay aware of moving customer desires.
2. ***Increment Straightforwardness:*** So as to construct trust and reliability in 2019, organizations should grasp progressively extreme types of straightforwardness. Blockchain and web-based social networking will be fundamental apparatuses.
3. ***Engage Purchasers:*** Driving organizations ought to put resources into building brand control by empowering customers to make manageable way of life changes that are both helpful and cost-aggressive.

2.3. SECURITY THREATS

Exchange wars, cybersecurity breaks, and environmental change undermine worldwide security and financial soundness.

The worldwide network is confronting difficulties on universal exchange, the effects of environmental change and the developing seriousness of digital fighting, which are all affecting advancement on reasonable improvement.

Governments and worldwide organizations are progressively powerless against cybersecurity breaks, debilitating their companies just as resident trust. Exchange pressures undermine a debilitating worldwide economy, while environmental change and different variables heighten clashes in the Middle East, Central America, and Africa and uproot millions.

2.3.1. The Cyber Battleground

From state-supported cyber-attacks, to psychological militant cells, and the developing advancement of solitary programers, the dangers of cyberwarfare are developing. Expanded digitization and mechanization, particularly IoT and distributed computing, make greater open door for cyberattacks. Hacking development keeps on outpacing the security incorporated with existing innovation. Government guidelines fall insufficiently behind.

The World Economic Forum's Global Risks Report 2018 recognized cybersecurity breaks as probably the most serious hazard to mankind. In its Top 10 dangers digital assaults are positioned third as far as Likelihood.

New deep fake innovation permits the production of carefully controlled recordings that can approach flawlessly copy anybody, from heads of state to military commanders.

Malevolent chatbots are getting progressively far reaching. Assaults presently start with fundamental content-based bots, however, could begin to utilize human discourse bots to capture exploited people over the telephone.

Year 2018 saw various prominent digital assaults hit enormous organizations including Facebook, Google+, British Airways, Marriott, and T Mobile.

WhatsApp, a mainstream auxiliary of Facebook, was utilized to spread disinformation by Russian programmers in the number one spot up to the 2018 Brazilian political race and may have assumed a job in the appointment of Jair Bolsonaro.

Confronting analysis over the abuse of its foundation during national decisions in Brazil, the US, France, and the UK, Facebook has declared designs to increment advertisement straightforwardness and safeguard against remote obstruction in front of the 2019 Lok Sabha surveys in India.

"Countries need to work together to tackle challenges that extend beyond their own borders. Countries should cooperate to reduce trade costs further and resolve disagreements without raising distortionary barriers.

Cooperative efforts are also essential for enhancing cybersecurity, tackling corruption, and mitigating and coping with climate change." International Monetary Fund, World Economic Outlook 2018 (Figure 2.3).

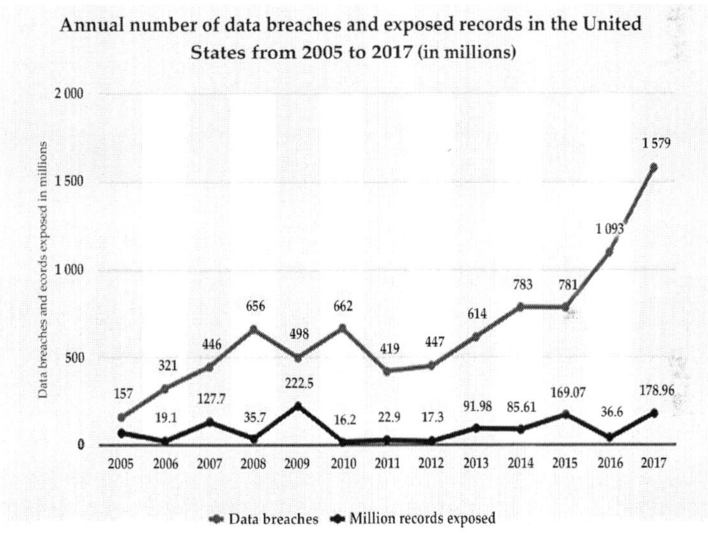

Figure 2.3. Data breaches.

Source: Identity Theft Resource Center.

2.3.2. Exchange Tensions Threaten Global Economy

The Trump administration is endeavoring to decrease imports from nations with which the US has an exchange shortage, upsetting exchange arrangements with the EU, Canada, and Mexico, South Korea, Japan, and, above all, China. Progressing pressure between the world's two biggest economies over exchange is expanding the probability of a worldwide financial downturn by 2020.

The breakdown of two-sided exchange talks and the acceleration of duties and other protectionist obstructions by the US and China is starting to hurt the two economies.

Exchange pressures could decrease universal development by around 0.5% by 2020, the IMF reports.

The CFO of Chinese telecoms organization Huawei was captured in Canada over potential infringement of US endorses on Iran, shocking China, and confusing exchange arrangements between the world's two biggest economies. As of composing, the US has made a deal to avoid following up on its ongoing danger to expand taxes on $200 billion value of Chinese imports from 10% to 25%.

2.3.3. Environmental Change Tops Global Security Threats

Environmental change is progressively perceived as the main worldwide security risk. Atmosphere-related security dangers incorporate effects to fundamental assets, for example, rural yields and drinking water, which can thusly intensify existing clashes, as has happened in Syria and Yemen. Further effects incorporate direct harm to foundation and networks from out of control fires, tempests, and flooding, and consequences for human well-being brought about by ozone harming substances, and related toxins. These effects can dislodge networks, expanding the number of worldwide outcasts and raising geopolitical strains.

Atmosphere-related dangers, for example, dry spell, crop disappointment, typhoons, and rapidly spreading fires, are huge supporters of contention and dislodging of huge quantities of individuals in Syria, Yemen, Kenya, and Sudan.

The most recent National Climate Assessment directed by the US government presumes that environmental change is "exhibiting developing difficulties to human well-being what's more, security, personal satisfaction, and the pace of monetary development" and accordingly presents noteworthy national security dangers.

Right now, more than 65 million individuals are uprooted internationally for some reasons counting struggle, starvation, and catastrophic events, which is the biggest number ever recorded by the UN Refugee Agency. The World Bank predicts that over 140 million individuals will be dislodged by environmental change alone by 2050.

2.3.4. What to Expect in 2019

The worldwide network will see much more prominent union of geopolitical and reasonable improvement motivation, with declining financial, physical, and computerized dangers in 2019. Environmental change impacts on worldwide security will turn out to be more conspicuous. The expanding number of cybersecurity breaks and exchange clashes are probably going to compound geopolitical pressures and cost the worldwide network billions of dollars. A potential worldwide financial downturn may slow advance on sustainability in the event that organizations decide to react by decreasing their sustainability spending plans:

1. ***Put Resources into Cybersecurity:*** The two governments and business are neglecting to stay aware of programers. All organizations need to expand interest in cybersecurity, and tech organizations specifically need to attempt to work all the more intimately with governments to assist them with sanctioning guidelines to all the more likely protect the two organizations furthermore, residents.
2. ***Draw in Governments on Exchange*****:** Enormous organizations need to cooperate, and with exchange relationship, to utilize their impact with governments and multilateral companies to endeavor to balance out the present unstable exchange relations between the US and other huge economies, most strikingly China.
3. ***Dissect Geopolitical Dangers*****:** Organizations that dissect geopolitical patterns will have the option to more readily envision, what is more, be readied, for interruption regardless of whether this comes in progressively capricious and entangled ways.

2.4. SAVING ECOSYSTEMS

Energy develops to handle plastic waste as biological systems are confronting phenomenal dangers. Our property and marine environments are confronting phenomenal dangers. Species are vanishing at disturbing rates, land corruption is undermining the prosperity of a large number of individuals, and compounding air contamination is costing a huge number of lives every year, and plastic contamination in seas and ashore is arriving at perilous levels.

China's choice to boycott plastic and e-waste imports has tossed waste and reusing markets into unrest, uncovering the greatness of plastic contamination, and raising the criticalness to lessen and reuse unmistakably more materials.

2.4.1. Biodiversity at Breaking Point

Appraisals of the Earth's biological system present a depressing picture. While mindfulness about biodiversity misfortune is developing, consideration paid by organizations and different companies to the issue stays restricted.

As per the most exhaustive evaluation of worldwide biological system well-being in late decades, biodiversity is declining at a disturbing rate crosswise over a large portion of the characteristic world. Species are vanishing multiple times quicker than their common rate of termination.

In its Living Planet Report, WWF finds "detonating human utilization" was the primary purpose for a monstrous drop in worldwide sustainable life populace in later decades. Somewhere in the range of 1970 and 2014, misfortunes in vertebrate species—warm-blooded creatures, fish, and feathered creatures, creatures of land and water, and reptiles—found the middle value of 60%.

Air contamination levels are arriving at basic levels. WHO evaluates that 9 out of 10 individuals inhale air containing significant levels of toxins, and around 7 million individuals bite the dust each year from presentation to contaminated air.

In excess of 75% of land, zones are currently considerably debased, which adversely impacts the prosperity of more than 3.2 billion individuals.

Sustainability specialists accept that the worldwide network has made constrained progress on SDG 14: Life below Water and SDG 15: Life on Land. They are among the sustainable development goals (SDGs) that get minimal consideration from business and different companies.

"Earth is losing biodiversity at a rate seen only during mass extinctions" Living Planet Report, WWF (Figure 2.4).

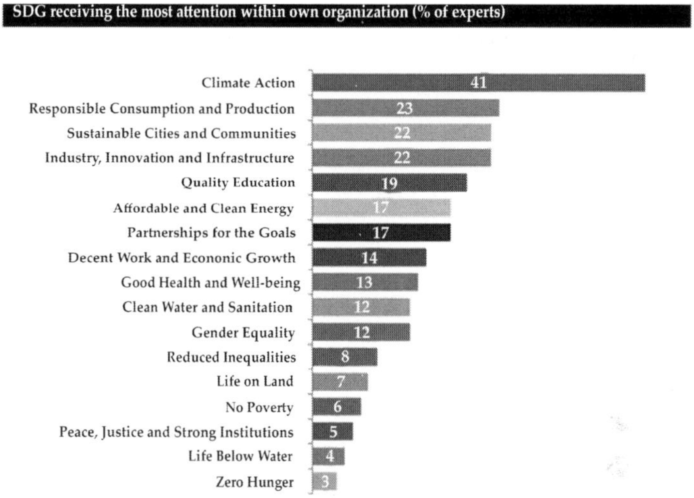

Figure 2.4. SDG 14: Life below water and SDG 15: Life on land is currently among sustainable development goals that receive the least attention by businesses and other organizations.

Source: Globe Scan-Sustainability Survey.

2.4.2. Waste and Plastic Hit Headlines

Worldwide mindfulness about plastic contamination and its effect on our biological systems proceeds to develop. A few significant worldwide alliances have been declared to handle the issue. Organizations are encountering developing weight from customers to diminish plastic waste.

Before reporting a boycott in January 2018, China imported more than 66% of the world's plastic waste. Nestlé is working towards plastic waste issue by making an Institute of innovative science research, which will concentrate on improving recyclable, biodegradable, and compostable bundling. The New Plastics Economy Global Commitment unites organizations, government, and common society behind a dream for accomplishing a round economy for plastic. The 290 companies that have marked the responsibility speak to 20% of all plastic bundling delivered all around. UNEP's Global Plastics Platform means to drive cross-fringe joint effort and learning among nations and urban communities. Marine plastic issues are increasing expanding unmistakable quality in Asia. Course Capital what is more, Ocean Conservancy reported at any rate $150 million of venture capital for waste and reusing advancements that keep plastic waste from entering the sea from Asian nations. WWF reported a 3-year, $7.5 million No More Plastics in our Ocean activity supported by the Norwegian government to propel a worldwide administration answer for marine plastic contamination (Figure 2.5).

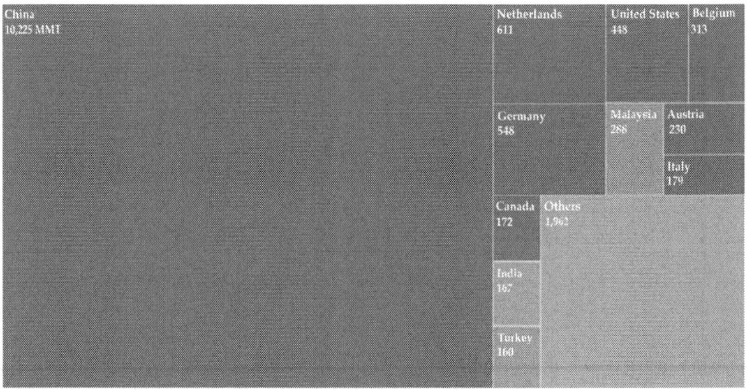

Figure 2.5. Plastic waste imports, millions of metric tons, 2016. For many years, China was the main importer of plastic waste, which changed in 2018 when it announced a ban.

Source: National Geographic.

2.4.3. What to Expect in 2019

Worldwide mindfulness about waste and plastic contamination will keep on developing. A number of coordinated efforts have just been reported however a lot more prominent exertion will be required to handle the issue. China's choice to boycott wastes imports will proceed to put pressure on governments and organizations to search for fundamental arrangements on a worldwide scale. While mindfulness about biodiversity misfortune contrasted with other practical improvement issues has been low, a developing number of NGOs are attempting to transform it. Open and private companies the same will confront developing desires to have an increasingly dynamic influence in saving area and marine biological systems.

1. ***Address Plastic Waste Over the Whole Value Chain:*** Organizations crosswise over numerous ventures—not just the ones legitimately capable for the greater part of plastic waste (nourishment and agribusiness, retail, and so on.) yet additionally those less related with plastic contamination (innovation, pharma, and so forth.)—will confront developing pressure by governments, clients, and

different partners to address plastic waste. Organizations need to investigate their whole value chain to execute arrangements that would diminish waste and plastic contamination.

2. ***Biodiversity as a Material Issue:*** Not many organizations distinguish biodiversity as a material issue, yet as mindfulness about land and marine environments emergencies develops, organizations will be relied upon to investigate their effect—and reliance on biodiversity.
3. ***Put Resources into Round Arrangements:*** Putting resources into round arrangements along the whole value chain gives one of the best pathways for organizations to address waste issues and improve the sustainability of their tasks.

2.5. NEW LEADERSHIP

Urban areas, locales, and business keep on sloping up authority as trust in national governments struggles. Worldwide governments are bearing a continuous emergency of trust. Non-state entertainers, for example, city and provincial governments and the business network, are venturing into the authority void and making a move to make a progressively manageable, impartial future.

2.5.1. Doubted Governments

Crosswise over significant European powers, the US, Canada, Russia, Australia, and Latin America, trust in governments stays low. This has been filled by expanding political polarization and deficient reactions to issues, for example, disparity, and environmental change.

Trust in national governments in a lion's share of European nations stays low, counting the UK, Germany, France, Spain, Italy, and Russia.

Latin America likewise has low degrees of trust in government with Brazil, Argentina what is more, Colombia all scoring under 50%.

The US Administration is bearing an immense emergency of trust—the first occasion when that such a huge decrease in trust has happened outside of a monetary downturn or national calamity as indicated by Edelman Trust Barometer.

In China, state-controlled assessments of public sentiment demonstrate high trust in government, yet this information has been raised doubt about by specialists who express that the administration's dictator control has brought about expanding doubt and loss of social capital.

Specialists evaluated national governments as having the least fortunate performance on tending to sustainable advancement out of any worldwide organization.

2.5.2. Urban Communities and Regions Lead

With worldwide pioneers neglecting to make a satisfactory administrative move on a scope of issues—counting atmosphere alleviation and adjustment, sea plastics, waste, and well-being—urban areas, what is more, provincial governments are assuming the job of sustainable advancement pioneers.

In the US, trust in neighborhood governments is at its most elevated since 2008. California leads subnational endeavors to control environmental change, with objectives to move to 100% sans carbon power by 2045 and to become carbon impartial by the same year.

Around 27 worldwide urban communities, including London, New York, Sydney, and Rome, have as of now arrived at top outflows and have effectively diminished their emanations for the most recent 5 years while keeping up powerful monetary development.

San Francisco now occupies 80% of its loss from landfills. It additionally joins New York, London, Dubai, and 20 other worldwide urban areas in having an objective a zero-waste objective. Company for Healthy Cities is another coordinated effort between a worldwide system of urban communities, WHO, and Bloomberg Philanthropies to spare lives by anticipating noncommunicable ailments and wounds.

In excess of 20 worldwide urban communities including London, Los Angeles, Paris, Mexico City, Seoul, and Tokyo have promised to guarantee a significant region of every city is zero emanations by 2030 and to buy 100% zero-discharge transports from 2025 onwards. Ukrainian urban areas have built up an objective of moving to 100% inexhaustible energy by 2050, in an offer to address environmental change and increment energy autonomy.

2.5.3. Business Leadership Is Increasing

Business is progressively venturing into the void left by worldwide governments, setting aggressive new social and sustainable objectives, and participating in radical straightforwardness endeavors that help to fabricate trust and believability with the two shoppers and workers.

In excess of 500 worldwide organizations are making a move on science-based atmosphere targets. Innovation organizations including Salesforce, Autodesk, Lyft, and Arm have framed the step-up coalition with the objective of using rising advances to lessen ozone-depleting substance emanations overall industry areas.

Driving Japanese insurance agency Sompo Japan Nipponkoa has set SDG targets for each territory of its business, including an objective to create products and administrations identified with fiasco avoidance and alleviation.

Around 150 organizations have focused on 100% sustainable power source through RE100. What is more, 23 multinationals have resolved to zero outflow vehicles through EV100.

Google as of late met its 100% sustainable power source objective, joining Apple furthermore, Microsoft.

Illustrious Dutch Shell has declared that it will interface official compensation to its carbon decrease objectives.

"With several governments dialing back from global commitments and reducing environmental protection, we need- and are seeing-the non-state actors step up to the challenge. We need a New Deal for nature and people." Kavita Prakash-Mani, WWF (Figure 2.6).

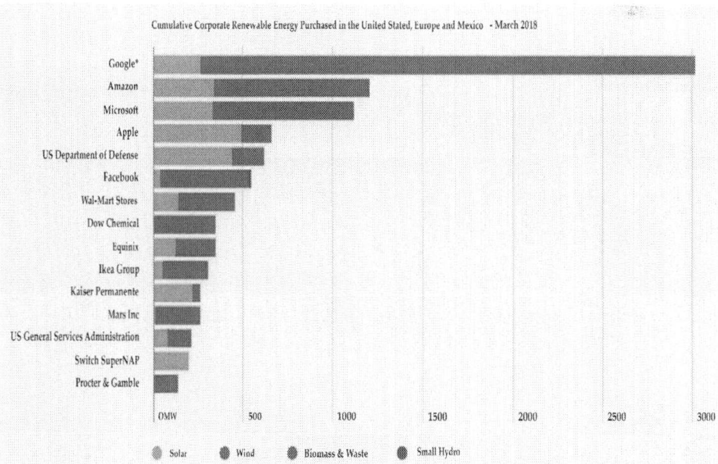

Figure 2.6. Royal Dutch Shell executive remuneration and carbon reduction goals.

Source: Royal Dutch Shell.

We hope to see proceeded with low degrees of trust in national governments and fortifying authority and aspiration of urban communities, provincial governments, and organizations. Proceeding with vulnerability in Europe due to Brexit and expanding polarization in the US is probably going to additionally hose trust in the political frameworks.

Buyers will be expanding hoping to organizations to act in agreement to their qualities and all the more effectively advocate on social and environmental issues.

Set intense objectives: Business should keep on inclining up administration and aspiration on conveying social and environmental advantages to society by setting and providing details regarding execution against intense sustainability objectives.

Increment straightforwardness: One of the best approaches to build trust is making information—on everything from decent variety to official compensation and carbon discharges—open and available to the general population.

Chapter 3

Small and Medium Enterprises

CONTENTS

Small and medium-sized enterprises (SMEs) may consider CSR/sustainability as not of their business. Proprietors maybe think these trendy expressions are simply pertinent to huge organizations who have the cash, individuals, and the methods for a more modest business, the authoritative and monetary expenses surpass the advantages.

In any case, SMEs that effectively bring sustainability issues into their business improvement methodology can have different advantages. From diminished dangers (across their supply chains, for example) to advancement opportunities, higher operational efficiency, lower costs, or a positive brand affiliation, an all-around executed corporate social obligation methodology can be of incredible incentive to SMEs.

SMEs are the foundation of both public economies and the worldwide stock chains of bigger companies. Alone, their effect is little yet, they have a colossal effect as they represent about 90% of business. In this manner, it is significant that SMEs join the sustainability change.

3.1. SUSTAINABILITY IN SMALL AND MEDIUM ENTERPRISES: GET EMPLOYEES ABOARD

How about we start by taking a look at the positive side. It is likely simpler and quicker to install sustainability into a little medium organization than into a huge one. SMEs have more straightforward structures (with respect to space, staff, or relationship with partners) and change can be executed all the more rapidly.

Then again, SMEs have a more restricted measure of assets (for example, staff or cash) which might be viewed as a solid hindrance to the advancement of a sustainability procedure. Be that as it may, sustainability related errands can be added (with thinking) to the current elements of workers.

Individuals need to be essential for an excursion to add to a superior climate and society-as it is most usually observed in corporate chipping in activities. So, in the event that they are gotten some information about their longing to contribute, clarified what that will probably mean, how it is dealt with their present undertakings and will make them train (there are free quality ones accessible): many will pull out all the stops and they will probably turn into such sustainability diplomats' enormous organizations have. This shared objective/excursion will likewise help reinforce the authoritative culture.

3.2. THE LOGICAL NEXT STEP IN DEVELOPING A SUSTAINABILITY PLAN IN SMES

As indicated by Steve Malkin from The Planet Mark™ sustainability confirmations, organizations need to zero in on decreasing carbon, energy, water, and waste. He says this can be refined by drawing in bosses to begin searching for upgrades in asset effectiveness-which costs just time.

By evaluating and lessening their carbon footprint, organizations decrease their operational expenses and can oversee better and all the more proficiently their day-by-day exercises, Malkin says to eco-business.

Understanding a company's effects is an essential piece of a sustainability procedure. Be that as it may, there is again and again an inclination to go toward any path and start any place with irregular activities, for example, publicizing new reusing containers. This is both tedious and misdirecting. Organizations need to initially quantify and afterward report: and really at that time, they will have the option to improve their tasks and notoriety. In any case, even before that, they need to outline the setting in which they do business.

3.3. BEGINNING A SUSTAINABILITY PLAN AND REPORTING IT IN SMES

Sustainability detailing, i.e., uncovering a company's most critical effects, should begin with SMEs sharing what is the issue here, how they work and how they are dealing with their effects. Regardless of whether they create a report, the accompanying rules can help set up an organized thought on where to begin and what to do.

The Global Reporting Initiative (GRI) recommends companies should begin by distinguishing, organizing, and characterizing their sustainability issues. They ought to do as such in light of four standards: sustainability setting; partner comprehensiveness; materiality; and fulfillment.

1. ***Sustainability in SMEs: Sustainability Context*:** SMEs ought to consider the setting around them: how might they contribute towards a surer future on a neighborhood or local level? What is their present execution and in which ways does it have negative social and sustainable effects?

   Thinking how sustainability subjects identify with the drawn-out hierarchical technique of a SME as far as business dangers and opportunities is additionally essential to begin with.

2. ***Stakeholder Inclusiveness***: It is significant that for a company to distinguish who are its partners, i.e., all the researches-from workers to NGOs, the media, or government bodies-keen on their exercises. This will permit a superior reaction to their desires, interests, and concerns.

   Cautiously planning the partners, a company considers it is responsible for ensuring the pertinent data from them is gathered.

3. ***Materiality Analysis: SMEs and Sustainability***: In the wake of surveying their unique circumstance, various dangers, opportunities, and effects will probably be distinguished. Amidst various potential paths to follow, it gets critical to distinguish which issues are generally pertinent to be tended to. Also, that is the thing that a materiality examination is for.

   Also, how to survey which subjects are sufficiently significant to be additionally considered and perhaps tended to and revealed? The appropriate response lies someplace in the middle of the issues that present a critical danger to a company and its zone of activity and the mains concerns and subjects of interests of the most applicable partners: which can be found by means of a materiality network.

4. ***Completeness of Sustainability Information in SMEs***: SMEs should think (and remember for their sustainability reports) about what their degrees and limits are. They ought to organize giving point by point data to partners with respect to the data they have/ are gathering, so their most critical monetary, environment, and social effects are precisely shared.

3.4. SUSTAINABILITY AND CSR CHALLENGES IN SMALL AND MEDIUM ENTERPRISES

In the wake of perusing the four standards above, building up a sustainability system may resemble an immense test for SMEs. Also, it is. Particularly from a viewpoint that these rules, along with numerous requirements (which help the cycle and give further validity), are costly and complex for the size of little medium ventures.

However, how about we keep present the possibility that SMEs, similar to all size organizations, can have huge advantages from embracing sustainable strategic approaches. In spite of the underlying significant expenses of incorporating and announcing sustainability-which can be diminished if representatives are propelled and included-the advantages may be more than counterbalanced by cost investment funds.

Decreased business chances, the capacity to meet the desires for purchasers, workers, and providers for mindful products and administrations and, thusly, a positive brand affiliation will probably make starting costs just a protected speculation. Additionally, start gradually and go greater as your SME picks up impact and energy and maybe at that point, bigger expenses with specific specialists or with a consultancy can be a protected (and more costly) subsequent stage.

Keep in mind: as SMEs measure their effects and incorporate sustainability into their center plan of action, they will begin getting verification of their sustainable and social execution. That separates from the opposition and gets another objective of shoppers progressively searching for capable organizations with a higher reason other than benefits. Start ASAP.

3.5. SMES ARE ESSENTIAL FOR DELIVERING MORE INCLUSIVE GLOBALIZATION AND GROWTH

In numerous nations, and specifically OECD nations, governments are confronting the difficulties of low development, frail exchange, and venture, and rising, or perseveringly high imbalance (OECD, 2016a). They additionally face a developing disappointment among residents with the present status of undertakings, which is too showing itself as a reaction against globalization and mechanical change. Against this scenery, there is a need to make the conditions that empower the advantages of open business sectors and innovative advancement to be improved and shared all the more comprehensively across the economy and society.

SMEs are vital participants in the economy and the more extensive eco-arrangement of firms. Empowering them to adjust furthermore, flourish in a more open climate and partake all the more effectively in the computerized change is fundamental for boosting monetary development and conveying a more comprehensive globalization. Across nations at all degrees of advancement, SMEs have a significant task to carry out in accomplishing the Sustainable Development Objectives (SDGs), by advancing comprehensive and sustainable monetary development, giving business and good work for all, advancing sustainable industrialization, and cultivating development, and lessening pay disparities.

In any case, boosting SME potential for partaking in and receiving the rewards of a globalized and computerized economy depends generally on favorable structure conditions and solid rivalry. Because of requirements inward to the firm, SMEs are excessively influenced by market setbacks and hindrances and shortcomings in the business climate and strategy circle. SMEs' commitments likewise depend on their admittance to key assets, for example, abilities, information organizations, and account, and on open interests in territories, for example, schooling, and preparing, advancement, and framework. Besides, for a huge number of SMEs, a helpful climate for the exchange of business possession or the executives speaks to a significant condition for guaranteeing business suitability after some time, with suggestions for occupations, speculation, and development.

These issues have picked up unmistakable quality in the strategy banter, as SMEs in certain nations proceed to battle with the drawn-out effect of the 2007–2008 worldwide crisis, which hit new and private companies excessively and denoted an augmenting of the gap in efficiency development among SMEs and enormous firms (OECD, 2017a, b). This gap is a significant driver of the noticed ascent in imbalance, including wage disparity, in numerous nations (OECD, 2016a).

The SME strategy space is intricate. It contains structure conditions; wide strategies that sway SMEs; and explicit focused on arrangements. These regions frequently cut across the limits of services and government offices, just as across levels of government. Since SMEs are frequently installed in nearby eco-frameworks, which speak to their essential wellspring of information, abilities, money, business opportunities, and networks, it is additionally imperative to consider factors influencing structure conditions at the nearby level, and how arrangements created at the public level are customized to nearby conditions, just as how they organize with strategies that are molded at the local or regional level (OECD, 2016e). Moreover, strategy methodologies should consider the adjustments in guidelines, markets, and innovations that happen across fringes which may influence SMEs' chances and execution.

The areas beneath inspect the chances and difficulties SMEs face in a worldwide and computerized economy, expanding on the OECD's huge assortment of examination directed across OECD Committees on SMEs, striving for account, development, tax collection, guideline, digitalization, work, aptitudes, exchange, internationalization, and global value chains (GVCs), climate, among others, just as on its interesting measurable ability.

Taken together, these discoveries present a solid case for building up a cross-cutting OECD Strategy for SMEs, which can propel the discussion and catalyze upgrades in structure conditions and SME strategies in Members and non-Members to convey more feasible and comprehensive development.

SMEs make diverse contributions to economic and social well-being, which could be further enhanced. SMEs assume a critical part in public economies around the globe, producing business and value. In the OECD region, SMEs represent roughly 99% of all businesses in the European Union (EU).

They are the primary source of employment, representing about 70% of occupations, and are significant supporters of value creation, producing somewhere in the range of half and 60% of economic value added (Figure 3.1) (OECD, 2016b).

In arising economies, SMEs contribute up to 45% of aggregate work and 33% of GDP. When considering the commitment of casual organizations, SMEs add to the greater part of work and GDP in many nations regardless of pay levels (IFC, 2010).

Likewise, SME advancement can add to monetary enhancement and flexibility. This is particularly applicable for asset rich nations that are especially defenseless against product cost changes.

The commitment of SMEs to development elements has expanded for many years, as pay development, more niche market interest and changing innovations have empowered SMEs to reinforce their relative preferences and diminished the underlying hindrances coming from asset requirements and restricted capacity to harvest economies of scale.

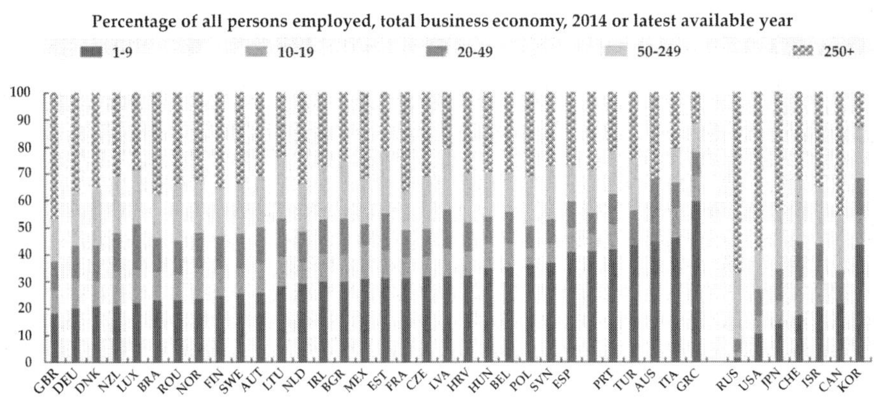

Figure 3.1. SMEs are the main source of jobs in the business sector.

Notes: For Canada, Switzerland, Israel, Japan, Korea, the United States and the Russian Federation, data do not include non-employers. Data for Korea and Mexico are based on establishments. Data for the United Kingdom exclude an estimate of 2.6 million small unregistered businesses. For Australia, Canada, and Turkey the size class 1–9 refers to 1–19.

Source: OECD (2017), Entrepreneurship at a Glance 2017, OECD Publishing, Paris.

While not all SMEs are innovative, new, and little firms are regularly the main impetus behind the kind of revolutionary developments that are significant for monetary development, since they can work outside of prevailing standards, abuse innovative or business opportunities that have been ignored by additional set up organizations or empower the commercialization of information that would some way or another stay uncommercialized in colleges and research companies (Baumol, 2002; OECD, 2010a). For example, SMEs represent about 20% of licenses, one proportion of development, in biotechnology-related fields in Europe (Eurostat, 2014). SMEs additionally add to interest creation by embracing development produced somewhere else, and adjusting it to various settings through steady changes, and by providing new or specialty products which react to assorted client needs. They additionally contribute by serving areas that do not have a huge enough scale to pull in bigger firms.

The information-based economy, an ascent in non-mechanical advancement and the development of open or organization-based methods of advancement have likewise empowered new and little firms to expand their commitments to development (OECD, 2010a). Development by SMEs is to a great extent impacted by information overflows, admittance to organizations and occasions to collaborate with different players, including bigger undertakings.

Globalization has expanded the significance of cross-fringe coordinated effort in development-both in getting contributions for advancement (purpose, money, abilities, innovations) from abroad and in misusing its yields (products and administrations, licenses, and so on) in unfamiliar business sectors. Nonetheless, a critical test for some SMEs is to distinguish and interface with fitting information partners and organizations at the nearby, public, and worldwide levels, just as to create fitting aptitudes and the board rehearses for coordinating information made by outer partners with in-house practices and advancement measures (Figure 3.2) (OECD, 2013b).

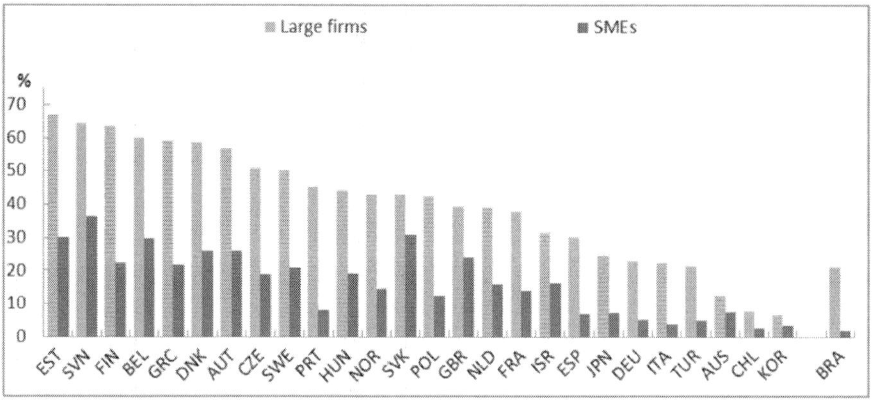

Figure 3.2. SMEs are less connected than large firms to international knowledge networks.

Source: OECD (2015), OECD Science, Technology, and Industry Scoreboard 2015, OECD Publishing, Paris, based on Eurostat Community Innovation Survey (CIS-2012) and National Data Sources, June 2015.

SME support in the progress to more sustainable examples of creation and utilization is essential for the greening of monetary turn of events. Despite the fact that the individual sustainable footprint of private ventures might be low, their total effects can, in certain areas, surpass that of enormous organizations.

Lessening the environment impact of SMEs by accomplishing and effectively implementing sustainability best practices, is a vital factor for success towards the green change. This is especially earnest for SMEs in the construction area, which represents a huge piece of the world's utilization of assets, air, and water contamination and age of waste (OECD, 2013a).

In numerous OECD nations, innovative SMEs assume an urgent job in the ecoindustry what is more, clean-tech markets. For example, in the United Kingdom and Finland, SMEs speak to individually over 90% and 70% of clean innovation organizations (Carbon Trust, 2013; ETLA, 2015). SMEs are particularly all around situated to take advantage of lucky breaks of greener stockpile chains in nearby clean tech markets, which might be ugly or impervious for huge worldwide firms, remembering for arising economies and low-pay nations (IBRD, 2014). Moreover, little "green business people," driven by monetary benefit joined with environment awareness, can drive a base up change and occupation creation, by growing new plans of action and spearheading green strategic approaches that impact mass business sectors and at last are received by the more extensive business network (OECD, 2013a).

Notwithstanding, the ability and capacity of SMEs to receive economic practices and hold onto green business opportunities regularly face size-related asset requirements, aptitude deficiencies and information impediments. Environmentally supportability upgrades in SMEs are frequently kept down by specialized complexities, weights, and expenses, just as absence of mindfulness about monetarily alluring chances.

Besides, an absence of proper aptitudes and mastery regularly keeps SMEs from following up on mutual opportunities, and asset limitations regularly lead to SMEs to be more danger opposed and less ready to contribute in new innovations than bigger firms (Mazur, 2012; EaP Green, 2016).

SMEs make open positions across geographic regions and areas, utilizing wide portions of the workforce, including low-gifted laborers, and giving occasions to aptitudes improvement. They likewise help uphold their workers' admittance to medical care and social administrations. SMEs that produce occupations and value-added are accordingly a significant channel for incorporation and destitution decrease, particularly however not only in arising and low-pay economies. In such manner, updating efficiency in an enormous populace of independent ventures, remembering for conventional sections and the casual economy, can help governments accomplish both financial development and social consideration goals, including getting away from low profitability traps and improving the nature of occupations for low-gifted laborers (OECD, 2009, 2017b).

Private ventures can likewise speak to a powerful instrument to address cultural necessities through the market also, give public merchandise and ventures. This is the situation of social ventures, which bring imaginative answers for the issues of destitution, social avoidance, and joblessness, and fill gap all in all interest administration conveyance (EU/OECD, 2016). In numerous nations, the financial load of the social and fortitude economy, in which social ventures work, has expanded consistently as of late, as a result of the worldwide crisis.

For example, in France, in 2014, the social economy represented 10% of the GDP. In the United Kingdom, in 2015, 41% of social ventures had made positions contrasted with 22% of SMEs (SEUK, 2015).

In numerous nations, corporate social responsibility (CSR) is progressively seen as a route for organizations, including SMEs, to add to cultural objectives.

By resolving to sound work and environment practices and great network relations, private ventures can add to sustainable and comprehensive turn of events, especially at the neighborhood level. CSR can likewise help improve the notion clients, financial specialists, and different partners have of the business, and upgrade their ability to pull in and hold qualified and persuaded workers.

Firm heterogeneity matters for development, profitability, work creation and comprehensive development. While huge contrasts exist among SMEs and huge firms, the SME populace itself is ordinarily made out of diverse organizations, regarding age, size, proprietorship, plans of action, and business visionaries' profile and goals.

SMEs assume a significant part in the more extensive eco-arrangement of firms. New companies and young firms, which are little or miniature firms, are the essential wellspring of net employment creation in numerous nations. Besides, business elements are a significant driver of profitability development (OECD, 2016b). Notwithstanding, most of new undertakings either fizzle in the main long periods of movement or stay exceptionally little (OECD, 2016c). High-development firms of various ages and areas additionally contribute lopsidedly to work creation (OECD, 2010b).

Set up of medium-sized undertakings that improve and scale-up are the main impetus behind development in numerous OECD economies, frequently guaranteeing the coordination, updating, and support in stock chains of more modest providers. For example, in Switzerland, medium-sized ventures (50–249 workers) speak to about 4% of the business populace, however represent 23% of work and 25% of significant value-added (OECD, 2016b). There are likewise numerous little ventures in mid or low-tech areas which are implanted in serious neighborhood creation frameworks, and which produce advancement, to a great extent gradual, also, add to work, social consideration, and regional attachment.

Simultaneously, some little undertakings do not go past little neighborhood markets. These organizations, which produce restricted advancement and do not have solid development yearnings, frequently stay little for the duration of their life cycle.

SMEs are a dynamic and advancing populace. Their organization differs broadly across nations what is more, areas, with suggestions for their capacity to flourish in and add to an open and digitalized economy. In all nations, miniature ventures (up to 9 representatives) overwhelm the business scene, representing 70% to 95%, everything being equal. For example, in the administrations area, their offer in work goes from over 60% in Greece to 20% in Denmark and Germany, while their offer in value-added goes from about 45% in Luxembourg to 15% in Switzerland (OECD, 2016b).

SME execution likewise differs across areas. In administrations, SMEs represent 60% or a greater amount of aggregate work and value included practically in all nations. Conversely, in assembling, albeit generally few in number, huge firms give an unbalanced commitment to work and value-added, in enormous part reflecting expanding re-visitations of scale from more capital-escalated creation, just as section obstructions identified with speculation. In certain nations, for example, Germany, and Mexico, huge assembling researches catch a critical portion of complete work and value-added. Notwithstanding, there are a few special cases (Figure 3.3). These incorporate more modest economies, for example, Latvia, and Estonia, just as bigger economies where SMEs have customarily ruled assembling movement, for example, Italy (OECD, 2017c).

A more profound comprehension of the commitments and difficulties of various sorts of SMEs (for example, a typology of firms) is expected to control underlying and focused on approaches.

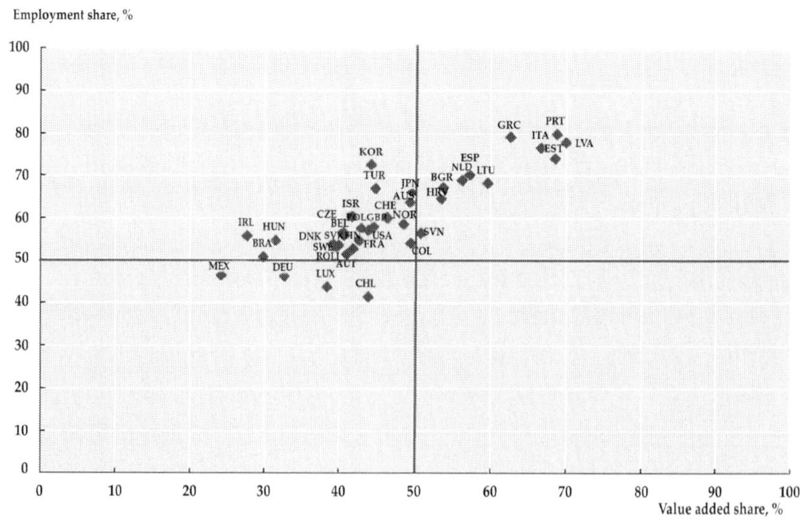

Figure 3.3. There are large differences in the SME contribution to employment and value-added across countries, particularly in manufacturing.

Notes: Size of SMEs: AUS: SMEs refer to < 200 persons employed; JPN, KOR: SMEs refer to < 300 persons employed; CHE, JPN, USA: data do not include non-employers. GBR data exclude an estimate of 2.6 million small unregistered businesses. For CHL, only enterprises with more than 10 employees are covered.

Source: OECD (2017), Entrepreneurship at a Glance 2017, OECD Publishing, Paris, forthcoming.

More grounded interest by SMEs in worldwide business sectors can assist with reinforcing their commitments to financial turn of events and social prosperity, by making occasions to scale up, quickening advancement, encouraging overflows of innovation and administrative skill, expanding, and extending the range of abilities, and upgrading efficiency. Likewise, more prominent adaptability and ability to tweak and separate products can give SMEs an upper hand in worldwide business sectors comparative with bigger firms, as they can react quickly to changing economic situations and progressively more limited product life cycles.

Some global business sectors are overwhelmed by SMEs, and creative little undertakings are frequently key partners of bigger multinationals in growing new products or serving new business sectors. Simultaneously, closer worldwide incorporation expands rivalry for SMEs in neighborhood markets, now, and again with disruptive effects, requesting improved market information and expanded intensity likewise for private companies that do not work universally.

In general, SMEs will in general be under-spoken to in global exchange. Across OECD and non-OECD Individuals, barely any SMEs send out straightforwardly, and for those that do, trades regularly speak to a lower portion of exchange turnover (comparative with bigger firms) and by and large objective neighboring nations (OECD, 2016b).

Upstream and downstream linkages with bigger organizations are fundamental for SMEs (OECD and World Bank Group, 2015). Advantages of these firm linkages run in both bearings, since the quality and responsiveness of particular providers, to a great extent SMEs or even miniature firms, can be vital for the intensity of whole inventory chains, at both nearby and worldwide levels, and of bigger bunches that are straightforwardly occupied with savage worldwide rivalry. In this regard, close company and coordination among enormous and private companies can be a significant wellspring of significant value and seriousness along supply chains (Figure 3.4).

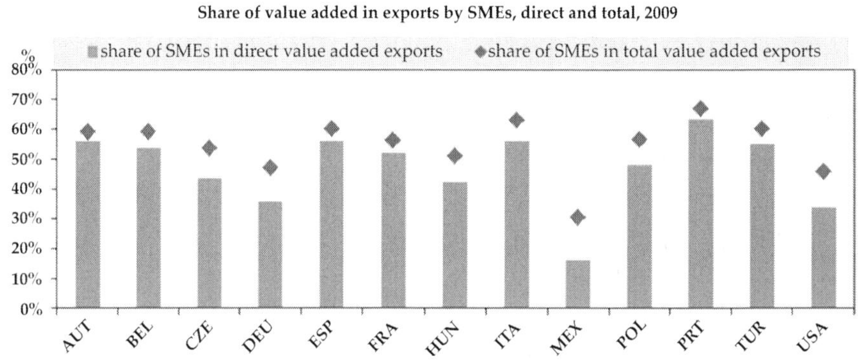

Figure 3.4. SMEs account for a larger share of value-added in international trade when indirect linkages are taken into account.

Source: OECD and World Bank Group (2015), based on OECD/Eurostat Trade by Enterprise Characteristics (TEC) Database; OECD Structural and Demographic Business Statistics (SDBS) Database; OECD Intercountry Input-Output Trade in Value Added (ICIO/TiVA) Database.

Interest in worldwide business sectors and value chains is lopsided across the SME populace. There are imaginative SMEs that are completely incorporated into worldwide business sectors ("little multinationals"), and a sizeable portion of SMEs that send out or are inserted in GVCs as providers of exporters. Simultaneously, for some, SMEs send out connections can be brief, with new exporters stopping to send out following a couple of years in numerous nations and, for longer-term exporters, successive exchanging of products and objections (Wagner, 2015). More modest and less experienced exporters are ordinarily more defenseless against a sharp drop in outside interest, for example, in the result of a worldwide crisis (IBRD, 2010; Beverelli et al., 2011).

Besides, ongoing proof recommends that non-industrial nation SMEs may battle to take a bit of leeway of new opportunities offered by the developing GVC scene. Numerous SMEs may coordinate GVCs at the low-interest end, where interfaces among MNCs and their nearby providers can be restricted and hard to create, including when the MNC has a business interest in building up a neighborhood provider base, effectively seeks after the target (OECD and World Bank Group, 2015). Truth be told, proof proposes that non-industrial nation SME roundabout fares may be lower than created nation aberrant fares (OECD, 2017d).

To create approaches that can uphold SMEs in capitalizing on the new chances offered by GVCs, a superior agreement is required of the association of SMEs with bigger firms and MNCs inside various settings and along various value chains, of the job of groups for SME support and redesigning, just as of how GVCs are developing, including as an outcome of the advanced progress.

Exchange and speculation receptiveness, just as exchange help, licensed innovation assurance, framework, and institutional quality, are critical to SME commitment in worldwide business sectors. SMEs are less capable than huge firms to confront the expenses of participating in global exchange because of their restricted assets and the executives' limits. Organizing straightforwardness and other great administrative works on, including the choice to decrease guideline, can handle administrative expenses and troubles and advance SME intensity in worldwide and developing business sectors. While conforming to different norms, specialized guidelines, and congruity evaluation methodology is exorbitant for bigger firms, it is conceivably restrictive for SMEs since huge numbers of the expenses to taking part in worldwide business sectors are fixed, and frequently sunk, paying little heed to a company's size or then again income. Unsurprising and productive traditions strategies and coordination administrations are particularly significant for SMEs, which may locate the connected managerial and monetary weights especially burdensome (OECD, 2015a; USITC, 2014). Public Trade Facilitation Committees as indicated under the new WTO Assistance Agreement can be a valuable instrument to look for SME input.

Moreover, limitations to bringing in maybe restricting the capacity of SMEs to exploit benefits emerging from more proficient sourcing. For instance, in Southeast Asia, an area which has grasped GVCs, SMEs will in general, source a lower portion of their value-added from abroad comparative with bigger firms (OECD, 2017d).

In a world in which without a moment to spare, conveyance is the norm, and in which travel is quick and capacity is costly, time is an essential driver of intensity. The nature of actual foundation, for example, streets, ports, and air terminals, just as the efficiency of the systems continued in the activity of these offices, are significant for organizations to enter unfamiliar business sectors and partake in GVCs. In arising economies, these are frequently the main unfriendly factors motioned by SMEs looking to hold onto worldwide opportunities (COMCEC, 2013). The advancement of an effective information and communication technology (ICT) framework, just as improved interoperability, and guidelines, are likewise progressively critical to get to worldwide business sectors, as they encourage data trade and correspondence just as interest in web-based business stages (BIAC et al., 2016; OECD, 2017a).

Digitalization offers new opportunities for SMEs to partake in the worldwide economy. Computerized innovations permit SMEs to improve market knowledge, arrive at scale without mass and access worldwide business sectors and information networks at moderate ease. The computerized change encourages the rise of private companies and gives new occasions to SMEs to improve their seriousness in neighborhood and worldwide business sectors, through product or administration advancement and improved creation measures. It additionally encourages the development of "lean new companies" that influence the Internet to lower fixed expenses and re-appropriates numerous parts of the business to remain light-footed and receptive to the market (OECD, 2017f). Besides, Big Data and information examination give a wide scope of chances for SMEs, empowering a superior comprehension of the cycles inside the firm, the requirements of their customers and partners, and the general business climate. The utilization of computerized advancements can likewise facilitate SMEs' access to workforce, through better work enlistment locales, reevaluating, and online undertaking employing, just as company with information systems (OECD, 2017f). It can likewise encourage upgraded admittance to a scope of financing instruments.

While digitalization offers new opportunities for SMEs to arrive at worldwide business sectors, actually countless SMEs have not had the option to receive the rewards of the mechanical progress. Proof shows that SMEs are falling behind in embracing computerized advancements. While, in many nations, the gap is tight for straightforward network and web presence, the gap widens while considering support in web-based business and, particularly, more modern applications. For example, across OECD nations, enterprise resource planning (ERP) programming applications to oversee business data streams are famous among huge firms (over 75% reception rate in 2014) yet less utilized by SMEs (under 20%).

In numerous nations, a huge selection gap is likewise noticed for distributed computing, for example, the leasing of PC power from an outer supplier, which can permit more modest firms to utilize Big Data, while beating a few of the boundaries related with the high fixed expenses of ICT venture (Figure 3.5).

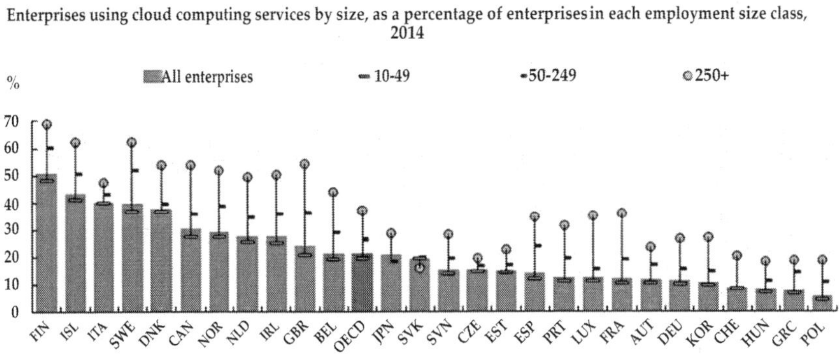

Figure 3.5. SMEs lag behind in the adoption of more sophisticated digital technologies.

Notes: Unless otherwise stated, sector coverage consists of all activities in manufacturing and non-financial market services. Only enterprises with 10 or more persons employed are considered. Size classes are defined as: small (from 10 to 49 persons employed), medium (50 to 249) and large (250 and more). For Canada, data refer to enterprises with expenditures on "Software as a Service" (e.g., cloud computing). Medium-sized enterprises have 50–299 employees. Large enterprises have 300 or more employees. For Japan, data refer to businesses with 100 or more employees. Medium-sized enterprises have 100–299 employees. Large enterprises have 300 or more employees. For Canada and Korea, data refer to 2012 instead of 2014. For Japan and Switzerland, data refer to 2011 instead of 2014. For Switzerland, data refer to enterprises with five and more employees.

Source: OECD (2015), OECD Digital Economy Outlook (2015), OECD Publishing, Paris.

The selection slack of SMEs is fundamentally because of the absence of interest in integral knowledge-based resources, for example, R&D, HR, hierarchical changes, and cycle advancement, and has suggestions for their ability to transform mechanical change into advancement and profitability development. For example, the absence of interest in in-house development measures and authoritative abilities restricts the limit of SMEs to exploit new innovations to improve data investigation and increment their investment in information organizations. Indeed, the ICT upheaval has made it simpler for firms to enhance through collective organizations with different organizations, including multinationals, colleges, and examination companies. Notwithstanding, this requires advancement skills, also hierarchical and the board abilities to facilitate with outer information partners and viably join information from outside sources.

Besides, for some SMEs, digitalization has brought about interruption of business sectors, including expanded contestability of nearby business sectors, fast outdated nature of information, abilities, and plans of action, and expanded unpredictability in the business climate. Whereby advanced advances take into account full and moment upscale of the triumphant product or thought, frequently at the worldwide level, could have broad ramifications for the dispersion of profits and support of new firms what is more, SMEs in business sectors. A more profound comprehension of the ramifications of all these computerized improvements for SMEs is required.

The business climate is basic to improve SME cooperation and profits by an open and coordinated economy. A sound business climate and a well-working enterprising "eco-framework" for business, counting at the neighborhood level, matter for nations and locales to cultivate interest of SMEs in a globalized economy. This is much more significant in the current setting, as expanded serious weights and the high speed of mechanical change request dexterity, imaginative conduct, remembering for public administration, furthermore, straightforward entry to vital assets. While system conditions influence in general business speculation, advancement, and development, a few measurements sway new and set up SMEs lopsidedly (OECD, 2017a).

Administrative vulnerability, intricacy, and irregularity influence SMEs excessively. SMEs are ordinarily less effective than huge firms in screening the administrative climate and managing important standards. Since they may need data or mastery in house, SMEs frequently bring about in other circuitous expenses, paying for outer consultants' aptitude or putting resources into explicit preparing of staff to agree to new commitments. Along these lines, the unpredictability of administrative techniques and conditions for administrative consistency are particularly significant for SMEs.

Moreover, for SMEs to take an interest in worldwide business sectors and GVCs, administrative difference across nations can force an extra layer of trouble. Wasteful bankruptcy systems limit business dynamism, rebuilding of suitable firms and admittance to outer account by SMEs.

In a few nations, on account of unincorporated miniature and little firms, the treatment of individual defaulters is severe, leaving full close to home obligation for a long-time past liquidation of the business (Bergthaler et al., 2015). Long and convoluted cycles can altogether influence the capital and notoriety of little business people, definitely diminishing the opportunity of beginning a business once more. Furthermore, legitimate vulnerabilities increment danger to loan specialists and compel the inventory of money to SMEs (OECD, 2017a).

Given a generous fixed cost part to burden administrative prerequisites and consistence costs (record continuing, documenting, and installment measures and so forth) at public, provincial, and city levels, little organizations are off guard as for huge undertakings. For young firms, which additionally will in general be little, high consistency expenses can intensify the asset and income limitations frequently experienced in the beginning phases of business advancement and may go about as a hindrance to formalization. Now and again, charge consistence costs for little firms may even surpass their duty money installments (OECD, 2015c; Eichfelder and Vaillancourt, 2014). Besides, certain parts of business tax assessment, including unbalanced treatment of benefits and misfortunes, the dissemination of tax collection among capital and work pay and the plan of R&D tax breaks and impetuses, can accidentally impediment some youthful and little firms (OECD, 2015c). Public area respectability and straightforwardness, policy management productivity and the nature of public administrations are fundamental for a level battleground.

Organizations communicate in numerous manners with policy implementation, whose uprightness, straightforwardness, and efficiency influence business creation and development. The expenses related to regulatory weights and formality are generally higher for SMEs than for enormous firms. Likewise, while absence of straightforwardness and debasement in the public area are impeding to all organizations, they present specific issues to SMEs, which frequently do not have the ability to adapt to a murky public area, plan, and actualize hostile to defilement procedures and anteroom for their requirements without a set up system for investment out in the open dynamic.

3.6. THE CAPACITY TO GET TO VITAL ASSETS IS BASIC FOR SME STABILITY

Explicit hindrances and market setbacks may keep SMEs from getting to vital assets, counting account, the board limit and aptitudes, and information organizations, setting them at a serious drawback in the worldwide and digitalized economy. For some, new companies and SMEs, admittance to back in the proper structures is hampered by a scope of request and supply-side hindrances.

Setbacks in monetary business sectors, because of uneven data and organization issues, commonly limit admittance to credit by SMEs and new companies, which are regularly under-collateralized, have restricted financial record furthermore, and may not have the skill expected to create refined budget reports (OECD, 2013c). This is a territory where the case for strategy intercession to address these setbacks is all around perceived. Credit imperatives are particularly serious in mid-and low-pay nations, where subsidizing gap are regularly the fundamental boundary to formalization and SME improvement. Across OECD and non-OECD Members, credit conditions for some, SMEs disintegrated in the result of the worldwide crisis, compounding the impacts of long-standing challenges, for example, absence of security and fixed expenses for banks in handling advance applications. The spread in the normal loan fees charged to SMEs and to enormous firms has significantly extended contrasted with the pre-emergency period, despite the fact that the expenses of financing have been diminishing consistently as of late, pointing to a higher credit hazard for SMEs (Figure 3.6).

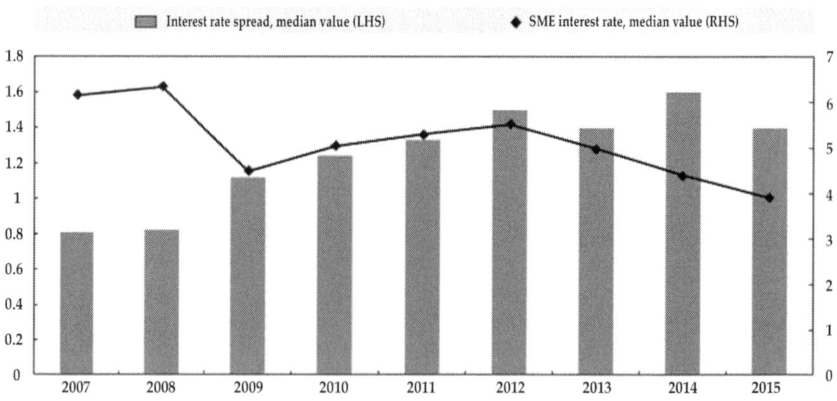

Figure 3.6. The gap in credit costs between SMEs and large enterprises has widened.

Source: OECD (2017), Financing SMEs and Entrepreneurs (2017). An OECD Scoreboard, OECD Publishing, Paris.

Perceiving that financing needs and limitations fluctuate broadly across the business populace and along the life-pattern of firms, the G20/OECD

High-level Principles on SME Financing call for reinforcing SME admittance to credit, while likewise supporting the expansion of their financing sources.

In truth, most SMEs, including new, innovative, and quickly developing firms, remain vigorously dependent on interior assets and conventional bank obligation. The absence of suitable types of account, particularly of the value type, remains conversely with enormous organizations, and is restricting passage, long haul venture, development, and advancement (OECD, 2015d).

The accessibility of bank loaning and of elective wellsprings of money is held back by a mix of interest side hindrances, most quite impediments in monetary information, key vision, assets, and in some cases even the eagerness or attention to effectively pull in sources, also as supply-side obstacles, for example, the general obscurity of the SME account market, an absence of leave alternatives for speculators in SME money markets, industrious administrative obstructions, for example, to the expanding of the financial specialists' base to retail and institutional speculators, and expenses of administrative consistency (OECD, 2016d). Abilities deficiencies, helpless administration practices and labor force preparing limit SME efficiency and development.

SME cooperation in the information-based economy is kept down by aptitudes deficiencies, poor inside administration practices and low degrees of labor force preparing. There is proof that SMEs have higher aptitudes lacks than huge firms and SME preparing exertion is on normal essentially more fragile per worker than in bigger firms (OECD, 2013b). SMEs regularly face difficulties in pulling in and holding profoundly qualified faculty and staff with applicable abilities and have more prominent troubles in recognizing laborers with sought-after abilities in the work market. Moreover, SMEs have all the earmarks of being generally behind in building up cooperation with schooling and preparing organizations, and in the utilization of organization-level learning systems, for example, the utilization of administrative practices and strategies that advance learning and self-governance (OECD, 2015b). Absence of interests here likewise restricts the take-up of computerized innovations and their compelling use to improve efficiency and access markets. Furthermore, the absence of innovative abilities may keep down change in accordance with and more prominent cooperation of SMEs and business visionaries in the "new universe of work" achieved by expanding digitalization and discontinuity of creation measures.

Unsuccessful administration rehearses, just as absence of a suitable corporate administration structure, likewise present difficulties to business advancement and the board change measures in numerous SMEs, especially family undertakings. Now and again, the executives' restrictions are compounded by financing requirements, administrative obstacles, regulatory, and taxation rates. This speaks to a developing strategy worry in numerous nations, especially where the business visionary populace is maturing quickly, yet restricted proof on business moves in numerous locales speaks to a hindrance to strategy activity.

Speaking to 33% of government expenses, public acquisition is an immediate wellspring of pay for organizations, including SMEs. While well-established strategies are endlessly embraced by OECD Members, substantial effects on the advancement of SMEs stay to be proven.

3.7. A CROSS-CUTTING POINT OF VIEW ON SMES IS REQUIRED

The drivers of the inconsistencies in firm execution, including inside the SME populace, and the ramifications of the computerized change for SMEs and their cooperation in the worldwide economy, are not yet completely comprehended. SMEs are regularly more reliant than huge organizations on their business biological system. Furthermore, because of their inner imperatives, are more helpless against market setbacks, strategy shortcomings and irregularities. While the lopsided impacts of these set backs on SMEs are very much archived, viewpoints contrast on how they should be handled and on the strategy instruments which are viable in evening the odds or tending to explicit hindrances to SME advancement, while advancing solid market elements.

Besides, while numerous administrations progressively perceive the requirement for a crosscutting viewpoint when creating SMEs arrangements and have made strides toward this path, the collaborations, compromises, and complementarities inside and across strategy territories, still lack the interdependency of approaches.

A significant exertion is expected to comprehend the joined impacts of underlying changes on the SME business climate, just as on the job and effect of arrangements focused to SMEs, including to cultivate advancement, support business dynamism, uphold abilities improvement, ease admittance to fund, and empower admittance to public business sectors. Such an exertion ought to consider the likely cooperative energies and compromises across assorted approach zones, including distortionary impacts that might be presented by some arrangement activities; perceive the heterogeneity of the SME populace; and recognize the multidimensional commitments SMEs make to the economy and society. It ought to likewise perceive those nations have various needs for various populaces of firms, contingent upon the particular public settings and conditions.

Extra work is additionally expected to create strategies across various areas and levels of government in a sound and commonly strengthening way. A comprehensive methodology is based on the grounds that the wide umbrella of "SME strategy" incorporates territories that cut across the limits of various services and government organizations, and that require close conference with different partners, for example, the business area, worker's guilds, and monetary foundations, among others.

Consideration likewise should be paid to how arrangements created at the public level can be custom fitted to neighborhood conditions, just as to system conditions also, arrangements that are formed at the provincial or regional level (OECD, 2016e). This is even more earnest to address the difficulties of the expanding combination of worldwide business sectors, the spread of worldwide value chains and the ascent of the computerized economy.

3.8. AN OECD STRATEGY FOR SMES CAN UPHOLD STRATEGY MAKING IN OECD AND NON-OECD NATIONS

An OECD Strategy for SMEs would bring value-added by conveying an exhaustive system, which would distinguish key switches for upgrading SME commitments to sustainable and comprehensive development, give direction to help strategy making in Members and non-Members and measuring sticks for estimating progress. Inside this system, it would likewise address focused on inquiries which have been distinguished as significant for SMEs in a globalized and digitalized economy. Along these lines, an OECD Strategy would uphold nations in building up their own systems customized to explicit public settings and conditions and various kinds of firms. It would likewise expand on the information picked up from encounters with planning and executing SME techniques at the public and supra-pubic levels. It would try to convey a more grounded proof base, by tending to SME information gap. Preliminary work would be attempted in 2017, including an itemized checklist for conversation in the significant

Committees, with the point of dispatching the advancement of the strategy in mid-2018.

The impending OECD Ministerial Gathering on SMEs in mid-2018 likewise offers a significant occasion to propel this work. Progress reports would be set up in 2018 and 2019, with the conveyance of the strategy in 2020.

The OECD is interestingly positioned to attempt this activity. For over 20 years, the organization has been at the bleeding edge of global SME strategy exchange and endeavors to give a proof base for more viable SME arrangements in both OECD and non-OECD members. It can use successfully its exceptional skill in creating, gathering, and understanding business insights across Individuals and non-Members, and expand on the solid establishment of strategy examination created across OECD Boards, treating for example topics such as SME accounting, development, tax collection, digitalization, business internationalization, GVCs, climate, and others, and give a compelling driving force to change. It can likewise utilize its broad organizations, incorporating with partners from the private area, and establish new involvement with creating cross-cutting arrangement systems. This broadness of skill and profundity of investigation offer an interesting occasion to address the complexities of the SME strategy space in various monetary and social settings. By supporting the improvement and execution of successful strategies for SMEs, the OECD can assist with leveling the playing field and empower SMEs to build their commitment to sustainable and comprehensive development.

Chapter 4

SME Sustainability Implementation Case Studies

CONTENTS

There are numerous approaches to decipher the term sustainability, yet whether it implies sustainable execution, corporate citizenship, long-term business viewpoints, or each of the three, it is a developing need for organizations. We addressed numerous little and medium-sized ventures (SMEs) to discover how more modest organizations can execute sustainable strategic policies to assist the climate, their networks, their clients, and their primary concerns.

There can be no uncertainty that sustainability has become a significant need for some organizations across Europe and North America throughout the most recent decade as driving organizations have perceived that fruitful sustainability execution means effective business execution. Be that as it may, sustainability implies far beyond lessening gas outflows or improving energy efficiency. It additionally implies organizations turning out to be more associated with their neighborhood networks and defining long haul objectives that go past the following quarter's monetary outcomes.

In 2010 the AICPA, CIMA, and CICA, which are all individuals from the Prince's Accounting for Sustainability Project (A4S), studied more than 2,000 top pioneers and met sustainability chiefs to decide the condition of corporate sustainability rehearses. Furthermore, the degree of account work contribution in corporate sustainability activities where more than 1,300 of the reactions were from SME organizations (under 1,000 representatives).

The significance of this more extensive, long haul point of view on sustainability is borne out by the contextual analyzes in the accompanying pages incorporated by CICA, CIMA, and AICPA. They show SMEs adopting totally different strategies to similar center issues and feature the discoveries of the 2010 overview, which diagramed the developing accentuation SMEs are setting on each part of sustainability.

The overview showed that 33% of more modest organizations have a characterized sustainability technique, and a further 23% mean to create one in the following 2 years. Their reasons for doing so may change, yet the central message is that sustainability is useful for business. In a few enterprises it bids to clients' evolving interests, it might fortify connections with providers, it can tremendously affect the situating of a brand as a decent corporate resident that works in amicability with nearby networks and the climate, and it can lessen the variable expenses of maintaining a business and, in this manner, drive benefit.

Conversations of these sorts of business advantage have frequently been outlined in the unique situation of huge, global organizations, yet more modest organizations are likewise putting forth incredible attempts to turn out to be more sustainable. Much of the time they can likewise lead the market and become victors of reasonable strategic approaches.

On the off chance that there was any uncertainty about how significant sustainability is to the SMEs, one need just looks at how their clients are changing their mentalities. Progressively, they are taking a look at the environmental performance of organizations from which they purchase, and are frequently attracted to firms that accentuate sustainable strategic approaches.

The contextual investigations that follow show that across various plans of action, there are some general certainties on which organizations unite. Some started with sustainability as the basic rule driving the organization, while others have consistently moved grounded organizations towards a more sustainable model, however all have discovered that underscoring sustainability improves their benefit, produces more noteworthy reliability and responsibility from representatives, and concretes companies with clients and providers.

Their experience shows that any SME, in any industry, can make important strides towards economic strategic policies and rapidly see benefits gather. From its work with bigger companies, the A4S has distinguished 10 components that are fundamental to implanting sustainability inside companies. These contextual investigations enlighten a comparative arrangement of components that are essential for SME organizations to execute economical rehearses in more modest companies.

4.1. KEY ELEMENTS TO IMPLEMENTING SUSTAINABLE BUSINESS PRACTICES IN SMES

4.1.1. Methodology and Arranging

- ***Take an Expansive Perspective on Sustainability*:** Comprehend the key sustainability drivers and opportunities for your company. However, significant as they may be, make sure to look past sustainable issues. Finding imaginative manners by which your organization can be a decent corporate resident to the advantage of representatives, clients, and providers will yield advantages to your business.

- ***Characterize in Detail How Sustainability Affects Your Organization*:** With a reasonable definition to which everybody in the organization can allude and clear achievement quantifies, any endeavors to put resources into sustainability or change strategic policies will zero in on the correct objectives.
- ***Connect All Partners*:** Converse with clients, providers, financial backers, and representatives about sustainability, so their voices can be heard in the discussion, and the system you create will actually want to address the entirety of their necessities. Incorporate them and get as quite a bit of their weight behind the methodology as could really be expected.

4.1.2. Execution and Arrangement

- ***Recollect That You are in Good Company*:** Public, global, and industry-wide activities exist that assist organizations with making it simple to implement changes. Draw in with these companies, tap into their insight and experience. Along these lines, actualizing a sustainability procedure will be speedier and simpler.
- ***Set up Obligation and Convey Generally*:** The conveyance of any technique is more effective if a company realizes who is accountable for it. Have senior administration drive the arrangement, designate sustainability advocate, and impart the significance of sustainability to each level of the organization.
- ***Make it Stride by Step*:** Turning out to be more economical is generally a cycle of advancement, not transformation. By rolling out little improvements now, an organization can influence critical change later on.
- ***Walk the Discussion*:** Any organization can discuss being more sustainable, yet in the event that it does not back up its words with important activities, its cases will rapidly be seen through. Clients and financial investors are astute to greenwashing, so never make the mix-up of considering sustainability to be an advertising exercise.

4.1.3. Execution and Announcing

- **Bind Sustainability to Benefit:** Turning out to be more sustainable regularly implies being more productive. Asset effectiveness, for example, benefits the climate and lessens the expense of maintaining a business. Make the connection between burning through less power, or producing less waste, and improving benefits clear inside your business.

- **Measure, Screen, and Audit:** Following advancement towards the objectives of a sustainability methodology is essential in advocating it to the board, and in completely understanding the business advantage it brings. Grow clear measurements, survey them consistently and whether progress is quick or moderate, continue to set sensible, achievable targets.
- **Put Resources into What is to Come:** Putting resources into sustainability does not generally need colossal capital use. Numerous SMEs say the greatest speculation is the executive's time.

4.2. CRITICAL ROLE OF THE FINANCE FUNCTION

In numerous SMEs, remembering those for the contextual analyzes that follow, the account work assumes a basic part in figuring and actualizing a sustainability procedure. It frequently characterizes the measurements that decide the system's objectives and screens progress. It continuously makes the crucial connection between interest in the technique and the business advantage that accumulates.

Financial experts are at the core of the information gathering measures that empower a company to show how well it is improving its presentation around explicit objectives. Moreover, the money work regularly has solid binds with all divisions inside a business, so it can viably coordinate the endeavors of the organization all in all. Thusly it is frequently the watchman of the sustainability system, yet it can likewise be its originator.

The most convincing message from our conversations with SMEs is that sustainability not just serves unselfish thought processes, but on the other hand, is acceptable business since it can convey higher benefit—both in the short and the long haul. A feasible business is more proficient, more vigorous and has nearer attaches with clients and providers—which is all music to the ears of the CFO, the CEO, investors, and, truth be told, the entirety of the partners in an organization.

Examples of how some SMEs implemented sustainability measures within their organizations are discussed in further sections.

4.3. UKOS

The finance manager of office hardware provider UKOS plc was uncertain about the advantage of accepting sustainability as a stage for the organization's more extensive business procedure, however lower costs and higher deals have made him a proselyte to the green plan.

For some SME's actualizing a sustainability system may appear as though a wellspring of extra expense while amplifying effectiveness is high on the plan. For those that attempt it, notwithstanding, the outcomes are frequently amazing. Sustainability can, indeed, be the way to efficiency and assist a company withholding its expenses down.

"We began our sustainability methodology on the grounds that a couple of years back I joined the Hertford-shire Resource Efficiency Club to check whether there were ways we could save money on assets like gas and power. From that came thoughts regarding corporate social responsibility (CSR) and we understood that we could separate ourselves from our rivals by being all the more harmless to the ecosystem," says Jerry Young, ACMA, Finance Director of writing material and office gear provider UKOS plc and individual from CIMA.

"We created a business frameworks manual that subtleties how every individual and every office ought to take care of their work. This encourages us to oversee workers and measure their presentation. It additionally implied we could apply for ISO 9001 and different accreditations. We understood that a sustainability methodology could make us totally different to our rivals, set aside us cash and give our clients valid justifications to purchase from us." The activity has brought about down to earth steps, for example, the Box4Life project, in which reusable, creased propylene boxes supplant expendable cardboard boxes. UKOS recently conveyed around 70,000 cardboard boxes each year, however has made significant investment funds on bundling materials.

"We set this up with clients that need it, gathering the purges when we convey every day. Clients like it since it credits their own environment systems. We additionally took a look at our conveyance courses. The business standard is 24-hour conveyance, yet for certain clients we can change this to ordinary conveyances three times each week. A few clients have changed their purchasing behaviors to accommodate our conveyance plan," says Young.

"We likewise took a look at our products. In our business there is a great deal of paper, so we took a look at what makes harmless to the ecosystem paper. We found an incredible support capable paper, yet discovered that it was delivered from Australia, which implied we did not pick it. We currently have a 'green' index of products."

UKOS plc additionally gathers recyclable waste—including cardboard, printer toners and plastics—from certain clients, as opposed to returning lorries void to the terminal after a conveyance. This costs the organization practically nothing, produces a modest quantity of income from selling the material and ties clients into the administrations given by UKOS.

Straightforward, shrewd thoughts like this are immensely affecting the organization. Among the tangible aftereffects of its sustainable technique are reserve funds on energy. UKOS has reduced its energy expenses by a normal of 5% year-on-year throughout the previous 4 years, and has decreased its utilization of cardboard boxes—which represent around 0.5% of deals—by 65%.

4.3.1. The Role of Finance

Estimating these effectiveness gains is crucial to demonstrating the estimation of any sustainability methodology and money assumes a critical part in social affair the applicable information and conveying the outcomes to the remainder of the company. Energy charts are used every month to show the effect of the sustainability technique, and there is a month-to-month audit of the measure of bundling materials utilized.

Close by the auditing cycle, account likewise has a focal part in setting key goals in regions, for example, eco-friendliness. With the correct measurements set up the advantages of the strategy become obvious, which goes far to advocating the underlying venture that is required.

"There is some speculation to be made, obviously, yet it is generally a venture of time instead of cash. The venture is driven by finance, while the administrator handles the advancement of the sustainability plan to clients and staff. The money division is vital. It delivers the estimations and results, and we have the order to do it consistently," stresses Young.

"You need to make it genuine, set targets, and let individuals see the outcomes. We have a green boss—generally somebody genuinely junior—who is responsible for basic things like ensuring the lights are killed. Furthermore, we permit our representatives to concoct smart thoughts."

An illustration of worker contribution to sustainability is the propensity the organization's drivers have created of estimating the miles per liter they accomplish on every conveyance run. They contend to be the most productive. Getting to the stage where sustainability is important for the day-by-day schedule of each worker requires consistency and responsibility at each level, however particularly among ranking directors.

"You need to make it genuine, set targets, and let individuals see the outcomes."

"The thought is not difficult to offer to staff on the off chance that you look after it. You should do this forever. The greatest test was to get it going and get the entirety of the division heads to compose the business frameworks manual. I expected to persuade them regarding the positives that would come toward the finish of the interaction," says Young.

"The business frameworks manual constrained us to take a look at all the pieces of our business. I went into the asset efficiency club as a doubter, yet now I am a believer. Our sustainability technique is setting aside us cash, expanding deals, and improving benefits, which we would not have predicted."

- Key Learning Points:
  - Get engaged with local area or industry activities to launch a sustainability drive.
  - Codify commonsense measures for sustainability in a record that everybody in the company can get to and comprehend, as UKOS plc's business frameworks manual.
  - Put set up measurements to gauge the presentation of workers and the organization overall on sustainability.
  - Look for ways by which sustainability can decrease costs, instead of expanding costs.
  - Work with your clients to discovers lines of work by which purchasing behaviors and supply practices can turn out to be more asset proficient.
  - Invest time at the board level and get their approval and commitment to lead on support capacity.
  - Build a feasible methodology that has a drawn-out point of view.
  - Set clear, practical targets and offer data about advancement all through the company.
  - Appoint 'green bosses' to install sustainability in the company.

4.3.2. About UKOS

From its development in 2000 UKOS has set up itself as an organization that stands separated from its rivals with regards to client support, value, and dependability. Offering office writing material and business supplies from the United Kingdom UKOS was granted first spot by The Sunday Times Best Green Companies a year ago, and included in a dedicated supplement, distributed in May 2010.

4.3.3. About Jerry Young, ACMA, Finance Director, UKOS

Jerry was an establishing individual from UKOS in 2000 and is liable for all money, legitimate, organization secretarial issue and furthermore HR obligations. Before UKOS, Jerry stood firm on various senior monetary footholds inside the workplace products industry, getting done with being the Finance Director of Guilbert UK. Jerry is a certified Chartered Management Accountant and an individual from CIMA.

4.4. ROCKY MOUNTAIN FLATBREAD

4.4.1. Little Organizations Can Start Large Change

New organizations that are established on sustainability as the crucial core value that drives each part of their business have the ability to begin an interaction that can change whole ventures.

Private companies have extraordinary force. Some get the opportunity to construct a business without any preparation on the foundation of sustainability. Others have more spryness than huge multinationals to roll out significant improvement and show the advantages that can build from support capable strategic approaches.

"Private companies are driving the route as far as molding how business will be later on," says Suzanne Fielden, fellow benefactor of Rocky Mountain Flatbread.

Established 7 years prior in Vancouver, Canada, Rocky Mountain Flatbread is a brand that contains a pizza café, a discount business, a versatile cook, and an educational society. Established by Fielden and her significant other, who had both been fruitful as initiative and the board specialists in the UK managing change and authority the executives, the organization exemplifies their insight about coordinating social and sustainable plans into corporate technique.

The organization exists not exclusively to produce benefit, yet additionally to make a positive change on the planet by acting locally to address the worldwide issue of sustainability.

"In the UK, we acquainted sustainability with a ton of organizations and distinguished the business opportunities that it introduced. We worked in schools, as well, on tasks like changing business waste into usable, value added products. One compound side-effect is as yet used to de-ice planes at Bristol Airport," says Fielden.

"At the point when it came to making a brand, we needed it to be founded on our support capable standards. We picked the pizza business since it is regularly done seriously. We did a great deal of examination and took a look at many plans of action, and we incorporated our experiences, which is the reason we have an instructive society working with nearby schools just as an eatery."

To endure, any café needs great food and incredible help, so the organization got a Red Seal cook, Oliver Zulauf, as an accomplice to make and normalize the menu and set high assistance guidelines to guarantee that the business had a financially practical stage. From that point, the objective was to incorporate manageable practices into all aspects of the plan of action. It made a zero-waste menu, for instance, and each dinner served is carbon nonpartisan as far as possible its outflows and purchases carbon credits to counterbalance what remains.

It focuses on steady improvement to its products, however has a basic way to deal with measurements. Prime supporter Dominic Fielden takes care of the money capacity, and his dad David, a Chartered Accountant who has worked for any semblance of American Express, 3i and SG Warbug, sits on the board to give exhortation on money and system.

The organization tracks its carbon impression and puts forth a cognizant attempt to diminish it consistently, and it keeps a nearby watch on the quantity of local area projects with which it draws in, meaning to expand this number each year.

4.4.2. Sustainability as a State of Contrast

"Individuals are searching for importance, for organizations that are accomplishing something positive. Sustainability separates us. We utilize something like 90% neighborhood produce, including vegetables from the schools where we show kids how to develop food. This year we turned into the primary organization to change to biogas, which is caught by the neighborhood sewage plant and put into the gas framework. We use it to fire the entirety of our broilers. We have likewise arrived at 100% treating the soil of all our food," says Fielden.

"Our methodology additionally establishes a positive workplace. We save individuals for quite a long time in an industry that is famous for high staff turnover. The standards of the organization make individuals pleased to work here."

"Individuals are searching for significance, for organizations that are accomplishing something positive. Sustainability separates us."

One of the key apparatuses the organization has used to coordinate economical practices is the frameworks thinking approach created by Gunter Pauli, originator, and overseer of Zero Emissions Research and Initiatives. Among the numerous ramifications of this way to deal with business is groups of organizations or enterprises cooperating, which is incompletely why Rocky Mountain Flatbread stresses systems administration and commitment with nearby companies, for example, Vancouver Aquarium's Ocean Wise program on support capable fish, the green table network, and instructive company Sustainable Step.

"We are very much organized. Discover who can help you locally. In the event that you need to change an industry and roll out sure improvement, you need the ethos that permits you to roll out little improvements. Local area is vital to us, which is the reason we go into schools and show kids developing food and making sound bites. We talk with metropolitan grounds-keepers and we store local area projects. We interface with anything that advances food security and sustainability," clarifies Fielden.

The inspiration is mostly the charitable craving to be a decent corporate resident and have an effect on the world, however this is not to the detriment of long-haul commercial achievement. The organization has prevailing with regards to making a benefit, some of which is put towards local area projects. Clients' perspectives are changing, and they are progressively searching for organizations that are environmentally and socially mindful.

"In the event that you need to change an industry and roll out certain improvement, you need the ethos that permits you to roll out little improvements."

"Sustainability and productivity are portions of a similar methodology. Individuals are less Toler insect of organizations that are barely out to amplify benefit. They are progressively searching for organizations that need to make the planet a superior spot. That is a positive advance, as it powers huge organizations to take a look at their environment strategies and local area projects," trusts Fielden.

"Sustainability and benefit are portions of a similar methodology."

"Regardless of whether you cannot siphon billions of dollars into sustainability, do what you can do. Zero in on it now, regardless of whether the financial circumstance is troublesome. Try not to put it off till later. Each little advance considers long as it is a positive development. Try not to surrender to present moment pressure to expand investor interest, take a look at the higher perspective. Having assorted objectives makes an organization vigorous. Discover the spirit of your organization."

- Key Learning Points:
  - Identify how all that you utilize or make in your business, even waste, may be transformed into a value-added product;
  - Consider how feasible strategic policies can expand efficiency, yet additionally separate your organization from its rivals;
  - Network with neighborhood companies that share feasible objectives to pool information and co-ordinate exertion;
  - Recognize the force of little upgrades in sustainability and how they accumulate over the long haul to make significant change;
  - Believe that private ventures have the ability to set the plan for sustainability and change the conduct of huge organizations and entire businesses;
  - Consider how reasonable standards can propel your labor force and do right by them to work for your organization.

4.4.3. About Rocky Mountain Flatbread

More than 7 years prior, Dominic and Suzanne Fielden conceptualized how they could make a business from values they were enthusiastic about—food, family, local area, and nature. The end was pizza pie! Pizza was a food that families ate routinely yet had gained notoriety for utilizing inferior quality fixings with minimal dietary benefit—an ideal food to rehash. The entryways of their first café opened in Canmore, Alberta, and they got rave surveys for their healthy pizza from pundits and clients. Simultaneously

Suzanne and Dominic dispatched a progression of imaginative school projects to help youth in being mindful residents and business visionaries—understudies mastered significant fundamental abilities including how to develop their own food, lessen their carbon impression and make heavenly and nutritious dinners and tidbits. The most recent couple of years have seen two carbon impartial cafés; a pizza discount business which disseminates to more than 200 wellbeing stores and supermarkets all through Western Canada; a general public which has permitted more than 2,000 understudies to take part in their school ventures, and they have joined an organization of like-minded individuals supporting the cultivating and conveyance of neighborhood sustainable food sources.

4.4.4. About the Partners of Rocky Mountain Flatbread

Dominic Fielden, Co-Founder, is responsible for money in the organization and his dad, David Fielden, is a Non-Executive Chairman and Chartered Accountant. Suzanne Fielden, Co-Founder, has both High National Diploma qualifications in Business Studies and an Honors Degree in Business Studies and Anthropology from Oxford Brookes University, Oxford.

Accomplice culinary expert Oliver Zulauf is a red seal cook from Switzerland. He built up our menu, guaranteeing it was delectable, and he is likewise splendid at systemizing all the plans so we can make predictable products and stay inside our food and work costs.

4.5. ENVIRONMENT FIBERS, INC.

4.5.1. Based on the Bedrock of Sustainability

For the individuals who accept sustainability is another idea in business, the time has come to reconsider. Some fruitful organizations have been established on biologically solid standards for quite a long time, and their experience holds significant exercises about the developing significance of sustainability as a fundamental element of good business.

During this previous decade there has been an emotional push to focus on economic practices across all enterprises. There are numerous instances of organizations—from huge multinationals to little, family-possessed organizations—that have gained extraordinary ground in embracing action plans that are kinder to the climate, better for representatives and more incorporated inside networks in which they work.

At times, standards of environmentally solid and dependable business have been an organization's establishment from which it characterizes their products. One model is Ecological Fibers, Inc., established in Massachusetts in 1972 as a materials treatment company. In 1979, it gained a covering office in Rhode Island, which was the spring-board for its venture into the worldwide commercial center, and it has since become a main maker of extravagance covered covers for books, writing material, security reports, and extravagance bundling. Under their business trademark Rainbow®, they give environmentally stable covers that are made regarding the climate, yet additionally focusing on the prosperity of its labor force.

"At the point when our proprietor bought the RI office each organization in this industry was utilizing solvents to cover paper. They were hurtful to the climate and to workers and perhaps the end clients. Sustainable built up a water-based covering arrangement that utilizes no unsafe segments. He was keener on ensuring the climate and his workers than in setting aside cash. The push of the organization is similar now—we need to be sustainably stable," says Eric Buchholz, CPA, CFO of Environment Fibers.

"The organization was comparatively radical—a pioneer in the business. It did not publicize its sustainable qualifications, it just did it on the grounds that the proprietor thought it was the best thing, yet now those issues have gone to the cutting edge. A portion of our products are produced using 100% post-consumer waste (PCW), which a portion of our clients needed yet couldn't discover," he adds.

"Environmental Fibers, Inc. is a world chief in changing over paper products. Our elite covering measure utilizes just 100% watery, self-cross-connecting, pigmented acrylic polymers. EFI's solid obligation to earth mindful assembling processes reject the utilization of solvents, perilous air poisons, or unpredictable organics, while simultaneously keeping up the great guidelines and qualification for use necessities of our clients. These endeavors have been perceived and granted by the US Environmental Protection Agency and EFI will keep on giving just Environmentally Sound Cover Solutions at the most serious cost."

"The organization was relatively revolutionary—a pioneer in the business. It didn't promote its sustainable certifications, it just did it in light of the fact that the proprietor thought it was the best activity, however now those issues have gone to the bleeding edge."

"It costs more to do what we do, the way we do it. It requires some investment and exertion to make what we make. However, the pattern is for sustainability, especially sustainable issues, to be a greater issue for our clients. They may have an inward push on sustainable issues, and there have been a ton of requests as of late about what amount of reused paper we use and about the absence of solvents in our cycle. We have numerous new clients that can't discover what they are searching for elsewhere," clarifies Buchholz.

4.5.2. Account and Sustainability

The part of the management office in driving the organization's biological plan of action, just as its benefit, is basic. Yet, in contrast to numerous different organizations, management is not fundamentally worried about following measurements that outline enhancements in effectiveness or progress towards sustainability objectives, yet with guaranteeing that current systems are clung to.

One of its primary errands is to guarantee that the chain of guardianship is not broken between requesting paper and accepting it. This guarantees that the production network meets the exacting sustainability models that Environment Fibers has set down, and is accomplished through the Forestry Stewardship Council's chain of care affirmation, which tracks material from the woodland to the customer. Management additionally guarantees that, where conceivable, waste returns to merchants for reusing, or is discarded in a way that is thoughtful to the climate.

"We utilize numerous material substrates; however our greatest products utilize two unique kinds of paper. The first is latex-based, the other is Kraft-based. Our loss from Kraft paper is 100% reused into new runs. The latex paper was a test, yet now we have partnered with an organization that takes that paper and uses it as biomass fuel," says Buchholz.

"The part of management is vital in guaranteeing that the organization keeps up its biologically stable tasks. However, all offices cooperate towards the objective of making a harmless to the ecosystem product."

The biological rule that supports the organization's plan of action may not mean each business, but rather Environment Fibers additionally takes a look at issues that do identify with any organization, including energy efficiency. It has, for example, changed to energy-efficient lights and introduced movement sensors so that lights sustainably go off in regions where there is no development. It has supplanted gas stoves used to fix the tone on to the paper with more productive infra-red broilers. The heater has been changed from oil to gas, which is cleaner and more productive, and has altogether cut the organization's energy bill. Additionally, with the assistance of outer specialists, it has discovered approaches to purchase gas at better rates and from 'greener' providers. They additionally have exploited innovative work tax breaks with the entirety of the R&D they do to ensure their products are biologically stable.

"The job of money is vital in guaranteeing that the organization keeps up its biologically solid tasks. Be that as it may, all divisions cooperate towards the objective of making a harmless product to the ecosystem."

Biological Fibers has taken a look at sustainability integrating it within its structures and has demonstrated what started as a moral guideline has additionally been sound marketing prudence. It has shown that putting sustainable issues initially is not just useful for the climate, yet additionally useful for business.

"Our biological arrangement was accomplished for its own reasons, however it wins clients and produce deals, so it drives benefits," says Buchholz. "Sustainability plagues all that we do."

- Key Learning Points:
  - Keep in sync with the sustainable activities that your clients and additionally providers may attempt.
  - Look at innovative understandings of the term 'reusing,' including the utilization of material as a wellspring of biomass fuel.
  - Call in outside experts to give a target see on how your organization can receive more manageable practices.
  - Look at the feasible certifications of energy providers and pick one that has better sustainable oversight.
  - Have the fortitude to make feasible standards the foundation of your business.

4.5.3. About Environment Fibers

Environment Fibers, Inc. was established in Lancaster, Massachusetts, in 1972 as a materials merchant to the book business. Through its 1979 obtaining of the Rhode Island coating office, Environment has ventured into a worldwide, head maker of extravagance covered covers to the book, writing material, security archive and extravagance bundling businesses. Under the trademark Rainbow®, we offer the biggest grouping of Environmentally Sound Cover Solutions and Bindery Supplies.

4.5.4. About Eric Buchholz, CPA, CFO, Environment Fibers, Inc.

Eric Buchholz is the CFO of Environment Fibers. Before this, he was the Corporate Con-trawler at Phoenix Media Communications Group somewhere in the range of 2003 and 2005. Buchholz moved on from Northeastern University in 1992 and is a certified CPA.

4.6. ARTOPEX

4.6.1. Paying Attention to the Call of Clients

At the point when an industry puts forth a deliberate attempt to improve sustainable strategic approaches, it is frequently in light of the changing requests of clients. At the point when such a move happens, no business can bear to be abandoned.

Sustainability is progressively a factor in clients' buying choices, regardless of whether those clients are end clients, vendors or different organizations contracting administrations. This pattern is simply prone to reinforce, so when contenders take a look at sustainable issues and CSR to fulfill clients, there is no an ideal opportunity to lose.

One organization that has reacted rapidly to the structure force behind support capacity is Canadian organization Artopex, which has been a supplier of excellent office furniture for more than 30 years and is reliably evaluated as one of the nation's best-man-matured companies.

"On the off chance that we need to work together, we should be engaged with all parts of sustainability. The huge producers in our industry in North America are all around connected with support capacity, and there is pressure from the market to be more dynamic. There is pressure from our clients, driven by the engineers and planners who impact the choices our clients make," says Jean Barbeau, a product expert at Artopex, who is responsible for the organization's sustainability activity.

In 2008, Artopex chose to focus on sustainability, starting with an arrangement to diminish its carbon impression. It started by taking a look at the business norms for discharges in the production of office furniture, however before long started to see sustainability in a lot more extensive setting.

"On the off chance that we need to work together, we should be associated with all parts of sustainability."

"We recruited a specialist to assist us with understanding what sustainability was. At that point, we required a year to devise our arrangement, which was dispatched in fall 2009, to set up measures to follow markers like energy and water use. Presently, we are going to compose our first sustainability report," remarks Barbeau.

"Up until now, we have incorporated sustainability into our business introductions and preparing materials, as schooling is a significant piece of our methodology. We have opened communications with the entirety of our partners, including the vendors that are our clients and furthermore our providers, with which we can go about as an accomplice in testing new materials or better approaches to move merchandise. For example, we met with transport organizations and said that we needed enhancements for emanations, and they showed us their thoughts. Those conversations, and the sharing of data, are large changes," he adds.

The task has brought about changes in product plan, selection of materials, transport, and coordination to lessen emanations and improve productivity. Having acted rapidly on environmental issues, one of the vital exercises to rise out of the commitment of an outer specialist is that a manageable business should likewise appear to be a decent manager and a decent corporate resident.

4.6.2. Social Inclusion

"Other significant fixings are sponsorship and social inclusion. We turned out to be touchier to those things. We were at that point doing extraordinary things for the nearby local area; however, we began to nail it down and center around it more. We were supporting clinics and companies in medical services, like hospices for the critically ill, so we settled on a choice to intentionally zero in on wellbeing," says Barbeau.

"We turned out to be more aware of the effect of the cash we put resources into the local area and that makes energy. Individuals are certain about it. The more we share, the better we become," he adds.

The organization's keener spotlight on sustainability is kept up through the administration board, which unites 12 senior individuals in the company. They address various features of the organization, including HR, promoting, and manufacturing. Money is addressed on the board of trustees by the organization's leader, who works with the VP of Production to characterize and follow the fitting measurements to guarantee Artopex is improving its environment and practical accreditations.

Among the main measurements are energy and water use, paper utilization, waste generation and the utilization of reused materials.

"We turned out to be more aware of the effect of the cash we put resources into the local area and that makes energy. Individuals are extremely certain about it. The more we share, the better we become."

Unmistakably, a portion of these estimates target sustainable objectives, for example, emanations reduction, however they likewise center around human components. The prosperity of the labor force, and the local area wherein it works, are fundamental to the organization's arrangement.

To some extent, the measurements are characterized by the prerequisites for ISO 14001 accreditation, which pays specific concentration to reusing and waste. However, there is unmistakably a more extensive core interest.

Artopex is mostly going to outer experts to participate in preparing from the base up to teach the labor force in sustainable strategic policies and CSR.

Up until this point, the venture Artopex has made has fundamentally been as senior management time, despite the fact that there have been some particular monetary speculations. It has, for example, changed all lights to more energy-efficient options, which has brought about a 16% saving money on energy use.

"There is some venture of cash, and a great deal of speculation of time for research and characterizing projects. In any case, the reserve funds take care of the entirety of this speculation," notes Barbeau.

The core value of the organization's sustainability drive is business advantage. "One of our principle explanations in our sustainability plan is tied in with being a 'human' company that considers its representatives and about the local area. The other is ecotechnology. We have put more than $7 million in new, more proficient creation gear over the most recent 3 years. The intention was to be more profitable and serious against imports from Asia, however it likewise causes us to be more sustainable. It was a financial choice that assists with sustainability," comments Barbeau.

"There is some speculation of cash, and a ton of venture of time for researches and characterizing projects. Be that as it may, the reserve funds take care of the entirety of this venture."

"We have incorporated sustainability into our everyday choices. Now what we do on sustainability is not just about the climate and social duty, yet in addition about benefit.

- Key Learning Points:
  - Engage outside aptitude to guarantee the organization considers each part of sustainability, not simply environment issues;
  - Open conversations with all partners, including clients and providers;
  - Be willing to impart data to partners to promote innovative solutions to decrease discharges and increment effectiveness;
  - Build on the exercises in which your organization is now elaborate that can have more impact in the field of sustainability;
  - Invest time and capital in innovation and cycles that convey both business advantage and sustainability gains.

4.6.3. About Artopex

Artopex has gone through more than 30 years building quality office furniture in Quebec and building strong connections all over North America.

Artopex Inc. is an exclusive partnership with its base camp in Granby, Quebec. The organization is involved four plants adding up to more than 500,000 square feet of production limit, upheld by more than 400 representatives, with display areas in Montreal, Toronto, and Calgary and a North American dissemination organization.

4.6.4. About Jean Barbeau, Product Trained Professional, Artopex

Jean Barbeau experienced childhood in the Montreal district in Quebec (Canada). Propelled by the imaginative part of engineering, he settled on furniture configuration, pulled in by the scale and the idea of the product to reexamine. He moved on from L'ecole du Meuble et du Bois Ouvre (school of furniture and lumber wood) of Victoriaville in the furniture configuration program in 1986.

He went through the initial 10 years of his profession functioning as a furniture originator of dental cabinetry and office furniture for various makers, continually searching for creative plan. He turned into an expert individual from the Association of Canadian Industrial Designers (ACID) just as the Association of Quebec Industrial Designers (ADIQ).

At that point an instructor, he functioned as an advisor in product plan for a very long time prior to joining Artopex, a Canadian maker of office furniture.As a product application expert at Artopex, he utilizes his innovative abilities to create ideal application arrangements in the workplace climate with salesmen, planners, and inside architects just as end clients.

Tested by the sustainable and social issues of the new economy, he was as of late appointed by Daniel Pelletier, President of Artopex, to be accountable for the coordination of sustainability in the business technique in a way that would mirror the special estimations of the organization.

4.7. BILLINGTON STRUCTURES LTD.

4.7.1. The Establishments of Good Business

The construction business is as a rule firmly examined considering sustainability and providers have realized that the correct accreditation can be an approach to win more business. However, to be a business advantage, it should be major to the plan of action, not an additional extra.

Any great business reacts to the necessities of its clients, and in the construction business, that implies committing to strict environment performance requirements. Fulfilling characterized guidelines for sustainability and accomplishing suitable accreditation.

"We got into sustainability on the grounds that the establishing CEO of our previous parent organization was energetic for all auxiliaries to go down the course of the ISO 14001 environmental administration framework standard. In this way, the auxiliaries were advised they needed to do it, yet did as such with energy for business reasons," says Peter Hart, ACMA, Financial Director, Billington Structures Ltd. furthermore, a CIMA part.

Billington Structures makes underlying steel for the construction business—an area that is zeroing in like never before on productivity, cost-cutting, and feasible business practices. The organization's customers are searching for capable providers, and a straightforward method to pass judgment on them is to take a look at the environment, wellbeing, and security and CSR accreditations they have accomplished.

"We comprehend that sustainability gives us a business advantage on the off chance that we are early adopters of ISO 9001, which we were the first in the business to get, and ISO 14001. It has an exceptionally certain appeal to customers," says Hart.

Billington likewise chose to think about its business in contrast to the sustainability contract spread out by the British Constructional Steelwork Company Ltd. (BCSA), which suggests the ISO guidelines that the organization has accomplished. It additionally requires an obligatory, bar listed sustainability strategy; a program of company with the nearby local area on social issues; checking of progress towards better sustainability with explicit management focuses on; an organized program for preparing, improvement, and correspondence; a distributed moral exchanging strategy; and an arrangement to oversee energy and vehicle fuel use.

"We comprehend that sustainability gives us a business advantage."

"We received this sanction early and experienced the review cycle, which brought about us getting gold accreditation. As far as we might be concerned, it was not really about money saving advantages, despite the fact that there are a few. Crude material steel is our greatest expense factor—around 40% of the expense base—and our cycles do not create a lot of waste. There are issues of energy use and transport, yet we discovered we had genuinely no place for cost investment funds in those regions. "It was more about the allure of sustainability to our clients and winning new business," clarifies Hart.

"It was more about the allure of sustainability to our clients also, winning new business."

"Our customers need us to have ISO 9001, ISO 14001 and the Investors in People accreditation. We likewise have ISO 18001 wellbeing and security accreditation. The BCSA sanction incorporates these rules, as well. We needed to roll out humble improvements to our business to get the highest quality level. We needed to take a look at our arrangements and roll out some minor improvements in practice. The most significant of those was tied in with guaranteeing that our providers consider environmental issue."

4.7.2. Sustainability Revealing

In embracing the norms set down in the sanction, Billington needed to be a decent corporate resident and fabricate the certainty of customers. To do as such, it needs to screen its performance and outline its encouraging towards manageable objectives. It has an environment strategy as a component of

ISO 14001, and consistently the organization does a yearly sustainability report.

A few targets are unmistakable, for example, the decrease in utilization of materials like shot impact, which is utilized to get ready steel. Different targets cannot be followed exact measurements, however are regardless critical to either improving sustainability or appearing to clients that feasible issues are central to the business. One model is Billington's transition to modernize its preparation records.

This progression is significant in light of the fact that the organization utilizes numerous individuals past its everyday labor force for on location tasks and these should be enough qualified. Tracking preparing and capabilities in automated structure saves money on paper and printing, yet in addition makes it simpler and faster to check and convey the pertinent data to customers.

"We need to show our customers those individuals we utilize have the correct capabilities. We should show them that we are a mindful provider. All the more comprehensively, we additionally need to guarantee we are improving the abilities inside the business. The entirety of this is required from the point of view of the business, yet additionally has a CSR point," comments Hart.

Billington's way to deal with sustainability is formalized. For example, it utilizes an environment director to supervise the specific components of its sustainability procedure. The organization has additionally put forth attempts to guarantee that the message about sustainability penetrates the whole business. The contribution of the account work has been central to its system from the beginning however, generally due to Hart's own commitment to sustainability.

"Sustainability is about the drawn-out strength of the business. It is about CSR and an organization's position locally. At that point, there are the environmental issues, such as reusing, which for us for the most part implies scrap the executives, for which we previously had measures set up for business reasons. A spotless workspace implies better wellbeing and security and more prominent productivity. What we needed to do was pull our support capacity system and our approaches together," says Hart.

"Sustainability is about the drawn-out strength of the business. It is about CSR and an organization's spot locally."

"I wear the sustainability identification inside the organization; however, it could similarly stay here in account or with creation, faculty or some other division. Sustainability is not something that is laid on top of the business. It does not need to be a different issue. It is simply essential for being a decent business."

- Key Learning Points:
  - Look at industry-wide activities to expand on the information on different organizations and industry affiliations;
  - Map official accreditation for sustainable administration and feasible cycle quality to your own business measures;
  - Consider sustainability inside your own organization, however across your organization of providers;
  - View sustainability in a more extensive setting, not simply regarding sustainable issues;
  - Clearly characterize who has obligation regarding sustainability inside the company;
  - Remember that sustainability ought to be a center component in being a decent business, not only an extra.

4.7.3. About Billington Structures Limited

Billington Structures Limited has been planning, manufacturing, and raising underlying steelwork for the construction business since 1947. Their accomplished labor force can handle projects from basic structure casings to the most perplexing constructions more than 6,000 tons. With plants in Barnsley and Bristol, the organization has the ability to handle 25,000 tons of steel for every annum and can support customers all through the UK.

4.7.4. About Peter Hart, ACMA, Finance Director

Peter, an individual from the Chartered Institute of Management Accountants, has 19 years' experience with Billington and had recently worked in the mining apparatus and aviation ventures. He is additionally Chairman of the Trustees of Dosco Overseas Engineering Ltd. Annuity Scheme and an individual from the BCSA Sustainability Working Group.

4.8. CIRTRONICS

4.8.1. Making the Best Choice

More modest organizations can assume a major part in supporting nearby networks through volunteering and donations. Such exercises may make representatives glad to work for the organization, and give the business a superior status locally or among providers and clients. For a few, these advantages are not significant in light of the fact that sustainability is just about making the best choice. At the point when organizations plunk down to work out the business advantage of turning out to be more sustainable, there is regularly an ¨aha second¨ when they understand that they can make significant cost reductions from decreasing their energy utilization, for example, or reinforce their companies with clients or providers. For different organizations, the advantages of sustainable business standards are so theoretical they are practically difficult to quantify. For them, sustainability is tied in with confiding in standards like beneficent giving, contacting the neighborhood local area through collaboration projects and giving workers responsibility for volunteering.

"More modest organizations regularly give more than large organizations. Their possession is nearby, so they give additional time and cash to neighborhood local researches. That forms the local relationship strong, which is vital. There is a constructive outcome on the organization and its workers of building more grounded, better networks, yet we do not have to see a substantial return. We simply need to realize that we are doing acceptable," says George Mandragoras, an accomplished public bookkeeper who is currently CFO of agreement producing organization Cirtronics.

Situated in Milford, New Hampshire, Cirtronics is associated with prototyping, PCB get together, box-assemble, test, and satisfaction administrations for different cutting-edge areas. The focal point of its activities is not exceptional, however its way to deal with business is altogether different to that of its rivals. It frames close relationships with its clients, also the value framework that is center to the organization sees workers' commitment to the business dependent on their individual qualities as opposed to customary occupation jobs, regularly shaping cross-utilitarian groups to best address their clients' issues.

The organization's way to deal with promoting the best from its labor force mirrors its attention on drawing in representatives in the business. It has, for example, changed 39% of the organization since 2002 into an employee stock ownership plan (ESOP) program, in this manner making the representatives the proprietors of the business. Proprietor and president Gerard Ferlin's accepting this choice as a component of her conviction that the strength of the organization is in its kin, their responsibility, feeling of local area, and want to serve and constantly improve.

"It depends on the guideline of 'give a man a fish and you feed him for a day, show him how to fish and you feed him for a lifetime.' In an entrepreneur society, it is not about the fish, but more about who claims the boat—that is the manner by which abundance is made," says Mandragoras.

This feeling of local area, and of the job of the organization as a corporate resident, characterizes the sustainable exercises wherein Cirtronics is included—in particular corporate giving, worker volunteerism and environment stewardship.

"We have a ton of environment endeavors, like reusing, improving our bundling and limiting our energy use, however sustainability is a lot more extensive than that. As far as we might be concerned, it is an all-encompassing methodology. We give individuals downtime to do chipping in, regardless of whether that is going on a field outing with their youngster's school or clearing garbage from the parkway. We will likely give 10% of our benefits as beneficent commitments, which is the thing that is permitted under US charge law. A few years we hit that target; however, it depends on what the organization can manage," says Mandragoras.

"We have a ton of sustainable endeavors, like reusing, improving our bundling and limiting our energy use, however sustainability is a lot more extensive than that. As far as we might be concerned, it is a comprehensive methodology."

"We would prefer not to pick an excessive number of leaves from the cash tree, so we should watch out for keeping up benefit and putting resources into the organization. We do what we can while ensuring that everything is in synchronize as long as possible. Over the long haul, everything returns to you," he adds.

With regards to concluding how to help the nearby local area through gifts of time, assets, or space, there is an unmistakable spotlight on improving the existences of youngsters. The designation of assets is chosen by the Cirtronics Community Out-Reach Program (CCORP) board, which has a pivoting enrollment of representatives.

"Neither I, nor the proprietor, have at any point sat on the CCORP council. It is comprised of people on the assembling floor. It's anything but a PR practice run by senior administration. Our workers realize their profit are going to their cohorts through the corporate giving cycle," clarifies Mandragoras.

Notwithstanding his experience as a bookkeeper and his job as CFO, Mandragouras isn't centered around estimating the compensation from the organization's endeavors to be a reasonable business. While he assumes a part in deciding how much the organization's corporate giving can add up to every year, he doesn't choose where it goes. Nor does he have set up an exact arrangement of measurements to quantify the advantage that the organization gets from such exercises.

"Magnanimous giving of benefits influences the estimation of the organization and its offers, and a few people inquire as to why we don't put that cash into the organization. In any case, working here isn't tied in with seeking after the 'omnipotent buck.' We can put resources into the organization and provide for the neighborhood local area. The organization feels firmly about it; however, we do not know how the advantage returns to us. We should essentially believe that it does," comments Mandragoras.

"We draw in with sustainability paying little mind to the advantages. There is an advantage, however we cannot quantify it. We realize that supporting nearby researches benefits our workers, their families, and cohorts, and constructs more grounded networks. Do you need substantial proof to realize that what you are doing is having a constructive outcome? We know the expense; however, we cannot quantify the monetary advantages, however it may move different organizations or help nearby youngsters. Regardless, it is the perfect activity."

- Key Learning Points:
  - Engage representatives by giving them responsibility for organization and an immediate job in characterizing sustainable exercises like altruistic giving;
  - Keep a drawn-out viewpoint on the harmony among sustainability and productivity;
  - Trust that sustainable strategic policies are carrying advantage to the organization, regardless of whether those advantages are theoretical and difficult to gauge.

4.8.2. About Cirtronics

Cirtronics was brought into the world in 1979 with the vision that an organization can stretch out past itself to really serve its clients, representatives, and providers, just as the climate and the local area. Cirtronics Corporation is certainly not a regular agreement producer. The establishment of the organization is based on its value framework. Representatives add to the company dependent on their individual qualities versus conventional occupation jobs. Cirtronics is a privately held organization, which permits them to oversee activities and settle on choices to the greatest advantage of their clients versus outside investors and Wall Street.

4.8.3. About George Mandragouras, CFO Cirtronics

George has been employees at Cirtronics for a very long time as the Chief Financial Officer. He got a BA in Business Finance at UMass Amherst and went through 13 years out in the open bookkeeping preceding joining the organization.

George works with numerous companies inside and outside of Cirtronics. He is presently the Treasurer for the Boys and Girls Club and is an establishing individual from the NHBSR (New Hampshire Businesses for Social Responsibility).

4.9. RAINBOW NIGHTFREIGHT LTD.

4.9.1. Productivity First

It has become all the more generally comprehended that focusing on economic aspects brings productivity gains for most organizations. A few organizations, nonetheless, have demonstrated that the rationale of that condition can be turned around and that by expanding effectiveness a business performs better regarding sustainability.

In a business that must choose the option to make fossil fuel byproducts by consuming fuel and which conveys merchandise that fundamentally require bundling materials, it might appear to be that any endeavors to improve CSR—the establishment of economical business—may have restricted impact on sustainable issues. However, one organization has shown that its plan of action is proof that sustainable execution can be superior to the business-standard.

Rainbow Nightfreight, the coordination and inventory network activity of the WA Rainbow Group, works a multi-client Nightfreight administration that limits utilization of vehicles and distance of movement on outbound and inbound routes. Contrasted with the fleet activities of its bigger rivals, this offers an affordable option, since it can take loads from various clients on each leg of each course, so it has less unfilled excursions. Subsequently, its plan of action is an incredible driver of its attention on sustainability since it separates it from numerous contenders and utilizes its vehicles.

"The underlying impulse came from my company in advancing the organization's new site, particularly the CSR pages. Our own is an industry that is under the spotlight for its utilization of fuel and bundling materials. We do produce outflows—it is essential for the business—and we know that our greater rivals like FedEx, DHL, and UPS are looking at sustainability," says Rob Smith, ACMA, Finance Manager at Rainbow Nightfreight and CIMA part.

"Active vehicles and return vehicles can be full. Contrasted with a committed organization with its own fleet, we can do less miles and utilize less fuel and, hence, produce less emanations for everything we convey. Our administrations can accomplish something beyond A to B on every individual excursion, so the model we work is normally more productive than a common supplier," he comments.

The organization keeps a center and talked framework for working its vehicles, which incorporates provincial terminals, and has more prominent adaptability in arranging its routes and vehicle loads. From that premise, endeavors to improve sustainability have more impact.

"The plan of action is all the more harmless to the ecosystem and, along these lines, more feasible, yet we likewise do what we can from a productivity and discharges point of view. For example, we have guarded driver preparing programs, which center around foreseeing risky circumstances and driving all the more securely, yet in addition cover issues like eco-friendliness, brake wear and ideal tire pressure, anticipating every individual excursion," says Smith.

Among its endeavors to advance sustainability inside its industry, Rainbow Nightfreight has been campaigning government to support multi-client organizations. It has clarified the advantages of its plan of action to the Department for Transport's Low Carbon Supply Chain Steering Group.

The organization has likewise included environment specialists in the plan of its new East Midlands stop, a task to keep up to date with the most recent improvements in reusable and recyclable pack-maturing materials. It is additionally observing the improvement of electric vehicles (EV).

"We are in a rest stage as far as our fleet. Two years back, we discarded three warehouses and had surplus vehicles, so we carefully chose the best ones. Along these lines, it will be an additional 2 years before we take a look at vehicle substitution, yet when we do, we will consider environment contemplations. We could go for electric or crossover vehicles, and may go past what is needed by sustainable enactment," remarks Smith.

"We have additionally deliberately taken a look at the bundling side and explored various plans. The clients are responsible for giving the bundling of the products we convey; however, we may support that were fundamental. We can prescribe travel packaging to clients to ensure their merchandise, and when we do, we should take a look at asset effectiveness and consider green issues."

4.9.2. Observing and Estimation

A restrained way to deal with checking progress against characterized sustainable measurements is likewise advancing inside the organization.

"We have been ascertaining our emanations since a year ago. At the point when we have an energy or fuel charge, we record the KWh per liter to figure our yearly carbon impression. We are likewise in a situation to compute outflows for our clients on the conveyance component of their business in the event that they ask us to, much the same as DHL does on its abroad conveyances," says Smith.

"We haven't set carbon impression targets yet, yet for our industry a decrease of even 1% would be something to boast about. It would be a significant accomplishment. In spite of the fact that we have explored it, we have chosen not to go into the carbon credits market since it is viewed as purchasing right out of an issue," he adds. Smith, as account director, started the organization's endeavors to improve sustainability. Subsequently, the money work assumes a significant part in checking and improving performance, yet Smith has the ear of the other board individuals and has discovered it moderately simple to collect their full help.

"The primary venture expected to improve sustainability in the business is the board commitment," he pushes.

What Smith has noticed is that the advantages of economical techniques can build regardless of whether being greener is not the organization's main goal. Seeing what is useful for business execution can bring about practices that advantage the climate and different components of CSR, and the other way around.

"The primary speculation expected to improve sustainability in the business is the board time."

"We approach effectiveness first and we have sustainability benefits because of that. We are aware of sustainability, which is imbued in the business now, so we are cautious about things like turning the lights off to save energy, yet the attention is on being an expense effective business," Smith clarifies.

"Sustainability is imbued in our business. It is not done under the pennant of being green. It is driven by efficiency."

- Key Learning Points:
  - Identify and expand on the components of your current plan of action that advance reasonable exercises and practices;
  - Make clear connections among sustainability and productivity, and among efficiency and cost investment funds;
  - Keep up with the most recent exploration on the best way to improve sustainability in key territories of a business, for example, eco-friendliness, and the decrease of bundling materials, and apply those exercises for all intents and purposes;
  - Devise fitting measurements and screen execution on key boundaries, similar to eco-friendliness;
  - Set reasonable objectives for execution improvement;
  - Involve sustainable specialists in the plan of new capital tasks.

4.9.3. About Rainbow Nightfreight Ltd. (WA Rainbow Group)

Rainbow Nightfreight Ltd is a business cargo network having some expertise in off-kilter shapes and sizes yet additionally handles standard packages and beds. The coordination and production network activity of the W A Rainbow Group, it is principally UK-centered yet additionally has a global presence. The organization utilizes around 100 staff and creates yearly incomes of around £7 million.

4.9.4. About Rob Smith, ACMA, Finance, and General Management

Burglarize Smith is responsible for Finance and General Management at Rainbow Nightfreight Ltd (WA Rainbow Group). Before that, Rob was the Financial Controller/Director at Dengel and Barker. Beforehand he had been Chief Accountant at Davidson Packaging (BPB Group) and Systems Manager at TI Parkray (Tube Investments—TI Group). Ransack is an individual from CIMA.

4.10. ZIONS BANCORPORATION

4.10.1. Talking the Discussion and Strolling the Walk

At the point when a monetary foundation handles sustainability, it cannot just glance at the environmental impact of its own activities, yet can likewise offer sponsorship to different organizations and private people hoping to make their own upgrades. One bank in the Western US is doing both to incredible impact.

Each industry can draw in with the sustainability plan and monetary administrations is no exemption. A few banks have, indeed, took advantage of the chance to situate themselves as 'green,' focusing especially on the environmental parts of sustainability. They offer, for example, paperless records that are run altogether over the Internet. Others, be that as it may, have gone above and beyond.

Zions Bancorporation, which includes various associate banks across numerous western US states, is putting its capital behind sustainability by dispatching another division, which has been inactivity for almost a year, committed to financing private business or even little utility-scale energy projects that identify with both sustainable power age and changes that improve energy productivity in homes or organizations.

Its loaning group is searching for financing opportunities that will get to advance ensuring billions of dollars from the Department of Energy and Department of Agriculture, and other government-upheld programs. There has been a ton of interest and tangible projects are now set up.

Collaborating with the City of Phoenix and a nearby utility, the National Bank of Arizona (NBA)—which is essential for Zions Bancorporation—has just made a $25 million reserve for private activities under the Solar Phoenix project. Different undertakings incorporate work with the Davis-Monthan

Air Force Base in Tucson, Arizona, where the bank is financing a 3MW sun-oriented force establishment to give energy to a considerable lot of the houses that lie behind the doors of the base.

"We have a decent connection with the utility on energy productivity upgrades, as well. We assist with advances from $5,000 upwards for purchasers to make changes to their homes. We are engaged with a Department of Energy award that will give $20 million to business energy effectiveness projects. We are additionally taking a look at a utility-scale undertaking, and we are helping public bodies like schools with credits to create elective force sources," clarifies Craig Robb, CPA, Managing Director of Zions Energy Link.

"There is a ton of interest in credits among shoppers for private conveyed generation projects to bring down utility rates by up to 20%, and public organizations are exceptionally intrigued, as well, as they are adequately purchasing a support against long haul ascends in energy costs. Be that as it may, there is an even spread between these sorts of borrowers and organizations or property designers searching for financing."

The bank's recommendation is just incompletely philanthropic. Its activities demonstrate that there is business interest in sustainability. Despite the fact that there is unquestionably a moral point to its choice to back practical undertakings, giving subsidizing to help mortgage holders, networks, and businesses become more manageable bodes well.

"This isn't tied in with appending ourselves to the green message in a thought up manner. It is not following a trend. All the advances we make are financially practical. Most importantly these advances bode well for the bank. There is a positive financial consequence from the bank's own endeavors on sustainability and from the advances it makes. We are not situating ourselves as a green bank from an advertising viewpoint—that isn't our fundamental objective," stresses Robb.

"Our credits are innovative in their methodology; however, we utilize similar basic financial standards we have consistently utilized. We take a look at financial soundness and how much value is in the arrangement, so despite the fact that the innovation may be a cycle distinctive the lone contrast in our interaction is the time allotment a credit is extraordinary. These activities frequently need a more extended term advance."

The bank is not just risking its capital for the sake of sustainability, it is doing as such from an educated point of view. It has made changes to its own business for the sake of energy productivity, giving a guide to its clients and different organizations.

"This isn't tied in with connecting ourselves to the green message in a devised way. It is not following a trend. All the credits we make are economically suitable. Basically, these advances bode well for the bank."

One significant task was the establishment of sun-based boards on another stopping structure at the central command of the NBA in Tucson. Covering the new structure with photovoltaic panels produces around 400 KW of power, which gives around a 4th of the force utilized by the 130,000 sq ft banking focus.

"We began our sustainability drive when things appeared at their hardest in the monetary business sectors, yet we viewed at ourselves as a drawn-out sustainable company, incompletely from a sustainable perspective, yet additionally on the grounds that when the world is by all accounts self-destructing, we are a company that has a drawn-out faith in itself," says Robb.

"The sun-based force projects at our corporate focus and different areas have great compensation, and the financial aspects of them are vital. We have a huge structure here that was planned during the 1980s with a ton of glass, and which is not extremely effective, yet with sun-based force we have diminished our force utilization by 40% in 2 years. That shows the estimation of it from our own record thus we can show others the advantage of doing something comparable."

"We began our sustainability drive when things appeared at their hardest in the monetary business sectors, be that as it may, we viewed at ourselves as a drawn-out economical company."

Urging clients to take a long point of view on change is basic to the recommendation of Zions Energy Link, and the bank makes a decent attempt to show others how it has done.

Each member of the bank inside Zions Bancorporation has command over the turn of events and conveyance of its own interior sustainability strategy, yet at NBA, Robb steered as CFO. With a forward-looking CEO and an executive with a proactive position on sustainability programs, the money work had the option to anticipate the long haul and separate the procedure into singular undertakings, similar to the sun-oriented influence activities at its corporate base camp.

"A drawn-out view is foundational; it is essential for what our identity is. Zions was framed in the last part of the 1800s, so it has been around for quite a while as of now, and it desires to be around for quite a while to come. Any sustainability undertaking may require a long time to take care of, however on the off chance that you have that drawn-out view it winds up adequately costing nothing in real money terms due to the efficiencies it brings," says Robb.

"Somebody needs to roll out an improvement and take on something like a little sun-oriented force application. When you get the ball going, it builds up speed."

- Key Learning Points:
  - Assess the advantages of sustainability projects from a drawn-out point of view;
  - Engage senior administration in characterizing a sustainability procedure that looks past the following quarter's monetary outcomes;
  - Make little switches that develop to have a tremendous effect on effectiveness after some time;
  - Lead as a visual demonstration, drawing in clients, partners, and providers in your excursion towards turning into a more reasonable business.

4.10.2. About Zions Energy Link

In November 2010, Zions Bancorporation and its auxiliary NBA reported the dispatch of Zions Energy Link, a division that represents considerable authority in the sustainable energy financial area. Zions Energy Link gives straightforward, smoothed out and practical financing answers for energy productivity and sustainable power projects in Arizona, California, Colorado, Idaho, Nevada, New Mexico, Oregon, Texas, Utah, and Washington. It has a large group of expert banks in these 10 expresses that are information capable in government awards material to sustainable power age projects. Energy Link is focused on effectively checking on subsidizing chances of both huge and little ventures, with current activities in the pipeline going from under $10 million to more than $100 million.

4.10.3. About Craig Robb, CPA, Managing Director of Zions Energy Link

Craig Robb is the Managing Director of Zions Energy Link, another division of the bank having some expertise in the sustainability financial area. Craig has been in charge of the bank's endeavor into a portion of the state's most huge private and business support capacity programs. Under his administration, NBA, an auxiliary of Zions Bancorporation, has become a perceived head of financing for energy efficiency and inexhaustible activities. Preceding his arrangement as the Managing Director of Zions Energy Link, Craig was the Executive Vice President and Chief Financial Officer of NBA. He regulated all monetary parts of the bank just as the two Facilities Management and Risk Management. Preceding joining NB|AZ in 2002, Craig worked for Desert Mountain Properties as Senior Vice President of Operations. He got a BS in Accounting from Arizona State University and is a Certified Public Accountant.

4.11. AÉROPORTS DE MONTRÉAL (ADM)

4.11.1. A Flying Beginning for Sustainability

The aeronautics business is under the magnifying lens for its effect on the climate, yet while the spotlight has to a great extent been on the fuel utilization of carriers, air terminals are additionally making an offer to improve efficiency and lessen asset utilization to improve the sustainable profile of the business all in all.

Among the businesses that have been most vigorously reprimanded for their discharges of ozone-depleting substances, the flying area is perhaps the most conspicuous. It has additionally been among the most receptive to issues of sustainability. Truth be told, aeronautics represents just 2% of worldwide CO_2 discharges, yet the business is focused on improving innovation and operational cycles to build productivity and diminish its environmental effect.

Carriers and airplane producers have put forth attempts to improve eco-friendliness—and in the process have exemplified how cost reserve funds and improved sustainability go inseparably. Air terminals, as well, have accepted the message about sustainability and integrated it within its structures.

Aéroports de Montréal (ADM), a not-revenue driven company responsible for the management, activity, and improvement of Montréal-Pierre Elliott Trudeau and Montréal-Mirabel global air terminals, is among the administrators putting forth a submitted attempt to offset business goals with the manageable plan. ADM states its missions as a mix of three objectives: perform efficiently, free from any and all harm air terminal administrations that are predictable with the necessities of the local area; cultivate financial advancement in the Montréal zone; and exist together incongruity with the general climate, especially in terms of sustainable assurance.

"ADM intends to turn into an air terminal director positioning among the best on the planet, and to arrive at that objective necessitates that we embrace a manageable vision and set up feasible practices. The triggers for our procedure are the essential chance to create and develop our air terminals, the potential for cost investment funds and the expanded readiness of the business lately to adopt a more sustainable strategy, especially by lessening ozone harming substance discharges," says Philippe Rainville, CA, VP Finance and Administration at ADM.

In 2008, ADM joined the worldwide aeronautics industry's Commitment to Action on Climate Change, and has embraced an unmistakable corporate target on reasonable turn of events.

Its approach will bring the entirety of ADM's numerous activities under a similar umbrella and expand sustainability past environment issues.

4.11.2. Sustainable Certificate

"Our objectives and targets have been embraced as a component of the ISO 14001 sustainable certification. ADM has been certified since 2000, however meeting these objectives implies having a constant improvement approach," says Rainville.

"Economical improvement should be considered not to be a cost yet as a venture. In drafting the economic improvement strategy, money is included all through. Likewise with all substances in the company, account should be included straightforwardly in the design approach," comments Rainville.

"Sustainable advancement should be considered not to be a cost however as a venture."

ADM has characterized various measurements to diagram its environment presentation, including energy utilization, pace of waste reusing, ozone-depleting substance outflows, and the quantity of workers utilizing elective methods of transportation. In any case, sustainable boundaries are not by any means the only pointers it tracks. There is a solid spotlight on HR markers, including staff preparing levels, turnover rate, and non-attendance.

In any case, sustainable contemplations have a prominent, part of the way since that is the zone wherein ADM's clients express the most interest. ADM has diminished its energy utilization with different tasks like the establishment of mechanized "brilliant" blinds that consequently open and near keep an ideal degree of characteristic light in the terminal structure, and the supplanting of sliding entryways with spinning entryways which diminishes the requirement for warming and cooling.

"Likewise with all elements in the company, money should be included straightforwardly in the sustainable advancement approach."

Its most remarkable achievement, be that as it may, has been the improvement of an elite heating plant, which has been intended to recuperate energy. It burns through various types of energy, focusing on power, at that point petroleum gas and afterward fuel oil. "The heating plant at Montréal-Trudeau air terminal, charged in 2003, is an energy productivity feature. ADM engineers created and applied innovative ideas for the new plant, which won acknowledgment grants from key energy productivity companies. The new heating plant accomplished 70% energy effectiveness improvement over the bygone one," says Rainville.

In 2010, ADM turned into the main air terminal power to sell carbon credits on the intentional market, addressing 24,205 tons of CO_2 same. "The offer of carbon credits is an unmistakable and material performance of the endeavors embraced over the most recent couple of years to diminish our discharges," he adds.

The reserve funds and efficiencies such undertakings have brought to ADM have enlivened the company to expand the extent of its sustainability drive to cover each part of its present activities and its future improvement plans. The following thing on the plan is to obtain a fleet of energy-effective vehicles. Approximately 20 vehicles are as of now being changed over to utilize propane gas rather than petroleum. ADM has likewise taken part in a preliminary research to test hydrogen advancements including energy units to control vehicles at Montréal-Trudeau.

"The three focal points of economic advancement are not really contradicted however are integral. For instance, energy productivity measures have brought about expense reduction measures. The utilization of electric as opposed to gas boilers outside pinnacle hours decreases discharges on account of Québec's hydroelectric organization, and diminishes energy costs."

For Rainville, the accomplishment of any sustainability drive requires responsibility from senior administration, who should get a handle on the significance of the issue presently to guarantee it is engrained in the business later on.

"Economical improvement is significant for our workers—they consider it to be a need. For the future, sustainable needs remain, however there is developing worry over social issues. ADM has gained some great ground however manageable advancement is a continuous excursion that requires the co-activity, everything being equal," he says.

"Sustainable improvement is significant for our workers—they consider it to be a need."

- Key Learning Points:
  - Embrace industry-wide activities and draw in with peer companies to accomplish economical objectives;
  - Share best practices with companies that face similar difficulties concerning sustainability;
  - Engage all partners in your drive to improve sustainability, including providers and clients;
  - Remember that improving sustainability is a progressing interaction, not an erratic exertion;
  - Open clear lines of correspondence to connect with the responsibility of workers all through the company;
  - Remember that commitment of workers begins with the responsibility of senior administration.

4.11.3. About ADM

ADM is a not-revenue driven partnership without share capital and is liable for the administration, activity, and advancement of Montréal-Pierre Elliott Trudeau International Airport (once in the past Montréal-Dorval International Airport) and Montréal-Mirabel International Airport under the particulars of a 60-year rent endorsed with Transport Canada in 1992.

4.11.4. About Philippe Rainville, CA, Vice-President, Finance, and Administration, and Chief Financial Officer, Aéroports de Montréal (ADM)

Mr. Rainville joined ADM in January 2008 as Vice-President and Chief Financial Officer. He is associated with all parts of corporate administration, especially money, data frameworks and acquirement.

Chapter 5

SME Competitiveness Through Sustainability: An Academic Case Study

CONTENTS

In light of different scholarly and public approach work, it is generally recognized that small and medium-sized enterprises (SME) are a motor for development and business, in both major league salary and agricultural nations. The supporting instinct for this center is genuinely direct. SMEs represent the greater part of the ventures in an economy (Ardic et al., 2011), and for a significant portion of work and public pay (Ayyagari, 2007).

SMEs are frequently treated interchangeably with advancement and business, which is progressively seen to be a significant wellspring of development. For instance, SMEs are believed to be a wellspring of Schumpeterian-style imaginative obliteration, in which creative new firms are destined to retain assets from inadequately performing firms. Especially in the midst of high unemployment and serious rivalry from a scope of new contenders (driving numerous enormous firms, especially in cutting edge economies, to decrease staff), zeroing in on SMEs is viewed as an alluring model.

Due to these and numerous different reasons, SMEs have gotten an expanding portion of strategy consideration as an expected motor of monetary development and improvement over the previous decade. In both industrial and non-industrial nations, generous speculations are being made by public governments, worldwide organizations, and contributors, in gathering information on SMEs, undertaking strategy situated SME research, and executing a wide scope of strategy and spending activities on SMEs.

It is essential to guarantee that SME strategy is all around adjusted and centered to guarantee that it makes the top-level development to public financial execution. The point of this case study is to give some organized direction to strategy designers regarding two key inquiries: what is the individual commitment of SMEs versus different firms, and how might SME strategy best be designed?

This case study continues in three stages. The first is to all the more likely comprehend the financial commitment of SMEs. A moderately little gathering of SMEs-the gathering of competitive SMEs that develop firmly over the long haul-make a lopsided commitment to financial execution. This proposes that shrewd strategy should address key difficulties and empower the development of competitive SMEs. Most of the existing strategies include helping the foundation of SMEs, and general enhancements in the business climate.

This examination supplements the current arrangement center and takes it further to focus on a more explicit management of development drivers to empower organizations-the competitive SMEs, while staying comprehensive and maintaining a strategic distance from market twisting.

The subsequent advance is to build up a point of view on how best to supplement the strategy center around competitive SMEs with that on bigger firms.

Competitive SMEs that are dynamic and innovative do make a sizeable commitment to the public economy. Be that as it may, enormous firms likewise make a material commitment to advancement, work, and generally profitability and pay development. Furthermore, there is a significant reciprocal connection between competitive SMEs and enormous firms. Policymakers need to structure strategy properly to build up a sound eco-arrangement of firms.

The third step is to make this examination noteworthy by policymakers. To do this, we build up an underlying SME strategy analytic. What are the variables that management ought to consider in building up a feeling of the needs for strategy activity; how significant is the SME commitment in their nation setting, and what kind of strategies ought to be sought after to catch this value? What are a few models on how a few nations have just started approaches that help competitive SMEs? We accept that a superior comprehension of how to support SME development can possibly make a considerable commitment to public financial execution.

5.1. DEFINITION OF SME

The meaning of SMEs changes from country to country, and frequently even inside nations. For instance, the IFC MSME Country Indicator analyzes the officially enlisted micro, small, and medium-sized enterprises (MSME) in 132 economies, out of which 12 have no accurate definition on MSME, and 26 economies have more than one MSME definition (for example various definitions among measurable foundations, monetary establishments, and government agencies).

The SME definition in many nations regularly incorporates the accompanying factors:

- Number of representatives (the most widely recognized quality, utilized in 115 of the 120 economies).

- Assets/Turnover/Capital speculation (regularly utilized related or as supplement to the quantity of representative's characteristic, being utilized in 61 out of the 120 economies).
- Industry (meaning of SMEs contrast across various enterprises in 26 of the 120 economies).
- Others (a few nations likewise have different quirks in characterizing SME, like possession).

While every economy characterizes SME diversely with their individual legitimate or administrative contemplations, we endeavor to normalize the definition for examination and investigation reason. Given that number of workers gives off an impression of being the most widely recognized and clear factor utilized in characterizing SME, we propose the accompanying standard definition for micro, small, and medium undertakings dependent on number of regular works:

- ***Micro:*** Less than 10 representatives (82 of the 120 economies characterize "Micro" with 10 as edge interest ($<$ or $\leq$ 10 workers).
- ***Small:*** 10–49 workers (75 of the 120 economies recognize "Small" and "Medium" with the edge estimation of 50.
- ***Medium:*** 50–249 workers (46 of the 120 economies utilize 250 as upper headed for medium-sized ventures. Other edge interests like 100, 200 are utilized less habitually).

This meaning of SME is the most widely recognized one, and furthermore reliable with that utilized by the European Union (EU), however EU definition likewise incorporates company's turnover and resource interest.

5.1.1. SMEs Gathered Structure a Significant Mainstay of an Economy

SMEs, as a gathering, represent a critical portion of financial movement anytime. They likewise uphold financial development in a critical manner through firm efficiency development. Anyway, SMEs are extremely different, and seeing them aggregately conceals significant experiences. In this segment, we will see that just a little level of SMEs represents a lopsided portion of SME's commitment to an economy.

5.1.2. SMEs Represent Critical Portion of Monetary Action

Firms that utilize under 250 full-time employees (FTEs) represent a critical portion of an absolute number of endeavors in an economy, all outnumber of occupations and gross value added. While definite numbers change across nations, as an outline, we present the proof from Europe as assessed by Ecorys for the European Commission (EC). In light of big business information of 27 European nations in 2012, SMEs all in all records for 99.8% of the ventures, 67.4% of work and 58% of gross value included the locale (Table 5.1). Information from less developed nations show a comparable example: United Nations Industrial Development Organization (UNIDO) gauges that SMEs address more than 90% of personal business and offer more than 50% of work and of GDP in most African nations. The miniature firms (under 10 FTEs) represent a sensible portion of monetary movement-92%, everything being equal, 30% of occupations and 19% of gross value added.

Table 5.1. SME Estimates of EU-27 (2012)

	Micro (<10 FTE)	Small (10–49 FTE)	Medium (50–249 FTE)	SMEs (<250 FTE)	Large	Total
Number of enterprises	19,143,521	1,357,533	226,573	20,727,627	43,654	20,77 1,281
Percent of enterprises	92.2%	6.5%	1.1%	99.8%	0.2%	100%
Number of Employment ('000)	38,396	26,771	22,310	87,477	42,319	129,796
Percent of employment	29.6%	20.6%	17.2%	67.4%	32.6%	100%
Employee per enterprise	2.0	19.7	98.5	4.2	969.4	973.6
Gross value-added (GVA) (billion EUR)	1,307	1,144	1,136	3,588	2,592	6,180

Source: European Commission.

SMEs uphold monetary development through firm profitability development notwithstanding representing a significant portion of financial action at some random point, SMEs additionally drive the GDP and the efficiency development of the economy. In the first place, the creation and exit of firms that makes an economy dynamic, principally occurs in the little and medium-firm environment. Furthermore, and as we will see all the more critically, inside firm profitability improvement among some SMEs is a significant driver of efficiency development in the general economy.

5.1.3. Creation and Exit of Firms

One of the striking discoveries from the examination of firm socioeconomics in numerous economies is that there is a serious level of change. Longitudinal proof shows a predictable example across nations of a high extent of firms entering or leaving each year. For instance, as per Singapore's Department of Statistics, 22,826 organizations were framed in Singapore during 2012 and 22,497 organizations stopped activity in a similar period. There were almost 154,000 organizations in the country in 2012. This infers almost 30% of all organizations are either entering or leaving at a given point.

The creation and exit of firms are the thing that Joseph Schumpeter had at the top of the priority list as far as the cycle of imaginative obliteration, where assets are redistributed from ineffectively performing firms who exit to more beneficial new contestants. This cycle positively affects public level results. An observational investigation utilizing firm-level board information from Taiwanese Census of Manufacturers (Aw et al., 2001) additionally bolsters that firm turnover adds to industry efficiency development.

Numerous organizations do not get by for more than a couple of years. Across a wide scope of nations considered, around 20–40% of recently settled firms come up short inside 2 years and just 40–50% of new firms get by for over 7 years (Bartelsman et al., 2003). Especially in nations with low expenses to firm section, like the US, there is a great deal of experimentation-the fruitful firms remain while the ineffective exit.

A couple of enormous firms additionally flop either fantastically or progressively and are regularly rebuilt or converged at the same time. In any case, the passage and exit of firms stays high for little firms.

5.1.4. Inside Firm Profitability Development

Profitability acquires that come from 'inside firm' efficiency development is a higher priority than assignment impact accomplished through passage and exit of firms. Baily et al. (1996) assessed that the total factor productivity (TFP) development contributed half of TFP development in the manufacturing area during the 1980s, though net passage represented distinctly around 25%.

Also, the OECD (2004) found that the commitment of passage and exit of manufacturing firms represented around 20–40% of work profitability development in a few OECD economies, and that inside firm efficiency development was the more generous driver. There was some variety across nations, however this was a steady finding.

5.1.5. There Is Huge Variety in Firm Profitability Development Across SMEs

With regards to SMEs, there is nothing of the sort as a normal or delegate firm, even inside a particular industry subject to similar outer conditions. There is a significant measure of firm-level variety inside an industry (Bartelsman et al., 2009). SMEs represent a blend of new and old firms, developing, and static firms, miniature, and little or medium, and high and low profitability firms. With regards to firm efficiency development of SMEs, we have two perceptions. To start with, there is a generous variety across the SME group regarding their development profile.

Second, SMEs that develop vigorously after foundation are a little subset of all SMEs, yet contribute excessively to generally speaking economic performance. In view of an investigation of US firms by the US independent company affiliation, it was discovered that a small subset of all SMEs delegated high impact companies (HIC) representing 6% of all US firms outperformed the net positions made by the entire economy (Figures 5.1 and 5.2). In the event that we additionally incorporate HIC delegated huge firms, these 6% firms made 184% of net new opportunities made in the country over a long-term period. A big part of these came from little and medium firms. Rest of the 94% firms-dominant part of them are SMEs-lost 4.9 million positions during the long-term time frame.

Number of net New jobs (6mn) created by 6% of US SMEs surpassed the total net new joba (5.8 mn) created by the whole economy during 2004-08

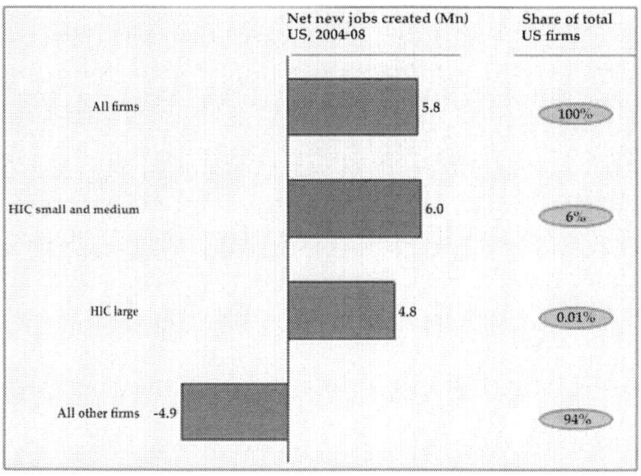

Figure 5.1.Number of jobs created per company size.

Source: US Small Business Administration.

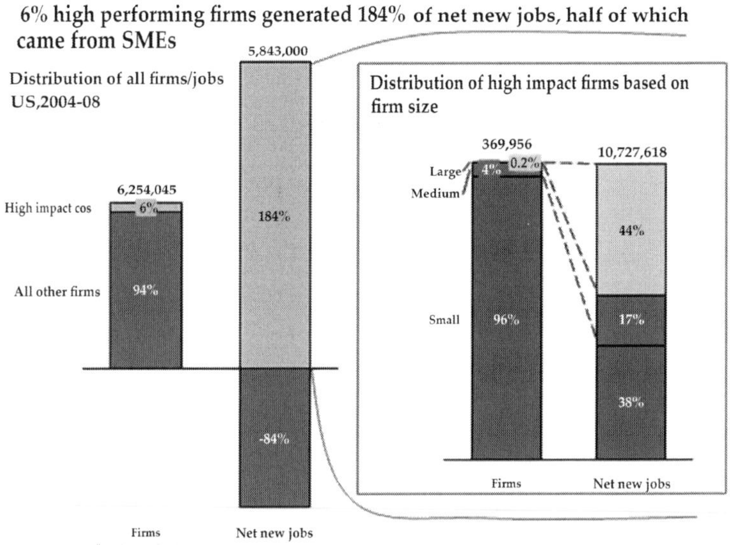

Figure 5.2. Distribution of high impact firms based on size.

Source: US Small Business Administration.

5.1.6. This Contrast Across SMEs Is Clarified Through the Distinctive Development Ways SMEs Take

What clarifies this tremendous disparity between occupations made by a bunch of SMEs and occupations obliterated by another set? Figure 5.3 fills in as a calculated representation on the development way that endeavors regularly experience. A critical portion of all new endeavors exit early and the excess enduring firms additionally follow diverse development ways. We sort these organizations into three researches: the ones that stay little (independently employed or way of life firms); the ones that develop decently (moderate or covered development firms); and the ones that show high development (high development or established firms).

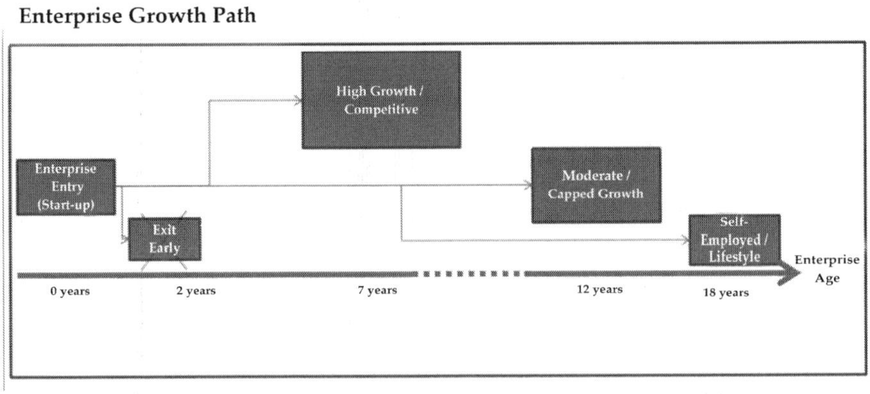

Figure 5.3. Enterprise growth path.

Source: US Small Business Administration.

5.1.7. Independently Employed or Way of Life Firms

Numerous organizations are created by individuals who need to have the option to practice more command over their working life, however have no goal to develop- or to enlist extra staff. They may get by for a longer time, however they decide to stay little both as far as staff strength and deals income. These organizations are recognized as the "Way of life" by Hanks et al. (1993), the experimental investigation finds that these organizations do not develop much since their commencement, however, they may remain in business for a moderately prolonged stretch of time (normal around 18 years).

The subjective proof is that numerous SMEs do not have important development goals. Numerous SMEs are viably independent work circumstances. They have no genuine development plan past their unique level. Proof from the Global Entrepreneurship Monitor (GEM, 2011) finds that freedom and independence is a solid spark for dispatching firms (pay and development inspirations were a lot of optional). As a side note, this is the reason proportions of entrepreneurialism are vital, however, not adequate since they just catch the foundation of firms, not their ensuing development (which is amassed in just a little extent of firms). Be it by decision or by incidental requirements, firms in this classification stay little regardless of whether they make due for long.

5.1.8. Firms with Moderate or Covered Development

This research incorporates SMEs that develop unassumingly past their foundation size over a time of 5–7 years. A new US study found that organizations utilizing under 20 individuals were gathered in administrations areas like bookkeeping, retail, and land, where the base proficient scale was very low (Hurst and Pugley, 2011). The overview proof detailed finds that the majority of these organizations serve a current market with a current product (instead of putting up an advancement for sale to the public), and have restricted development yearnings. Like the "Covered development" recognized in Hanks et al. (1993), these organizations may create higher income and stay in business for more when contrasted by new firms, yet their development in work is lower because of incidental reasons.

5.1.8.1. High Development or Established Firms

The last group of SMEs are the high-development firms; those with a CAGR of 10% more than 7 years. As per Hanks et al. (1993), firms experience critical development and accomplish development in around 7 years. It is ordinarily these organizations which go through gigantic development in the initial not many years and would develop to a lot greater scale to turn into a medium-enormous measured venture. It is not amazing that the dominant part of firms in this gathering are small and medium organizations given the way that SMEs represent the biggest share of firms in many economies. We call these Competitive SMEs.

5.1.8.2. Defining "Competitive SMEs"-Little Subset of Firms That Excessively Add to Occupations and Efficiency

From the point of view of financial commitment, it is this gathering of dynamic, youthful developing SMEs that are specifically compelling, and we term them as 'competitive SMEs.' Given enormous contrasts in meaning of SMEs around the world, it is normal that various governments and different researches would characterize competitive SMEs diversely dependent on nearby conditions. The grouping and distinguishing proof of competitive SMEs is dependent on the accompanying three measurements:

1. ***Firm Age:*** Young firms (for example, under 7 years of age)-on the grounds that the proof reliably proposes that firm age is a solid indicator of development possibilities. It is considerably less likely that old firms will begin to become competitive late in their lives.

2. ***Historical Growth of Firm:*** Firms that have filled (in headcount) by in any event 10% p.a. over in any event the previous long term time frame. It very well might be contended that credits other than work, like income and profitability, are likewise significant markers for organization development. In any case, with regards to young firms, we accept that critical expansion in work shows an increment of solid interest of the organization's products or administrations. Thusly, for straightforwardness purpose, we are of the view that development in employment is a decent sign of solid development of the firm.
3. ***Growth Prospect of Area:*** The organizations ought to be in areas (or economies) with projected development rates that may proceed with development paces of at any rate 10% per year on a supported premise. In the event that the firm is in an around the world uncovered area, we need to take a look at worldwide area development rates. Meaning of area here ought to be just about as granular as could be expected. The purpose behind not zeroing in on serious firms in any case stale areas is on the grounds that these organizations commonly increment their piece of the overall industry with restricted effect on market size.

These characterization grids are not intended to be prescriptive and authoritative. It fills in as a demonstrative rule for government to survey their own country's firm socioeconomics and financial elements.

5.1.8.3. Only Around 5% of Firms in a Cohort of SMEs Become Serious

The critical variety seen in SME execution by sectioning the little and medium-firm populace, is profoundly unpredictable-with heterogeneity in firm size, specialization, and execution. Numerous SMEs fall flat inside a couple of long stretches of foundation, and large numbers of the enduring SMEs do not develop much past their beginning size. Taking a look at information across OECD and Latin American agricultural nations, utilizing auxiliary sources and Enterprise Survey information, we find that by the 7th year since firing up, 60% of firms have left, around 20% stay independent work or single-owner firms, 15% are little and medium firms yet with low or deteriorating development (Figure 5.4). This little gathering of firms called Competitive SMEs make an unbalanced financial commitment and are ground-breaking motors of new development and advancement.

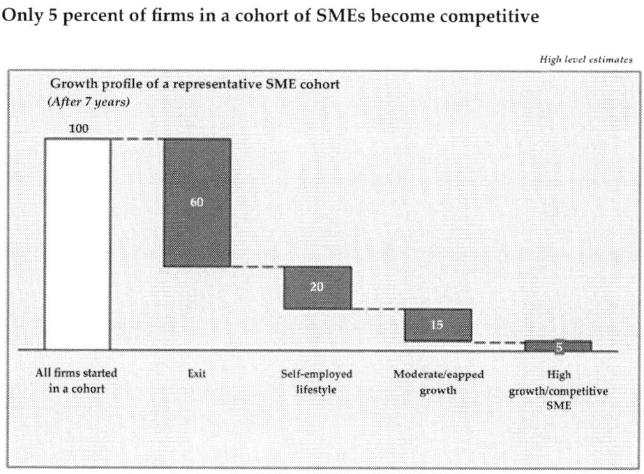

Figure 5.4. Growth profile of a representation SME cohort.

Source: US Small Business Administration.

It is hard to exactly assess the proportion of firms in a partner of SMEs that exit, deteriorate, or stay in independent work circumstances due to wide contrasts across nations and absence of accomplice astute information (a large portion of the SME information is enumeration information). The exact appropriation will change contingent upon the time span, the economy, the business area, and numerous different elements. Subsequently, these evaluations are significant level. Nonetheless, there is sufficient proof that these are directionally right, which ought to be adequate for policymakers to use the knowledge of competitive SMEs to refine their present SME procedures.

The extent of SMEs encountering high development following 7 years is assessed to be in the range of 3 to 5%. For example, the percent of firms in a cohort that become serious past 7 years to be 3.2% in Mexico and 4.8% in Argentina. Additionally, an examination was directed by Statistics Canada in 2006 to survey work creation corresponding to firm development and firm size, in light of firms that opened or shut during the time of 1993 to 2003. The examination shows that just around 4% of firms experienced hyper-development (characterized as development of 150% more than 4 years or total yearly business development pace of about 10.5%), and they added to around 45% of the net occupation creation during the time frame. The information on American firms, shows that 6% of SMEs were distinguished as high development firms. For the moderate or covered development firms, in view of a similar investigation of the World Bank Enterprise Survey as verified above, it was assessed that organizations in this classification establish around 12–16% of the whole SME associate, with middle around 15%. By allowance from the past researches, the organizations in independently employed/way of life classification establish around 20% of the populace.

In outline, however, the specific numbers differ across time span and areas, one steady finding is that around 5% of all settled little firms in the economy show reliable high development, and make lopsided monetary commitment. The Global Entrepreneurship Monitor additionally noticed that the little gathering of 'high effect business visionaries' make an unbalanced measure of development (4% make 40% of occupations). Bartelsman et al. (2003) gauge that the normal US fabricating firm that has made due for over 7 years is around multiple times bigger than at foundation regarding headcount. Given the conveyance of development profiles, and that a few firms do not develop a lot, this proposes that some enduring firms develop at surprising rates over supported periods.

The SMEs that do develop competitively are additionally liable for a lopsided measure of advancement and new financial movement. These organizations are bound to contribute, to send out, to embrace R&D, and to drive change in the economy-bringing assets into profitable utilization and away from other, less gainful pieces of the economy.

Related evidence on the growth profile of firms also finds that it is not so much that small firms can grow quickly as much as young firms (who tend to be small). Young firms are more likely to grow than are old firms. Haltiwanger et al. (2010) present findings from the U.S. that it is the young firms that matter for growth in employment (it is not due to firm size). However, there is an indication that this relationship may be weaker in developing countries where there are some limitations on growth (which delays the growth process of intrinsically strong firms).

5.2. COMPETITIVE SME AND THE "GAZELLES"

Like most thoughts, the idea of "competitive SME" works from learning of the past. In the late 1970s, David L. Birch's 52-page report The Job Generation Process "originally threw out the possibility that numerous small however quickly developing firms are contributing extraordinarily to job creation. In the many years that followed, with expanding consideration on small firms among specialists and policymakers, Birch instituted the expression "Gazelles" to depict a little gathering of high-development firms that produced the greater part of the new opportunities in the economy. The expression "Gazelles" is utilized as opposed to "Elephant," which are firms with enormous work share yet scarcely any new opportunities; and "Mice," which are little firms with little development.

In particular, Birch et al. (1995) characterized Gazelles as "a business establishment which has achieved a minimum of 20% sales growth each year over the interval, starting from a base-year revenue of at least $100,000." There have been different varieties of this definition, however they are completely advanced around the idea of reliable firm development throughout some undefined time frame.

A considerable lot of the resulting concentrates on firm size, development, and commitment to work have upheld or broadened the thought on Gazelles, and showing that Gazelles are normally youthful and small firms, and as a little part of firms in the economy, they produce disproportionally gigantic measure of net new jobs. In light of a new report delivered by the US Small Business Administration (Spencer and Tracy, 2011), more than 4-year time spans from 1994–2008, 6.3% (roughly 350,000) of all US organizations are ordered as Gazelles, 99.5% of them has under 500 representatives (94% have under 20 workers), and they represent all the net new opportunities made in the economy.

Despite the fact that most meanings of Gazelles do not restrict the organizations to be SMEs, SMEs absolutely comprises a huge extent of these high-development Gazelles. Along these lines, there are regions of complementarity and a couple of contrasts in our concentration and approach opposite the Gazelles.

5.2.1. Relevance of Competitive SMEs to Policymaking

In this part, we present proof that public approaches matter, with regards to creating competitive SMEs. Competitive SMEs are more relevant as economies move from being low-income country to lower-middle-income country. Competitive SMEs likewise may confront difficulties that are explicit to their requirements and are not shared by a huge number of other SMEs on the lookout.

There is proof that public approaches matter, with regards to creating competitive SMEs. The proof on the dispersion of development profiles across firms has direct ramifications for policymakers. It proposes that, in numerous nations, SME strategy ought to guarantee sufficient help for the development of these competitive SMEs, as it is this gathering of firms that will make the most material commitment to monetary results. However, is there proof that such arrangements really work?

There is for sure proof that administration arrangements matter being developed by competitive SMEs. Nonetheless, it is suggested that some low income and lower-middle-income nations are lucky to be first seeking after expansive business environment improvement plan and fundamental changes. Figure 5.5 reports information from Bartelsman et al. (2003) for a scope of nations. The normal US fabricating firm that has made due for over 7 years is around multiple times bigger than at foundation regarding a number of works. This is about twofold the pace of development saw in the UK and Italy, and commonly more than the development rates insight in Germany and France. This considerable public variety in firm-level development recommends that public arrangement is likewise a factor. There is likely cross-country variety in administration limit and perspectives towards enterprising action, however it appears improbable to expect that these variables clarify the noticed contrasts. It is likewise essential to take note that the higher development rates in the US, when contrasted with Europe might be credited to the overall more modest beginning upsize in the US (because of lower expenses to passage).

Substantial national variation in firm-level growthsuggests that public policy is also a factor

Figure 5.5. Average growth of successful firms 1980-2000.

Source: US Small Business Administration.

In certain nations, the way to deal with SME strategy is excessively daintily spread, instead of zeroing in on the predetermined number of indispensable commitments that it can make. It appears to be that a huge portion of the arrangement exertion has been comprehensively centered around the entire SME area instead of more firmly centered around the subset of SMEs that are probably going to have a genuine effect.

Yet, note that this contention for strategy around competitive SMEs has more prominent power in center and top-level salary nations. This contention might be more vulnerable for low pay nations where there are critical boundaries to business entry (undertaking power is a lot of lower in less fortunate nations). In these lower pay nations, there is more noteworthy incentive in eliminating these obstructions to entry- and in permitting the casual economy to be formalized (Acs et al., 2008; de Soto, 2000).

There is more prominent profit by invigorating pioneering movement. Also, almost certainly, a more noteworthy level of public area limit is needed to operationalize a tight spotlight on competitive SMEs. But as countries develop through middle- and high-income status, an increased focus on competitive SMEs will become appropriate (Figure 5.6).

SME policy focus may vary by development level

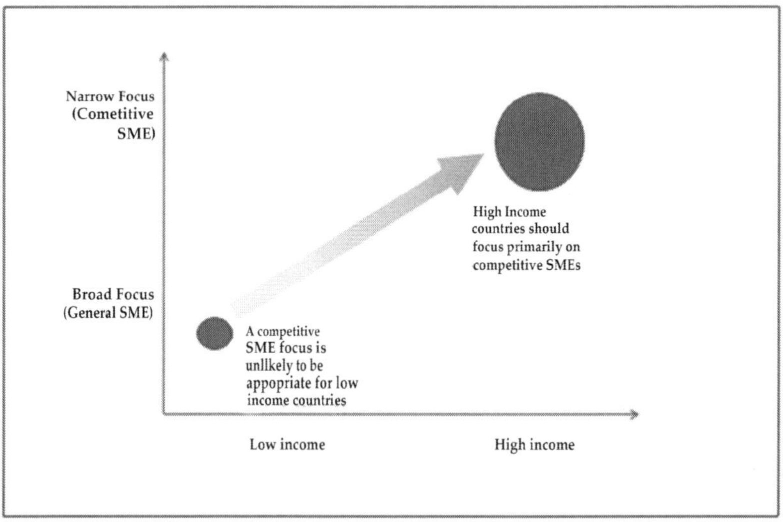

Figure 5.6. Types of Policy focus.

Source: US Small Business Administration.

There are explicit challenges looked by these organizations that little firms ordinarily do not confront, and henceforth there is a requirement for more educated government activity. Competitive SMEs, as we have characterized, are well-performing young firms with powerful development potential. They have more possibility for bank credits contrasted with other little firms. In any case, access to finance may in some cases be an issue for these organizations particularly in the beginning phase of their development (where banks are too risk-averse Secondly, while these firms generally have access to bank finance, sometimes there is a mismatch between the amount of fund they need to grow quickly and what banks, which are bound by their policies, are willing to provide. The second area where competitive SMEs struggle more than other small firms is on access to cutting edge knowledge and expertise related to internationalization. This is particularly valid for competitive SMEs in more modest nations where internationalization is a vital wellspring of development for firms that need to get away from the stagnation trap. Thirdly, in certain nations, these exploring firms do not have information and attention to top tier the board practices and most recent innovation, and take more time to arrive at their latent capacity.

5.2.2. Governments Ought to Build Up a Way to Create Policy and Initiatives to Develop Competitive SMEs

The response to this inquiry relies upon the nation setting. Three territories are covered which will illuminate how the legislatures can move toward approaches and activities to create competitive SMEs.

- First, examining the corresponding connection between enormous firms and competitive SMEs. Financial approaches zeroed in on competitive SMEs should be educated by the biological system in which these SMEs work, particularly their relationship with huge firms;
- Second, an indicative methodology for policymakers to all the more likely comprehend the lay of the land to advise last strategies;
- Lastly, we give a couple of topics and models that a few nations, for example, Singapore is receiving to build up their competitive SMEs.

5.2.3. The Integral Connection Between Competitive SMEs and Huge Firms

The past conversation has noticed the financial commitment that competitive SMEs can make, and the manners by which a more engaged SME strategy could possibly create monetary value. However, policymakers ought not to move toward SMEs autonomously of different pieces of the economy. Huge firms likewise make a significant commitment to the economy. Furthermore, there is an important, reciprocal connection between competitive SMEs and bigger firms. Policymakers should address configuration firm-level arrangement to guarantee that solid monetary commitments are being made by competitive SMEs and furthermore that the approach is organized such that the reciprocal idea of the relationship is caught.

Some portion of this is an issue of strategy balance, to guarantee that arrangement endeavors are being coordinated in the most ideal manner. Some fundamental math shows why this is significant: a nation needs monetary enhancements across a considerable number of (thousands) of SMEs to get a material improvement in public GDP, though similar development in only a couple enormous firms might be more critical. For instance, a 10% increment in the fares of New Zealand's biggest exporter is around 1% of GDP; it would take a huge number of SMEs to convey this size of monetary improvement. Furthermore, there are cutoff points to the limit of little firms to convey this improved performance, comparative with bigger firms. It is a troublesome, unsafe zone of strategy.

The correct equilibrium should be struck to make the most extreme expected commitment to public financial execution. In numerous nations, it will be the bigger firms that are all around set to make a solid commitment; each nation ought to survey the commitment that SMEs are probably going to make to financial and social advancement comparative with different kinds of firms, given the idea of the organizations that the nation has and what it is attempting to accomplish.

5.2.4. Large Firm Commitment

However, in spite of the fact that SMEs, and especially competitive SMEs, make a solid commitment to public financial execution, enormous firms additionally make an exceptionally generous commitment. What is more, strategy should be adjusted to perceive the material commitment made by these huge firms. Think about the accompanying perceptions.

5.2.5. GDP, Business, and Efficiency

In spite of the fact that there is some variety across nations, enormous firms regularly represent the greater part of business and GDP (regardless of representing a little portion of the quantity of undertakings). As specific illustrations, the Malaysian government noticed that 99.2% of Malaysian firms are SMEs, representing 56% of work and 31% of GDP; in Singapore, SMEs represent over 99.4% of firms and around 50% of significant value-added GDP. As a rule, as noted prior, firms utilizing in excess of 250 individuals represent under 1% of the quantity of ventures. What is more, around 80–90% of firms utilize under 20 individuals; yet this may represent just 15–20% of complete work in numerous economies.

Consequently, huge firms are significant drivers of economic performance. In the US, the McKinsey Global Institute (MGI) gauges that the MNCs that have developed more quickly than the non-MNC over the previous decade. Albeit the US MNCs represent under 1% of US firms, they contain 11% of US private area work development and 31% of genuine private area GDP development. They create solid work efficiency execution, and record for 74% of private area R&D spending. Moreover, these huge MNCs pay essentially higher wages than their more modest partners.

Also, the work efficiency of SMEs is lower than for different firms. For example, as demonstrated in Table 5.1, the efficiency (as estimated by income per representative) of huge organizations (with in excess of 250 FTE) are 1.5 occasions of the SMEs (with under 250 FTE), and multiple times of that of the miniature firms (with under 10 FTE). The lower level of work profitability probably reflects lower levels of capital force in SMEs, just as lower levels of TFP-human resources, hierarchical, and specialized best practice and so forth It additionally mirrors the sectoral creation of SMEs; there are fewer SMEs in the manufacturing area, which will in general have more significant levels of work profitability than the administrations area. Economies of scale and extension assist bigger firm with accomplishing higher efficiency.

To be sure, late examinations recommend that SMEs have not been a critical piece of the quick pay combination story in many agricultural nations. The latest examination by Dani Rodrik (2012) proposes that intermingling has been passed through the Manufacturing areas, as developing business sectors industrialize. Assembling will in general be relative scale escalated, which makes it less inclined to be overwhelmed by little firms. To this degree, all things considered, quick development has been driven by the bigger firms that will in general populate the Manufacturing area; these are the organizations that can retain and utilize unfamiliar innovation, and scale up as they venture into both homegrown and fare markets. This was valid for the East Asian tiger economies in the course of recent years, and is likewise the situation for China; albeit a portion of the neighborhood firms got going as SMEs, they scaled up quickly. The proof is likewise powerful regarding progressed economies. As an outrageous model, consider the size of the Walmart impact on total US efficiency-an enormous firm that pre-owned IT to update its conveyance framework immensely affected total US profitability development during the 1990s. What is more, the McKinsey report concentrated on profitability in Japan (Kondo et al., 2000) found that the enormous, internationally uncovered Japanese firms had profitability twice as high as the non-exchanged area (which is genuinely divided in Japan and dominated by little firms).

5.2.6. Research and Advancement

There is a blended picture in as for the connection between firm size and interest in examination and development. Regarding the more effectively quantifiable R&D spending, huge firms contribute significantly more. As indicated by the OECD's STI scoreboard, firms with under 50 representatives burn through 10% of the complete business spending on R&D regardless of representing a considerable portion of the quantity of undertakings.

There are a few conceivable purposes behind this. There is a component of fixed expenses to putting resources into R&D, which SMEs may battle to cover; there is a requirement for absorptive limit; and R&D is bound to happen more in manufacturing than in the administrations area (where SMEs are more normal). Be that as it may, huge firms spend more on R&D on the grounds that they are bigger; the connection between firm size (regarding incomes) and R&D spending is positive, however generally little.

At the point when development is characterized all the more extensively, be that as it may, competitive SMEs make an inexorably significant commitment. Lerner (2010) depicts the changing plans of action around advancement in the course of recent years, and the move away from enormous mechanical examination labs to a greater amount of an out-sourced models in which the new, problematic developments frequently occurred in moderately little, young firms- and which were regularly bought accordingly by the bigger firms. However, especially in areas like IT, it is the youthful, little firms that have created the advancement developments.

5.2.7. International Commitment

Worldwide commitment is likewise normally connected to firm measure; huge firms are significantly more likely than SMEs to take part in trading or to contribute abroad. Little firms think that it is harder to grow abroad than huge firms. A huge collection of subjective contextual investigation work distinguishes a few of the critical purposes behind this lower level of worldwide financial movement: absence of interest in unfamiliar statistical surveying, nonappearance of the board, the option to scale up to satisfy bigger orders, and the requirement for bigger accounting reports to adapt to the different threats (for example conversion scale instability).

The generally low degree of global commitment by SMEs is one contributing motivation to the moderately powerless work profitability execution that was portrayed above (as there is a causal connection between firm-level worldwide commitment and firm-level efficiency).

5.2.8. The Reciprocal Nature of the Relationship

So, SMEs, competitive SMEs, and enormous firms all make huge commitments to public financial execution. The general view in the writing is by all accounts that there is no deliberate connection between firm size and the monetary commitment that is made by firms. Or maybe it is significant that all pieces of the economy are making solid commitments; supported financial execution required a reasonable arrangement of development motors (as opposed to being excessively dependent on specific pieces of the economy). The blend will shift by country, as indicated by their specific conditions (there is no all-around proper solution).

Competitive SMEs can possibly make a significant commitment to the economy- and with fitting arrangement settings, it is conceivable that this commitment could be reinforced further. Notwithstanding the direct monetary commitment that SMEs make, their conduct and execution likewise can possibly make a more extensive commitment to the economy.

Right off the bat, SMEs are a wellspring of financial incentive to bigger firms in an assortment of ways. For instance, to an expanding degree huge firms utilize little firms as their advancement lab (they do their R&D in an out-sourced way, as verified previously). So, the commitment of little firms might be purchased and utilized by huge firms. SMEs can likewise be useful regardless of whether they are not the vehicle that conveys the improved monetary results.

Second, in light of the fact that SMEs represent a considerable portion of the economy, the presentation of these organizations matters for the general competitiveness of different firms. The administrations area, for instance, impacts on the intensity of the exchanged area- and it is significant subsequently that little firms in this area perform well all together for the huge firms to perform at top potential.

Relatedly, SMEs may give extra serious force, offering new products and management that contend with the bigger firms- and give a spike to them to stay profitable and to improve. Bartelsman et al. (2003) note that areas with the high pace of creation of new firms have various attributes, recommending that officeholders face a more prominent level of contestability. Also, SMEs can improve the nature of administration by giving contestability, and making it more outlandish for enormous firms to take part in lease looking for action. A dynamic SME sector lessens the odds of economic sclerosis.

Third, SMEs can give business opportunities that would some way or another not exist and might be a method of bringing adaptability into moderately inflexible work markets. SMEs may likewise help address local business issues in regions where different firms decide not to locate (SMEs might be the solitary wellspring of monetary movement). A portion of these advantages might be especially articulated in times of financial unpredictability of emergency, and to this degree may give some extra versatility.

5.2.9. Towards Keen Arrangement: A Proposed Analytic

Policy needs to be focused on competitive SMEs, particularly as countries graduate from low income to middle income status, and to encourage complementary contributions from these SMEs and from large firms. For most developing countries, a two-pronged approach to support competitive SMEs is recommended.

The primary pillar is a bunch of strategy topics that reward result and effect, while the subsequent pillar is about the interaction of strategy plan, conveyance, observing, and cycle. Models on the first pillar incorporate improving a company's methodology and execution through administration limit fabricating and improving the company's profitability and advancement. There are instances of competitive SME strategy improvement that policymakers can gain from. This could be a decent beginning stage; anyway, every nation should make its own decisions about how to move toward its SME area given the common conditions. Precise and country-explicit examination is significant in light of the fact that the fitting approach fluctuates across nations, contingent upon their monetary construction, strategy climate and level of improvement.

This is the place where the subsequent pillar comes in, which manages the interaction of strategy plan and conveyance. Specifically, this segment starts to build up a four-stage organized country diagnostic apparatus. These are inquiries to be posed; not every one of them will actually want to be replied with sufficient information uphold. Be that as it may, it gives an organized way to deal with contemplating SME strategy and fills in as a manual for the kind of exploration and information assortment needed later on (a forward examination plan).

A vital component of the diagnostic is to develop peer groups to empower reasonable worldwide benchmarking. Nations have various models, and there is no single model of best practice that all nations ought to imitate. The US model, for instance, exists in a totally different climate when contrasted with the European model, underlining models of troublesome development to a more prominent degree than Europe. At the end of the day, this is both a subjective exercise just as a quantitative exercise.

5.2.10. How to Develop a Firm Map?

1. ***Historical Materiality:*** Examine commitment to GDP, business, and profitability commitment from firms of various sizes. Additionally, break down the adjustment in commitment across a time frame. This examination should guarantee controls for area piece of the economy, as the commitment from firms in various areas will be firmly related with the kind of 'creation work' that the area has.

This commitment can be benchmarked universally to give a feeling of similitudes and contrasts in the segment structure. When looking at the SME's commitment across nations, it is critical to adapt for money trade and swelling utilizing proper country and area-level deflators. The selection of nations to be remembered for the benchmarking exercise is additionally significant. It ought to be noticed that more exploration is needed to decide if higher per capita pay is associated with higher SME commitment to GDP. More examination is likewise needed to comprehend if higher SME commitment to GDP is in reality attractive. One speculation is that convention drops with pay development and more SMEs are formally enrolled and considered piece of GDP, and subsequently their commitment may look higher.

2. ***Potential/Planned Materiality:*** By area, look at financial execution (especially profitability levels) and benchmark against worldwide information. Is there an efficient connection between profitability execution in explicit areas (comparative with significant benchmarks) and are little or enormous firms are over-addressed in that area? In the event that there is, this may recommend that there is potential for improved execution from a specific firm segment.

5.2.11. Information/Information Necessity for Diagnostic

To play out the proposed diagnostics, data may be needed at three levels: firm-level information that gives quantitative experiences of the firm attributes in the economy; overviews and subjective examination of firms that mirror the trouble spots of SMEs in the economy; and government approaches that permit us to comprehend the current vital heading and activities for SME advancement.

1. ***Firm-Level Quantitative Information:*** The accompanying information ought to be gotten for all little and medium-sized firms in the neighborhood economy. Sometimes, the modern statistics may just have the option to furnish us with the accompanying information for a huge however critical example, while in different cases acquiring firm-level information might be considerably more troublesome. In such cases, the corporate expense information base could fill in as a sensible source and intermediary for the majority of the factors we need.

Variable	Description
Sector	The industry sector/subsector that the firm is in. This information is required to categorize the firms and to apply controls for sector composition.
Location	The specific geographic location of where the firm primarily operates in. This would help to understand the distribution and concentrations of firms in a region, more specific location (e.g., based on postal code) would be preferred.
Firm inception year	The year in which the firm started operation. This information is used to determine the age of the firms.

Output	The annual production output (in monetary value or production quantum commonly used in the particular sector) of the firm. The firm's output value, i.e., the sales revenue is an indication of the firm's size and scale, relative to other firms in the same industry sector. The growth of output/output value should also be derived.
Number of employees	The total number of full-time employees in the firm. The firm's employee strength indicates the size of the company. Together with output, the firm's productivity can be derived as output / number of employees. The growth of employee number should also be derived.

All these information ought to be acquired as a stock figure, for example, as a preview of time. For yield and worker number, a chronicled base year figure or time arrangement information in the previous quite a while ought to be gotten to notice development design.

2. ***Surveys and Subjective Investigation (for example the World Bank Enterprise Survey):*** While the firm-level information gives quantitative proportion of profitability to all organizations in the economy, reviews of test firms may give more subjective experiences about the difficulties looked by the organizations.

   In such manner, the World Bank Enterprise Survey, which is a firm-level overview of a delegate test of an economy's private area, could be a decent wellspring of data. The studies cover an expansive scope of business climate themes including admittance to fund, debasement, foundation, wrongdoing, rivalry, and execution measures. The firm-level data of agent organizations gives more minute perspective on the organizations in the economy.

   Correspondingly, the World Bank Doing Business report would likewise give experiences on the business guidelines and their implementation at subnational or local level. It would likewise be a decent wellspring of data on broad business climate level, corresponding to the Enterprise Survey at firm-level.

3. ***Government Approach Plans:*** Clear comprehension of the current government strategies and activities structure a significant contribution to the diagnostic cycle and help decipher numerous discoveries from the quantitative and subjective investigation.

These commonly incorporate:

- Central government SME strategy, technique, and explicit activities (for example, Malaysia SME Master Plan, 2012–2020);
- Local government SME technique and activities;
- Central bank SME strategy and activities. Admittance to fund (working capital, term credits and value) is one of the center issues looked at by SMEs, and national banks commonly have expressed system, guidelines, and activities to help address this from a financial area perspective.

5.2.12. Defining and Distinguishing Competitive SMEs

The vital movement here is to characterize the measures for being shortlisted as competitive SME with regards to firm demography. We have demonstrated a three-section definition above dependent on age, development, and area possibilities. These can be changed with the goal that a reasonable number of high developments high potential little and medium firms are recognized. Whenever models are characterized, the rundown of a sensible number of Competitive SMEs can be made.

Some vital inquiries at this stage would include: what is the business blend of these organizations? Furthermore, how does this development direction contrast with different nations at a comparative phase of improvement? How enormous is the competitive SME area contrasted with nations at a comparative phase of advancement (regarding commitment to GDP, business)? In nations at a comparable phase of improvement, in which areas are competitive SMEs most usually found (for example, in IT)?

In the event that the public information does not exist, could do some outside-in determination to distinguish and estimate the competitive SME area dependent on the global experience.

5.2.13. Policy Needs to Help Competitive SMEs

The proof on SME development proposes a few key factors that sway on firm development. Benchmarking public execution on different measurements will give a sign of qualities and shortcomings, and help with focusing on arrangement activity on the most applicable requirements. Parts of this will be populated with 'hard information.' In any case, it could conveniently be enhanced by subjective overview work, to more readily comprehend the points of view of SMEs regarding the critical requirements on development.

The key variables include:

- Capital markets including the monetary profundity and the VC market;
- Internationalization remembering development for sends out by SMEs and size conveyance of trading firms;
- Business climate for SMEs including work market adaptability and consistence costs (how simple is it to enroll, work, and grow a SME).

The yield from the indicative will illuminate the plan and weighting regarding SME strategy. Figure 5.7 starts to outline the strategy objectives, asset arrangement and administrative accentuation independently for Competitive SMEs (Autio et al., 9). The information to populate this analytic may not be finished; addressing the arrangement of inquiries may require an interest in gathering information to more readily see firm development elements, the conduct and execution of competitive SMEs, and to distinguish the significant imperatives on firm development.

	SMEs Policy	**High-Growth Entrepreneurship Policy**
Policy Goals		
Objectives in relation to entrepreneurs	Entice more people to become entrepreneurs	Entice the right people to become entrepreneurs
Objectives in relation to entrepreneurial firms	Increase the number of new entrepreneurial firms	Increase the growth of entrepreneurial firms
Objectives in relation to operational environment	Facilitate the environment for small business operation	Facilitate the environment for entrepreneurial firm growth
Resource Provision		
Source	Mostly from public sources	Combination of public and private sources
Type of financial resources	Grants, subsidies, soft loans	R&D loans and innovation grants. business angel finance, venture finance, IPOs
Dominant service	Basic (standard) advice for firm creation, business planning, small business operation	Experience-based advice for venture finance; strategic planning. internationalization: organizational growth
Resource distribution principle	Ensure equal access for everyone (resource spread)	Select promising recipients (resource focus)
Regulatory Emphasis		
Life cycle focus	Remove bottlenecks to new business entry	Remove bottlenecks to entrepreneurial firm growth

Compliance bottleneck addressed	Reduce cost of compliance for small businesses	Smooth compliance requirements for growing firms
Fiscal regulations	Reduce VAT for small firms	Accommodate dramatic changes in firm scale; treat share options neutrally
Attitude toward failure	Avoid failure, bankruptcy	Accept firm failure and bankruptcy. but reduce the related economic and social cost
Links to other policy domains	Industrial policy, social policy, labor policy	Industrial policy, innovation policy, labor policy

Figure 5.7. Strategy objectives, asset arrangement and administrative accentuation for Competitive SMEs.

The critical thing here is for governments to think of comprehensive approaches while boosting financial and social effect from restricted government assets? As numerous examinations have appeared, Governments frequently fall flat on the off chance that they attempt to pick champs (firms that the public authority thinks will succeed) and furthermore increment risk of capture. A portion of this can be addressed by synchronous commitment with numerous organizations of an area, interest chain or bunch level. The risk can be further mitigated by dynamic planning, stage-gate funding and by leveraging new forms of media to inject greater transparency.

Another highlight note is that the activities are redundant all through open arrangements or government activities, as seen in numerous different occasions. Working with private areas or reinforcing private area limit may be more compelling and productive in conveying the outcomes.

For instance, a credit agency for SME could be set up to give an autonomous assessment of the monetary dependability of little firms, and it would assist with tending to a portion of the difficulties in getting to fund. A credit agency for SMEs will likewise run into the limitation of getting to such a large number of SMEs with restricted assets, and they might be most appropriate to begin their inclusion with Competitive SMEs.

Moreover, as Khan brought up in his exploration (Khan, 2009), for organizations to get serious, balance among cost and quality should be accomplished through securing "implied information" that must be learnt by doing, and the speed of retaining the implicit information relies upon the degree of exertion put in by the firm. The key for policymakers is that the financing instruments made accessible to firms should zero in on fulfilling, actuating, or requiring the organizations' degree of exertion and quality, and it should likewise be adjusted against political explanation and firm constructions.

Ultimately, as a "quality control agenda" for planning SME strategies, the following should be considered to guarantee the proposed strategy tends to the "competitive SMEs":

- Will the competitive SMEs (i.e., the 5% of firms) need and want the proposed initiative?
- Will the competitive SMEs be benefited from the initiative?
- Will the competitive SMEs be benefitted more than the rest of firms?

5.2.14. Monitoring, Assessment, and Motivating Forces to Help the New Methodology

The quantity of enlisted SMEs in many nations will in general be high. The number is likewise in motion with an enormous number of firms entering and leaving. For instance, the city-territory of Singapore, positioned 39 in the World by GDP, has roughly 154,000 firms. Of these, around 30% of firms are either pristine or are currently leaving-22,826 organizations were framed and 22,497 organizations stopped activity in Singapore in 2012.

Following and intently observing serious SMEs, is subsequently, a more viable route for government specialists to deal with the SME arrangement of the economy. It is likewise a basic advance to screen and assess Competitive SME arrangements.

We suggest that the short rundown of competitive SMEs be followed throughout the long term. The viability of government activities and foundations zeroed in on SME improvement could be estimated against the destiny of these organizations throughout the long term. This would likewise illuminate the public authority's future procedure for improving SME profitability. We repeat the point made in the past subsection that the approaches should stay comprehensive and the field ought to be level playing. However, given limited financial and human resources at the disposal of governments, it will help to track, monitor, and aim to make high potential SMEs globally competitive.

To take responsibility for examination and strategy plan, we likewise recommend that a project management office (PMO) be set up in a pertinent government organization. This arrangement regions cuts across numerous administration organizations, and coordination is required. What is more, without maintained and centered exertion, brilliant approach is probably not going to be completely powerful.

5.2.15. Concluding Comments

There has been reestablished strategy and exploration interest in SMEs over the previous decade or somewhere in the vicinity. This is welcome; SMEs can make a significant commitment to public financial execution. Be that as it may, this case study has contended for a more centered, better adjusted way to deal with SME strategy to augment the commitment to public monetary results. The objective is to guarantee that all pieces of the economy are set up to make a solid commitment to income, profitability, and business development.

Specifically, this case study has contended for a tighter spotlight on endeavors to help competitive SMEs. The controlling idea here is that firm-based approach should be guided by materiality; given restricted arrangement and financial assets, strategy ought to be firmly centered around the zones that will contribute the most extreme add up to in general economic performance; occupations, development, GDP, etc. This strategy exertion should be upheld by an examination plan: for instance, more noteworthy endeavors to amass analytic information on the most proficient method to evaluate the general significance of SMEs and the idea of the approach plan. Putting resources into applicable information and exploration to all the more likely illuminate these particular inquiries would add interest.

For most non-industrial nations, a two-dimensional way to deal with helping competitive SMEs is suggested. The main pillar is a bunch of strategy topics that reward result and effect, while the subsequent pillar is about the interaction of strategy plan, conveyance, checking, and emphasis. Government strategies should zero in on empowering high possible endeavors to develop instead of just expanding the quantity of firms in the economy.

Key approach subjects include improving a company's procedure and execution through management constructing, and improving the company's profitability and development. The idea of competitive SMEs requires the public authority to focus assets towards fewer firms since covering a huge number of firms is not pragmatic. Be that as it may, the last approaches and activities should stay comprehensive, reward execution alongside great administration, and maintain a strategic distance from capture and market contortion.

5.3. CASE STUDY: COMPETITIVE SME STRATEGY SUBJECTS AND MODELS, SINGAPORE

The problem statement for policymakers is to: how to get the most extreme effect from restricted government assets to create competitive SMEs, while staying comprehensive? As numerous investigations have appeared, Governments regularly come up short in the event that they attempt to pick winners (firms that the public authority thinks will succeed) and furthermore increment danger of capture. So, policymakers need to configurate savvy strategies that have careful distance, equivalent freedom, however open the capability of competitive SMEs.

While financial awards and appropriations are normal instruments that the public authority offices may convey, these are not by any means the only methodologies. For instance, a portion of the projects started by the Singapore government takes advantage of the assets and aptitude accessible on the lookout, making motivations for versatile and solid SMEs to develop.

Positioned No. 1 in the World Bank's "Working together" study, the Singapore government is popular for its business-accommodating arrangements and favorable to business mentality. Different government offices and legal sheets have projects and plans focused on various businesses with various goals. Following are a few models from Singapore that could fill in as reference for planning approaches and projects to help competitive SMEs.

1. ***Grants to Improve Profitability-Enhanced Mechanization Credit (MechC) Scheme:*** This award is available to all Singapore-enlisted development workers for hire, pointed toward assisting them with improving profitability and receive new innovation. Regulated by Building and Construction Authority (BCA) of Singapore, and as of late upgraded with higher cap and bigger subsidizing sum in 2013, this award repays project workers up to 70% of the costs caused in buying or renting gear that outcomes in profitability enhancements.

   This plan takes a look at compensating "throughput" as opposed to "sources of info," and it remunerates just the individuals who have just shown critical efficiency improvement (for example in any event, 20% labor-saving). Accordingly, it urges the organizations to turn out to be more profitable and consequently more serious simultaneously, and boosts the individuals who have accomplished positive outcomes. The plan has surely profited numerous little project workers, coming about in as much as 400% improvement in profitability for a few.

2. ***Equity Financing for Fruitful New Businesses-Startup Enterprise Development Scheme (SEEDS)*:** To help youthful (under 5 years) and planned (exhibiting high development potential with clear versatility for the global market) business people to develop, the plan gives co-speculation choices another outsider financial backers. In particular, SPRING SEEDS Capital (SSC), an entirely claimed auxiliary of SPRING Singapore, will coordinate the total contributed by outsider investor(s) dollar-for-dollar up to a limit of $1 million, in this manner taking a value stake in the investee.

   Government is not straightforwardly engaged with the private area capital market activities. Qualified VCs have full self-sufficiency to pick, are boosted to contribute more on account of better yields because of co-financing, yet need to bear the danger if the startup falls flat. It causes the planned SMEs to handle both the difficulties of admittance to back and admittance to aptitude. This plan has assisted numerous nearby new businesses with developing and extend in the global market.

3. ***Non-Monetary Help/Counseling for Global Development-IP for Internationalization Program*:** IE Singapore gives helps consultancy administrations on ensuring and augmenting protected innovation rights for Singapore organizations who wish to wander abroad, through procedure, exploration, preparing, and online assets.

   This program, among numerous others that supported by different Singapore government organizations, are planned to build up a pool of information and encounters in a specific space region (for example IP) that everything firms can tab on, or fill in as a typical stage to establish a more dynamic climate for hopeful organizations to develop.

   By giving all the more freely accessible assets needed by developing SMEs, no organizations are avoided from the advantages that administration offers, yet just the more serious ones will use these assets for their potential benefit to make more an incentive in the economy.

5.4. CASE STUDY: COMPETITIVE SME STRATEGY SUBJECTS AND MODELS, SOUTH KOREA

The South Korean economy has developed quickly into the tenth biggest economy power lately, and SMEs have made huge commitment. They represent 99.5% of the absolute organizations, 77% of individuals utilized and 50% of the value include the economy. There have been more than 100 SME approaches since the 1960s, with subjects moving as the economy created.

As of late, the emphasis has been on fortifying SME intensity, internationalization, and setting up mutually advantageous participation between enormous organizations and SMEs.

1. ***"Purchase-Guaranteed New Product Development Program" – SMBA*:** Through this program, the small and medium business administration (SMBA) upholds SMEs' new product improvement with up to 500 million KRW subsidizing in the wake of getting intentional interest from the public companies or enormous firms.

   The public authority (for example, SMBA) weds the interest and supply from enormous and little firms individually, organizing the coordinated effort in the reciprocal eco-framework. Government financing is gone through on product development with a market interest, to help SMEs that have shown versatility. As indicated by the SMBA's 2009 Report, this program has been powerful for SMEs in bringing down advancement cost and in subbing recently imported products with broadly created ones. Cooperation has consistently expanded with more than 170 buying companies partaking in 2008.

2. ***"Hidden Champion Initiative" – Korea Import-Export Bank (Exim bank)*:** As the authority trade-credit office of Korea, the Korea Exim bank built up this program to give strategy help to encourage high-potential SMEs' improvement towards turning into a main worldwide fare organization. As the state-run bank, Exim bank will give both monetary and non-monetary help to chosen SMEs all through the phases of business exercises including product improvement, creation, and abroad deals.

   Despite the fact that the determination interaction may be tested on the ground of decency and adequacy, the idea driving this activity is to concentrate on more serious firms on the lookout and give focused on asset help to encourage their development.

5.5. CASE STUDY: COMPETITIVE SME STRATEGY TOPICS AND MODELS, MALAYSIA

Positioned number 1 in simplicity of working together among 49 upper center pay nations by the World Bank Doing Business, Malaysia has genuinely a dynamic private area, and the Malaysian SMEs have been at the cutting edge of economic advancement even before the nation's freedom.

With the vision of "making worldwide competitive SMEs across all areas that improve abundance creation and commitment to social prosperity of the country" and to turn into a big-time salary country by 2020, the Malaysia SME Master Plan 2012–2020 plainly expressed 4 objectives and 32 activities to change the SME scene in the country. The way of thinking embraced in this ground breaking strategy is especially in accordance with the idea of competitive SME.

The four expressed objectives are:

- Increase business development;
- Expand number of high development and creative firms (like competitive SME approach);
- Raise efficiency (this objective is additionally installed in the competitive SME approach);
- Intensify formalization.

The accompanying two activities (from the 6 high impact programs (HIPs)) serve to outline how they accomplish the objectives of extending the number of high development and imaginative firms and of raising profitability. Despite the fact that these activities are yet to crystalize as explicit approaches, they are useful in mirroring the perspective of strategy planning.

Malaysia is building up the technology commercialization platform (TCP) to energize advancement. Under this program, the current hatching offices are incorporated under one public stage; program chiefs are boosted upon fruitful commercialization; and SMEs and potential financers are better connected. As we can notice, the plan of the TCP project centers around distinguishing the most serious and innovative firms. The subsequent model is the Catalyst Program, which plans to make local bosses through a focused-on methodology with help nearby financing, market access and human resources advancement. The program has straightforward determination measures and leave instruments and configuration underpins the advancement of the most serious firms.

5.5.1. Regions for Future Exploration

The case study endeavors to build up the idea and meaning of competitive SMEs, and proposes a step-by-step approach in contriving brilliant SME arrangements that focus on supporting the development of competitive SMEs while staying comprehensive. Given the wide distinction in the SME space across various nations, we deliberately received a conventional methodology for our investigation and indicative. Practically speaking, every country or area should characterize and analyze competitive SMEs explicit to winning conditions.

As the organizations contrast fundamentally in numerous viewpoints like geographic area, industry area, level of monetary turn of events, position in the value chain, their qualities, and requirements in approach they uphold shift significantly. More profound local examinations are needed to address appropriate inquiries on competitive SMEs, for example, where they are found and which industry area they are in, what are their requirements and what strategy measures have been demonstrated viable (and incapable).

According to the abovementioned, it may likewise be fascinating to investigate the connection between SME's commitment to work, GDP, and efficiency and the country's pay level, to comprehend on the off chance that it is ideal to have a higher portion of GDP come from SMEs in an economy, or if there is an ideal synthesis among little and huge firms.

Another significant zone that is not canvassed in this investigation is on the casualness of economy and business arrangement, especially in less developed nations. Casual organizations, which are regularly little, additionally add to economy and occupation creation. This is especially applicable for Africa, where their commitment to occupations can be huge. Formulating applicable arrangements and formalizing these organizations would likewise be a region of interest for future investigations.

All the more significantly, we accept that the future work around there ought to be done in an organization with a couple of customers both to profoundly contemplate competitive SMEs in a particular district and to create and test intercessions. The inside and outgaining from encounters of competitive SME strategy execution, like the usage plan, cost, and return, and effect assessment technique would likewise be of extraordinary incentive to numerous different customers.

Chapter 6

Greening SMEs: Europe Case Study: Opportunities and Difficulties

CONTENTS

6.1. DEFINITION OF SMES

The legitimate meaning of SMEs fluctuates by country and by industry. Notwithstanding the quantity of representatives, strategies used to arrange little organizations incorporate yearly deals (turnover), estimation of resources and net benefit (asset report), alone or in a blended definition. The definition in the European Union (EU) is that a SME is an endeavor of approximately 250 representatives, with a turnover beneath EUR 50 million or asset report complete not surpassing EUR 43 million. A private venture is characterized as having under 50 workers with approximately EUR 10 million monetary record, and a miniature business would have under 10 representatives and approximately EUR 2 million asset report.

Among EaP nations, the meaning of a SME regarding the quantity of representatives is indistinguishable from that of the EU in Armenia, Moldova, and Ukraine (in the previous two nations the turnover limits have been acclimated to the normal pay levels, which are a lot of lower than in the EU). Belarus characterizes miniature ventures as having up to 15 representatives, little organizations have up to 100 workers, and medium-evaluated firms to 250 (there is no turnover model). Georgia has set lower edges: 20 representatives for little ventures and 100 for medium-sized ones. In Azerbaijan, the limits for "little ventures" (a solitary classification) differ contingent upon the financial area: 50 workers in industry, 25 in agribusiness, 10 in administrations, and so on.

Simultaneously, environment administrative systems are planned around sustainable risks and not to address a specific organization size. No sustainable guideline explicitly targets SMEs, rather recognizing generally safe exercises and establishments, albeit administrative direction normally remembers specific highlights of independent companies. Environment authorization specialists are not efficiently mindful of the quantity of SMEs they manage and do not gather this data.

It is difficult to characterize generally safe to human wellbeing and the climate. Sustainable controllers in various nations have totally different risk tolerance, driven to some degree by their command and the institutional setting. Generally safe establishments are typically characterized "by avoidance," for example, as those that are not viewed as high-hazard. Danger appraisal rules normally identify with the environmental risk of a controlled office (its intricacy regarding impacts on various sustainable media, area concerning metropolitan and earth delicate zones, volume of contamination deliveries and potential for mishaps) and to its administrator's presentation (consistence record and sustainable administration rehearses).

The sustainable enactment of EaP nations characterizes an undertaking as having low, medium or high environment risk relying upon their monetary action and expected sustainable effect. For instance, in Georgia and Belarus financial exercises with high environmental impact are characterized corresponding to the necessity to go through an environmental impact assessment (EIA). Low environment impact may likewise be characterized regarding certain sustainable media: in Belarus, no air discharge limits are set for low-sway offices.

This Guide utilizes the term 'SMEs' as an all the more broadly acknowledged term, especially with regards to greening the economy and in acknowledgment of the particular guideline and consistence provokes identified with independent ventures. In any case, it centers around those SMEs that are considered by pertinent sustainable controllers to be okay establishments.

6.2. ROLE OF SMES IN GREENING THE ECONOMY

SMEs represent around 99%, all things considered (of which more than 90% of ventures are miniature undertakings) and 66% of work across the OECD zone. Albeit independent ventures' individual sustainable impression might be low, their total effect can, in certain regards, surpass that of enormous organizations. For instance, SMEs represent 60–70% of mechanical contamination in Europe (Miller, 2011). The key areas where SMEs have a huge climate sway incorporate animals cultivating, development, metal completing, waste treatment, food, and drink industry, material, and calfskin fabricating, and so on.

Lessening the sustainable effect of SMEs through accomplishing and going past environment consistence in both assembling and administrations is a key achievement factor in greening the economy. SMEs are significant for green development as key drivers of eco-advancement and central participants in arising green ventures. Developing freedoms exist in the administrations related to greener assembling. Exceptionally innovative and imaginative SMEs in the assistance business, for example, plan, and design firms or bio-energy arrangement suppliers, contribute progressively to eco-development across a wide scope of enterprises. New and young firms are especially significant for extremist green developments, as they frequently misuse mechanical or business opportunities which have been disregarded by more settled organizations or even test the plans of action of existing firms.

The "green change" is additionally a critical business opportunity for SMEs themselves as significant providers of products and enterprises. In reality, the key drivers for SMEs to embrace green practices are non-administrative and include:

- The rising cost of products and key crude materials;
- Potential cost reserve funds and upper hand;
- Market pressure from clients.

Nonetheless, the ability and capacity of SMEs to embrace feasible practices and take advantage of green business lucky breaks for the most part face size-related asset requirements, expertise shortfall and information limits. SMEs are frequently unconscious of numerous monetarily appealing chances for environment improvement. There is a far and wide misperception that ensuring the climate is related with specialized intricacy, weights, and expenses. In any event, when they know about the capability of better environment execution to improve a company's seriousness, an absence of fitting abilities and mastery ordinarily keeps firms from following up on mutually beneficial freedoms. Simultaneously, the absence of assets frequently prompts SMEs being hazard opposed and less willing to put resources into new advancements, incompletely as a result of the uncertainly about the restitution time frame.

The UK Carbon Trust survey found that 65% of customers need to buy products from earth mindful organizations. However, the greater part of SMEs consider a to be economy as a danger, about a portion of private companies accept that profiting by the green economy requires a ton of speculation capital, and just 22% imagine that putting resources into green products and administrations will prompt higher benefits (Carbon Trust, 2011).

For SMEs, becoming environmentally friendly is to a great extent a deliberate activity subordinate upon the vision and conviction of one or a couple of people. Numerous SMEs will put resources into more energy-proficient and harmless to the ecosystem measures, however they require dependable partners in financing their speculations and the privilege administrative structure. In any case, they regularly face deterrents in gaining admittance to back, with banks being hesitant to finance such ventures and without the specific staff expected to assess SME projects.

The expanding number of business relationship in OECD nations (for instance, the UK Forum of Private Businesses) are requesting that their legislatures offer help to SMEs in the progress to the green economy by ensuring that guidelines are straightforward and assess the necessities of independent companies; giving more clear data on the scope of green decisions accessible and their useful and monetary angles; and utilizing monetary impetuses to give independent companies certainty to put resources into green advances and the executives frameworks. To address these requirements, the EU has attempted various arrangement activities to help the green change of SMEs.

6.3. OBSTACLES TO IMPROVING ENVIRONMENT EXECUTION OF SMES

Late examination has shown that while SMEs represent roughly 64% of the modern contamination in the EU, truth be told, not many of them proactively take part in activities to lessen their sustainable effect: 3–4% of miniature organizations, 7–8% of little organizations and 6–7% of medium-sized organizations (Calogirou et al., 2010).

For the public authority, the environment guideline of SMEs addresses a significant test because of the variety of SMEs' exercises and particular sustainable issues, the generous number of administrators, and the absence of data accessible to the controller about their degrees of consistence. Most of SMEs are "powerlessly agreeable" (EC, 2002), as in they do not think enough about sustainable prerequisites to guarantee that they generally conform to every one of them.

What inspires SMEs and their proprietors is probably going to be totally different from what rouses huge enterprises. Notwithstanding their heterogeneity, SMEs have numerous basic qualities that impact their way to deal with environment issues and the execution of green practices; both in accomplishing and going past consistence (see likewise Table 6.1):

- Ownership and the board are focused on similar hands. The business person assumes a critical part in the undertaking and his own inclination is typically the most powerful factor when choosing about ventures and business procedures.
- This business visionary is probably going to experience the ill effects of significant time and assignment pressure, which leaves him with a brief period to think about deliberately future exercises

past the center business of the organization. This could suggest that speculations that are not identified with center business are viewed as optional and experience the ill effects of the absence of consideration.

- SMEs have a restricted limit (absence of assets, time, and aptitude) to ingest sustainable prerequisites and to consent to them, just as a low consciousness of the need to address their environmental impacts.
- The business visionary himself, for the most part is not very much educated about chances of the applicable green practices, their expenses, and advantages. Given this time and errand pressure, SMEs as a rule, depend vigorously on the assessment of their expert encompassing (exchange affiliations, providers, customers, managers, and so on), which regularly have a similar absence of data.
- The business person is frequently hazard disinclined given the moderately little monetary size of the undertaking. Vulnerability might be related with operational issues inside organizations, like the ability to retain and execute the change needed to improve sustainable execution. These incorporate vulnerability about the most fitting innovation to be utilized and the absence of information on the best way to join green practices into the center business arranging.
- The required compensation back for new speculations is regularly pretty much as short as 2–3 years (it is additionally an element of the expense of capital). For the most part, sustainable advances incorporate greater expenses temporarily though the additional advantages are acknowledged in the more drawn-out term, which prevents their reception by SMEs. Restricted admittance to back is additionally a key constraint. The most widely recognized sustainable issues for SMEs, like asset and energy reserve funds, which typically are not identified with the center business of the organization, are possibly tended to if activities are probably going to bring about a generous expense decrease for the time being.
- SMEs experience minimal outside strain to carry on in an all the more harmless to the ecosystem way. It is hard for NGOs or clients to relegate explicit negative sustainable results to at least

one SMEs, while it is a lot simpler to target enormous notable ventures. Besides, governments when all is said and done, try not to press SMEs by environment enactment.

Table 6.1. Internal Barriers in SMEs that Prevent the Adoption of Environmental Improvements

Resources	Attitudes and Company Culture	Awareness
• Lack of time to investigate issues or locate support or tools. • Severe time pressure in small enterprises. • Lack of resource allocation to address environmental issues. • Lack of investment in training. • Cost constraints on investment. • No employee allocated responsibility for environmental issues.	• Belief that SMEs have a low environmental impact and have no environmental issues to consider. • Mismatch between beliefs and actions: positive attitude toward the environment is not translated into actions. • Perception that environment has no relevance to the business: environment given no status as a business issue. • Skepticism about the potential cost savings and market benefits. • Prevalence of short-term business planning; belief that costs of environmental measures arise quickly while benefits accrue slowly.	• Low awareness of environmental legislation. • Low awareness of support organizations and information sources.

Source: EC (2002).

The most recent Eurobarometer overview of EU SMEs (EC, 2013) took a look at explanations behind inaction on asset productivity. Around 26% of European SMEs said that managerial or lawful systems were perplexing, and 24% said that the expense of environment activities was a hindrance. Also, 20% demonstrated that they were hampered by an absence of explicit environment ability, and 17% experienced issues in picking the correct activities for the organization.

A big part of SMEs in the EU (51%) does not wish to go past consistence with pertinent administrative necessities, while 22% are mulling over accomplishing more than needed by enactment, and 19% are doing so as of now (for 11% of respondents, sustainable concerns are essential for the organization's need targets). The bigger the SMEs, the almost certain it is to characterize sustainable worries as a need. More than 90% of SMEs in the EU are making probably a few moves to be more asset productive for absolutely financial reasons. Most basic activities identify with limiting waste, saving energy and crude materials.

6.4. CURRENT ENVIRONMENT STRATEGIES FOCUSING ON SMES IN EAP (EASTERN PARTNERSHIP NATIONS)

6.4.1. Regulatory Systems

Altogether EaP nations, similar system for setting environment prerequisites applies paying little mind to the office's degree of sustainable danger, which makes a weighty authoritative level for SMEs just as for controllers. The administrative framework is vigorously overwhelmed by single-medium allowing (for air emanations, wastewater releases, and garbage removal) which applies to each endeavor which has separate sustainable effects. Where general restricting guidelines ("specialized guidelines") with sustainable standards exist, they are not area explicit and do not recognize offices with various degrees of effect.

Be that as it may, the circumstance is beginning to change as sustainable controllers are beginning to zero in their endeavors on ventures to address the most elevated danger. For instance, Armenia is venturing out the broadening of sustainable administrative systems: the draft law "On environment impact appraisal and aptitude" visualizes the order of managed elements into three classes (A, B, and C) with various evaluation methodology for every classification. Armenia is likewise building up a law on environment self-observing which would separate self-checking and self-detailing necessities dependent on the administrator's sustainable effect. Moreover, in Ukraine just administrators with higher environmental impact are liable to air outflows self-checking and self-announcing.

In Azerbaijan, the draft of the new Law on EIA sets the requirements for endeavors dependent on their environmental impact, area, and kind of financial action. In Georgia, the administrative changes made during 2004–2007 fundamentally worked on the regulatory methods for all endeavors, including SMEs, by radically cutting the quantity of licenses and allowances, lessening the permit assurance period to not exactly a month, and presenting "one-exit shopping" for all grants and licenses.

Other EaP nations are likewise wanting to take comparative measures. Moldova's Small and Medium Enterprise Sector Development Strategy for 2012–2020 imagines changing the administrative structure to coordinate SME needs. Belarus' National Strategy on Environmental Permitting for 2009–2020 accommodates the disentanglement of the managerial strategies identified with sustainable allowance of endeavors with low environment impact by 2015.

The separation of administrative systems additionally concerns consistence observing. In some EaP nations, the recurrence of environment assessments has been separated between wide risk classifications. For example, Armenia is actualizing a risk-based arrangement of consistency checking. The 2011 alterations to the Law on "Coordinating and doing examinations in the Republic of Armenia" (No. 60 of 2000) and Government Decree No. 1562-N of 2012 specified that the recurrence of examinations ought to be founded on the surveyed level of the venture's environment risk. The degree of risk is resolved through a scoring framework considering the undertaking's area explicit and singular dangers. The review recurrence for generally safe offices is set immediately like clockwork.

6.4.2. Existing Approach Motivating Forces

EaP nations have commonly given little thought to the greening of private ventures, and do not have the lawful, arrangement, and institutional intends to upgrade the environmental performance of SMEs.

The climate services and their partner foundations give administrative data to the managed local area. Particular environment data habitats, normally connected with climate services, help with understanding sustainable necessities through phone counsel, workshops, and rules. For instance, in Georgia, the Ministry of Environment and Sustainable Resources Protection has set up an Environmental Information and Education Center in 2010 to give consistent warning administrations to organizations and people. A comparable Environmental Information Center exists inside Moldova's Ministry of Environment. Be that as it may, these data benefits infrequently arrive at more modest organizations.

There are a couple of instances of administrative motivators for getting affirmed to a sustainable administration framework (for example in Azerbaijan and Belarus). In Belarus, organizations sending an EMS ensured in agreement to ISO 14001, advantage from monetary impetuses while ascertaining environment expense on air outflows, wastewater releases and garbage removal. Generally speaking, notwithstanding, consistence advancement exercises are immature in EaP nations.

Simultaneously, governments in EaP nations progressively understand the significance of SME uphold approaches with regards to greening the economy. Services of Economy in both Moldova and Armenia are intending to bring environment contemplations into their essential records on SME uphold exercises, yet have not begun the advancement of explicit strategy measures.

At the point where a system does not have institutional proprietorship, it is probably going to stay that way. In Georgia, a "Green Business Support Strategy for Georgian Private Business Organizations" was created in 2011 by the Georgian Entrepreneurs Confederation with help from the German government. It suggested setting up an "Data place for green business," advancing environment administration frameworks, dispersing of best practices, creating suitable financing instruments, and so on, however has been executed just incompletely. The Georgian Green Business Award was declared by the Ministry of Environment and Sustainable Resources Protection in October 2013. The honor is made in the green organization, green product, and green structure classifications and looks to bring inspiration of business people up in climate security and social obligation. Be that as it may, numerous other approach instruments are as yet inadequate.

All EaP nations with the exception of Georgia have broad contamination charge plans covering many toxins. These duties are payable by all endeavors with separate contamination discharges; however, the duty rates are too low to even consider giving impetuses to sustainable enhancements. All EaP nations force burdens on earth hurtful products (like engine powers and vehicles), yet just a few of them (Armenia and Moldova) have product burdens commanded by environment enactment. The sustainable motivating force effect of these product burdens is similarly unimportant.

6.5. TECHNICAL AND MONETARY HELP FOR GREEN PRACTICES

The circumstance with government upholds for SMEs in EaP nations is still inconsistent. Governments frequently assume a detached part in advancing environment sustainability and best practices, and their company is by and large restricted to facilitating global contributor undertakings.

Services of economy in a few EaP nations execute different data and preparing programs for private ventures, yet they seldom get systematized. A positive model can be found in Georgia, where the Ministry of Economy and Sustainable Development has been furnishing privately owned businesses with dependable and noteworthy industry information and investigation, and creating them mindful of opportunities, among others, identified with the usage of economical business practices.

As indicated by 2014 SME reviews in Armenia and Moldova (OECD, 2015a, b), just 12% and 23.5% of the organizations that embrace asset productivity measures in the particular nations get some specialized or monetary help (Figure 6.1). The bigger the undertaking, the more probable it is to get some help, which never arrives at micro-organizations. The absence of government uphold seems to address the greatest gap, as a glaring difference with the degree of public help exercises in the EU (EC, 2013).

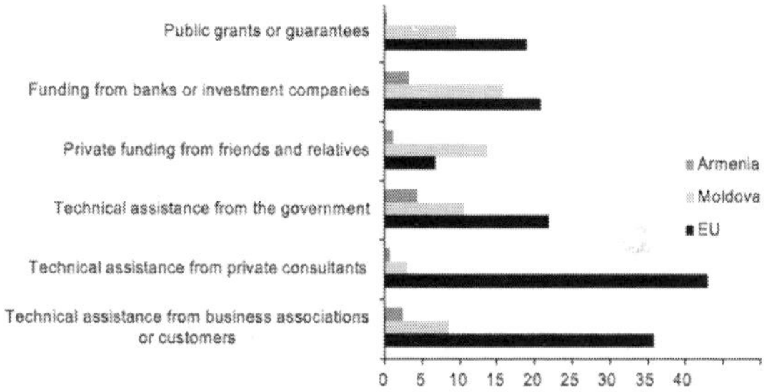

Figure 6.1. Percentage of SME receiving support for resource efficiency actions.

Source: OECD (2015).

Contrasted with public awards and advancement, private financing assumes to some degree the greater part in supporting asset effectiveness and in the creation of green merchandise and ventures in EaP nations. Be that as it may, the current private financing instruments are by and large restricted to credit lines given by International Financial Institutions (IFIs). Practically all IFIs dynamic in EaP nations have opened such credit lines. These incorporate the European Bank for Reconstruction and Development (EBRD), the International Finance Corporation (IFC), the European Investment Bank (EIB), the Asian Development Bank (ADB), the German public bank Kreditanstalt für Wiederaufbau (KfW), and the Development Bank of Austria.

EBRD is by huge the main agent in the area. Various IFIs economic pertinent environment exercises through credit lines principally committed to SMEs, like EIB and ADB. What is more, there are various multilateral offices and benefactor financed stages that have likewise given environment credit lines to nearby monetary foundations in the district that target SMEs (for example the Green for Growth Fund and the Global Climate Partnership Fund). In the Lviv locale of Ukraine, the territorial government finances loan costs of business credits for energy productivity projects in organization with five private banks. Worldwide benefactor supported activities to advance SME green improvement assume a considerable part in improving admittance to fund and expertise for SMEs. While they are not economical in the long haul, they add to building social and environmental duty in private banks. In Georgia, a couple of banks have set up sustainable administration units, and the Bank of Georgia has officially embraced an environment and social approach and individual methodology.

The positive part of the private area likewise shows itself through greening the store network activities. Azerbaijan is a genuine illustration of how bigger organizations can help more modest organizations to improve their sustainable presentation. In 2007, the Enterprise Development and Training Program (EDTP) was dispatched with financing from British Petroleum (BP) and its co-adventures. EDTP motivates and enables organizations to build up their business and become more serious and harmless to the ecosystem provider to BP, its partners and the oil and gas industry overall.

6.6. INSTITUTIONAL DIFFICULTIES

The absence of limit in environment specialists to create and execute explicit arrangements, the disregard of sustainable consistence advancement exercises, the shortcoming of the "green" part of SME uphold strategies and foundations, and the deficiency of assets (other than the restricted contributor subsidizing) for the help of green strategic approaches comprise the essential institutional difficulties in this space in the EaP district.

Environment experts in EaP nations do not have a particular unit which would be responsible for advancing sustainable consistence. The inspectorate is by and large not responsible for consistence advancement exercises. These capacities are here and there performed by a data community inside the climate service, which explains and scatters sustainable writing, instructive aides, bulletins, and other enlightening materials.

Services of economy are the main entertainers in the area in working with SMEs. Particular SME uphold companies under the protection of the service of economy have been set up in a few EaP nations. The SME Development National Center of Armenia (SME DNC) was made in 2002 to give state backing to SMEs just as to execute projects on SME area advancement utilizing state budgetary assets just as commitments from global benefactor companies. The SME DNC has a very much evolved organization of provincial branches and delegate workplaces covering all areas of Armenia and is composed by the focal office in Yerevan. The SME DNC furnishes organizations with data, counseling administrations and instructional meetings. It likewise runs send out advancement programs, upholds development and successful plans of action just as directs monetary advance certifications to new companies and working organizations. In any case, it is simply beginning to create exercises to advance asset efficiency among SMEs.

In Moldova, the organization for small and medium enterprises sector development (ODIMM) was made in 2007 as an exceptional office with the primary goal of encouraging manageable advancement of the SME area. Undertaking Georgia was set up in 2014 with a comparable order.

Neighborhood governments can likewise animate SMEs to improve their sustainable performance. On account of their neighborhood information, they are frequently preferable put over focal governments to offer custom-made measures for nearby SME advancement. Nonetheless, because of monetary imperatives and different needs, neighborhood administrations of EaP nations are not generally in a situation to utilize this possibility without limit. In Armenia and Moldova, neighborhood governments have legal obligations in the field of environment insurance and the utilization of characteristic assets, however they are not executing a particular project zeroed in on improving SME sustainable execution and consistence. Another major institutional test in the district is the shortcoming of business affiliations. The current business associations, like offices of trade and industry and bosses' affiliations, are overwhelmed by bigger organizations, do not offer need to serving the necessities of private ventures, and have little information on feasible creation issues. There are not very explicit exchange affiliations (particularly contrasted and their wealth in most OECD nations), and their SME enrollment is very restricted. Independent ventures do not see the advantage of teaming up with their rivals and do not get sufficient reasonable help from business relationship in return for participation expenses that they are approached to pay. This makes it a lot harder for the public authority to contact individual SMEs.

6.7. REGULATORY INSTRUMENTS

6.7.1. Simplified Allowing and General Standards

Controllers do not normally have procedures that apply just to modest offices-they essentially have less assets to spend on them than on high-hazard locales. In any case, an expanding number of sustainable controllers in OECD nations set up uncommon systems for generally safe establishments, by far most of which are SMEs.

While allowing stays a prevailing administrative system in most OECD nations, there is a fast development of standard principles, from improved allowing to action-based necessities without obligatory notice of the controller, to an enormous number of SME areas. More modest organizations, normally having not many or no in-house administrative assets, generally welcome a normalized, rules-based way to deal with setting sustainable prerequisites, which gives them more assurance about the best method to accomplish consistency than do individual, bespoke licenses. Most SMEs like to be determined what they need to do plainly and compactly. Rule-based systems additionally have different advantages, including diminished administration and expenses to the controller and the shortfall of effect fair and square battleground inside a mechanical area.

The pattern to improve on administrative prerequisites for SMEs is all around showed by the presentation in 2009 in France of another environment administrative system. Establishments that present a current danger sufficiently huge to legitimize its earlier assessment can be tended to through normalized administrative requirements. Before the finish of 2014, 35% of establishments recently covered by allowing prerequisites are intended to be moved to the enrollment system. This is accomplished for explicit movement areas (for example, distribution centers, gas stations, dry cleaners, little refineries), movement volume edges being applied were vital. The presentation of this new system was the aftereffect of a gap between the managerial convention of an announcement and the incredibly thorough cycle of authorization (allowing). The enrollment actually requires the accommodation of an application and an improved on open meeting, however it has expanded the consistency of the prerequisites and decreased the application handling time.

Another illustration of work on grants is found in England and Wales, where nearby specialists issue air contamination licenses to private companies. The Department of Environment, Food, and Rural Affairs (Defra) produces direction notes for every one of the 80 areas managed by nearby specialists. Created as a team with business companies by specialized working researches, these direction notes contain the portrayals of applicable best accessible methods and discharge limit interests. They are for the most part very prescriptive to keep a level battleground between nearby specialists all over the nation.

Administrative systems for setting environment necessities are normally coordinated in levels, contingent upon the level of an office's danger. In Scotland, SMEs that are not liable to incorporated allowing can be controlled by straightforward licenses/grants (with layout conditions), an enrollment system (including a notice with data on who is taking part in pertinent exercises), or green building ratings (GBRs) where lower-hazard exercises (release into a surface water waste framework, stockpiling, and utilization of excrement and composts, and so on) do not should be told to the sustainable controller.

While the streamlined allowing strategy consistently includes a conventional application from the administrator, which is affirmed by the administrative authority at the sub-public or neighborhood level (despite the fact that offices in numerous nations progressively utilize direct online application structures custom-made to singular areas), rules-based systems could conceivably require warning of, or enlistment with, the capable power. Decisions that expect administrators to tell, or enlist with, the skilled environment authority prior to taking part in an action are best regarding the controller's information on the directed local area and command over its possible sustainable effects.

There is no standard wording to depict rules-based administrative systems across OECD nations. Terms, for example, 'enlistment' and 'general restricting principles' mean various things in various frameworks. For instance, in certain nations (in the Netherlands for Type B establishments, Section 5.3) GBRs are characterized as standard conditions explicit to a sort of action or an area with mandatory warning of environment specialists prior to participating in a movement, while in others (for example in the UK) they do not force such a prerequisite. In the last case, the framework is like that of exclusion from allowing, where the controller does not have the foggiest idea who is taking part in a movement to which the principles apply and how much generally safe action is being directed overall. The following head models ought to be applied when the utilization of GBRs or different guidelines-based systems is considered for a fragment of the managed local area:

- Rules should cover an adequately huge number of controlled substances in a specific area to make this administrative system powerful;
- The condition of innovation and methods in that area should not be quick, as rules cannot be refreshed habitually; and
- The offices should have a comparative, environment impact.

Indeed, even a GBR system with obligatory warning does not generally give sufficient data to the controller. Establishments under the "presentation" system in France are dependent upon GBRs that are spread out in normalized pastoral orders (arrêtés-types). These prerequisites are connected to the proper affirmation of receipt of a presentation which is sent by the administrator to the administrator. Now and again, they might be made more tough by a request for the regent to reflect nearby conditions. Nonetheless, the investigation administrations do not ordinarily have a chance to audit an announcement or suggest dismissing it. There is an ensuing issue of the absence of information on generally safe SMEs by environment administrative specialists. The notice issue can be tended to by expecting administrators to routinely evaluate their own consistency with the standards and present an individual explanation to the skillful environment power. For instance, the Small Quantity Hazardous Waste Generator Education and Self-Certification Program in the US territory of New Hampshire (set up since 2003) requires the state's roughly 3,700 endeavors to direct an office appraisal at regular intervals and give an affirmation to the New Hampshire Department of Environmental Services that the organization is in consistence with the appropriate guidelines.

6.8. BETTER GUIDELINE ACTIVITIES FOR INDEPENDENT COMPANIES

Independent companies frequently grumble that staying up with the latest sustainable necessities is oppressive, especially comparable to understanding which prerequisites apply in their individual setting. Discovering direction and exhortation disclosing what they need to do to conform to given guidelines is troublesome. SMEs frequently feel that they are not upheld enough and are nonsensically expected to adapt to similar degrees of desk work and commitments as bigger organizations. Organizations, for the most part express help for a client centered connection among controllers and the directed with the essential objective of consistence instead of authorization. Improved data for directed substances has been reliably distinguished as the main factor for diminishing the authoritative weight on organizations (EA, 2011).

A new UK study (Defra, 2011b) proposes that miniature organizations invest more energy on exercises related to showing consistency (getting ready for examinations, finishing desk work, record-keeping) than genuine exercises to follow guidelines. Regardless of endeavors to decrease pointless duplication of reviews, business is still regularly needed to give a similar data more than once in exhibiting consistency with guidelines.

Additionally, the first of the UK Government's five standards of better regulation is the proportionality of guideline, which assumes controlling independent companies just were fundamental and with pragmatic exclusions. That will essentially affect private ventures, requesting their contribution at the drafting stage lessens possible unfriendly impacts. The US Small Business Regulatory Enforcement Fairness Act (1996) furnishes SMEs with an extended chance to take part in the advancement of specific guidelines. Some European nations require administrative organizations to plan uncommon articulations on the possible effect of proposed guidelines on private ventures.

Posting the full scope of guidelines that affect private companies in chosen areas assists with recognizing freedoms to diminish duplication in desk work or potentially measures among administrative specialists. Among various approaches to improve on the authoritative prerequisites for writing about environment issues and keep away from duplication of mentioned data are the production of cross-country data enrollment frameworks available by all able government specialists, the acquaintance of e-government with supplant desk work documentation, and the usage of the "one-window" approach for giving proper allows and licenses to organizations (for example through nearby specialists). Offering consistence related data to organizations additionally adds to better guideline by decreasing their exchange cost of consistence.

6.9. INCENTIVES FOR ENVIRONMENT ADMINISTRATION CONFIRMATION

While the fundamental driver for organizations to have a guaranteed environment administration framework (EMS) is market interest from clients and customers), sustainable specialists may offer extra administrative motivations:

- The selection of an ISO 14 001 EMS or a comparable standard may qualify administrators for specific advantages in the allowing interaction. In the Netherlands, EMS-affirmed administrators can apply for licenses that are less definite and prescriptive. A few EU nations (for example Italy, Slovakia) issue licenses with longer legitimacy periods and with diminished announcing prerequisites to EMAS-confirmed organizations (EC, 2004b).
- The US EPA's Small Business Compliance Policy permits independent ventures to get decreases in financial punishments if infringement is found by any deliberate methods, including government-supported nearby consistence help exercises or environment audits, EMSs, utilization of online consistency help apparatuses, and so on In Austria, regulatory fines are postponed for organizations with a guaranteed EMS in the event that they identify resistance during an inside review.
- The review recurrence may likewise be straightforwardly or by implication connected to the presence and nature of the administrator's EMS. Organizations with a confirmed EMS appreciate decreased investigation recurrence in Norway, and in France, establishments enrolled with EMAS (there were just 17 such establishments in April 2011) are excluded from routine consistence reviews. In Korea, "green organizations" assigned by the Ministry of Environment are absolved from routine sustainable announcing, and their examination recurrence is decreased.

  In any case, while there is some dependence on EMSs to encourage consistence, the experience of numerous controllers (for example in the UK and the US) is that an EMS is a long way from being an assurance of consistency (particularly since ISO 14 001 does not represent consistency). Along these lines, there may not be adequate explanation behind the unique treatment of EMS-guaranteed organizations in consistency checking.

6.10. SECTORAL WAY TO DEAL WITH CONSISTENCE AFFIRMATION

Administrative necessities (like GBRs) are normally determined by the sort of sustainable effect, despite the fact that they will in general influence explicit areas. Be that as it may, consistence affirmation when all is said in done and especially consistent advancement is transcendently area based. Independent ventures ordinarily react just to messages adjusted to their movement area, which makes the sectoral approach urgent in advancing consistence and green practices among SMEs.

A developing number of environment requirement specialists produce sectoral techniques that look to enhance the harmony between the three mainstays of consistence confirmation-consistence advancement, observing/evaluation and implementation-corresponding to the necessities and difficulties of a particular fragment of the controlled local area. Therefore, a huge portion of consistence checking/evaluation exercises is turning out to be area based, despite the fact that it keeps on depending on effect-based guidelines.

In numerous areas, themed, and exceptional examinations (assessment crusades) have been progressively used to screen modest destinations or exercises. Pivoting area explicit missions could be a technique for boosting the effect of restricted organization assets. Such missions can make the impression of a generous administrative capacity and danger of requirement, with an exceptionally restricted administrative asset responsibility. It is fitting to connect mindfulness missions and assessment crusades: the previous give organizations data to go along while the last mentioned, after a specific time frame, look to build up a level battleground through consistent observing and requirement. In any case, controllers partaking in such an investigation mission ought not zero in solely on topical risks yet additionally focus on location explicit risks and prerequisites.

Dependence on objections and reports from the public remaining parts is fundamental, given the asset imperatives, unavoidable piece of consistence observing of SMEs. Notwithstanding, while grievances can possibly reveal new risks and risk presenting organizations, they are regularly determined by quick worries that may not be identified with the controllers needs or even fall under its order, in this way disseminating office assets.

To enhance consistency checking of non-unpredictable, modest establishments, it is fitting for sustainable authorization specialists to help out non-environment controllers and private area companies in their assessment exercises. For instance, Scotland's Environmental and Rural Services (SEARS) organization of 8 Scottish controllers with capabilities over the cultivating and ranger service areas guarantees composed assessments and smoothed out detailing methods. Burns partners mastermind joint visits or endow a couple of the partners to investigate the angles that are typically under the other companies' ward. They likewise share data given by the ranchers and other significant organizations, along these lines decreasing the authoritative weight on the directed local area, and facilitate the treatment of client enquiries. The Scottish Environment Protection Agency (SEPA), the sustainable controller, trains staff of other accomplice organizations that lead normal site visits as indicated by their own commands yet additionally play out certain environment administrative duties appointed by SEPA.

Reevaluating of consistency checking to non-government bodies might be more fitting at the neighborhood level, where capable specialists frequently need the ability to appropriately practice this capacity. In Ireland, Dublin City Council has named a project worker to execute its Fats, Oils, and Grease program to diminish oil releases from food administration foundations (bars, cafés, inns, and so on), consequently forestalling blockages in the public seepage organization. The worker for hire's job is to distinguish premises that require a profluent permit, to exhort the administrator on best administration rehearses, and to assess the premises four times each year to guarantee consistency with permit conditions. In setting up such a course of action, the skillful legislative authority should set clear prerequisites for the project worker's performance and survey it occasionally.

6.11. INFORMATION-BASED INSTRUMENTS

6.11.1. Advice and Direction

SMEs, especially miniature organizations, have restricted capacity to comprehend and decipher guidelines, leaving them feeling confounded. Organizations are informed that they have an obligation to act in an environmentally capable manner, however it is regularly indistinct what this really implies, how a business can do it, and at what cost. Going past consistence addresses a considerably greater test, where the absence of consciousness of financially savvy opportunities is the key bottleneck.

Governments, as a team with business researches, can address these difficulties by giving SMEs data on green practices. Among data spread apparatuses, one can recognize exhortation and direction. Guidance is dynamic, direct commitment with a business eye to eye during investigation visits or reviews, noting phone, email or site help demands, just as tending to business delegates at classes and comparative occasions. Direction is the arrangement of data to managed elements, commonly in the composed (printed or electronic) structure. Direction incorporates, among others, email refreshes, site free-access direction pages, flyers, pamphlets, and different distributions.

6.11.2. Designing Successful Messages

Most of European SMEs act to turn out to be more asset productive to lessen costs (63%), while 23% are driven by the client interest. The developing number of SMEs making asset effectiveness moves says that their creation costs have diminished thus: 42% in 2013 contrasted with 35% simply a year sooner. More than 66% of SMEs are happy with the profit from their interests in asset effectiveness (EC, 2013).

Notwithstanding monetary advantages (Table 6.2), actualizing green practices may bring about business benefits (new business opportunities, favored provider status, and so on), authoritative advantages (got from upgrades in the nature of the board), correspondence benefits (positive public picture, better companies with clients, financial backers, and controllers), and expanded worker inspiration and confidence. These advantages are affirmed by independent ventures themselves: Scottish SMEs named diminished working expenses, a more persuaded labor force, decreased danger of indictment or fines, and improved client connections as key business gains from improving their environment presentation (NetRegs, 2009).

For miniature organizations, improved local reputation, expanded number of clients and staff spirit have all the earmarks of being the fundamental motivators for better environment practices (Defra, 2011b). Simultaneously, most independent ventures are worried that improved reputation or expanded deals are probably not going to result from consistency with environment prerequisites since clients do not know about a business' operational practices and, consequently, this does not impact their client decision.

Table 6.2. Cost Savings from Environmental Improvements in SMEs

Areas of Improvement	**Sources of Savings**
Process efficiency	Optimizing the performance of existing processes (or introducing more efficient new ones) minimizes the use of raw materials, energy, and water and the production of waste. Proper maintenance of equipment minimizes costly downtime and resource waste associated with shutdown and start-up periods.
Product design	It may be possible to re-design a product so as to reduce the amount of resources it contains while still maintaining the level of service it provides.
Waste disposal	Improving process efficiency reduces the amount of waste that a process produces. Once waste has been generated, it is often possible to reuse it or pass it on to other companies that can use it, and thus avoid the costs of its disposal.
Source of raw materials	Changing the source of raw materials in a particular process by switching to recycled materials can result in cost savings.
Infrastructure	It is possible to generate savings by making efficiency changes in the company's infrastructure: installing energy-efficient lighting, insulating buildings, improving the efficiency of heating systems.
Packaging and transport	The reduction of packaging volume and finding local suppliers and customers to decrease transportation distances can be major sources of cost savings.

Source: Starkey (1998).

Notwithstanding various exact examinations which have shown that improving the environment presentation of a firm likewise improves its monetary performance, numerous SMEs actually dread that improving their sustainable presentation will cost cash and that there will be a contention between their craving to secure the climate and the need to hold down expenses and maintain a fruitful business. The test is to persuade SMEs that green practices really decrease expenses and make for better business.

By far, the greatest worry of SMEs is the transient monetary benefit, selling that sustainable administration can set aside cash, diminish expenses and increment efficiency is generally welcomed by entrepreneurs. Subsequently, whether or not the goal is to improve consistency, impact the take-up of environment innovations or increment the reception of EMSs, sustainable data focusing on private companies should make the "business case" and outline the monetary advantages of environment upgrades.

Most private companies look for clear and steady data on the base necessities for consistency. Translation of text-hefty direction can be hard for a SME: there ought to be a straightforward message about the issue, its answer (bit by bit direction) and where to go for more data. The most effective method of giving exhortation and direction to organizations is to consider the full set-up of guidelines that apply to them, not simply environment guidelines. Administrative necessities that are conveyed to independent ventures ought to be very much organized across government.

To stay away from exorbitant or pointless expenses for organizations, direction ought to plainly express the base lawful necessities. As the volume and intricacy of both compulsory and intentional (great practice) direction develop, organizations are worried that it is getting harder to separate between the two and that deliberate direction can some of the time be treated as obligatory practically speaking. Deceiving counsel could prompt over-consistence and a superfluous expansion in the administrative weight. To dodge this, consistency, and great practice direction ought to be obviously recognized.

Organizations like consistence direction to be legitimately solid (absolving them of possible approvals if the direction is precisely followed). Helpless direction which is not adjusted to the requirements of independent companies leaves entrepreneurs stressing that they are accomplishing something incorrectly and that when they attempt to make the best decision, they can be punished for not getting it totally right. Then again, a lot of counsel and direction may confine advancement in discovering arrangements that are financially savvy for the administrator's particular conditions, conceivably putting more modest organizations at a serious burden.

It is significant to underscore that what is acceptable in environment terms may likewise be useful for the monetary primary concern. For instance, the prescribed procedures control for carports created by the Irish EPA's National Waste Prevention Program is designated "Keen Garage Guide: Save cash and improve the performance of your carport." Utilizing a similar methodology, the EPA's Green Business Initiative (www.green business. ie) dispatched in 2006 looks for basically to empower organizations to evaluate their own asset use effectiveness, especially as for waste and water, by utilizing online review/appraisal devices. The Green Business pages additionally offer tips and contextual investigations on the most proficient method to set aside cash by lessening asset use.

In making the "business case," it very well might be especially helpful to introduce instances of other comparable organizations getting business benefits because of the sustainable administration upgrades being referred to. Contextual investigations ought to ideally be neighborhood to expand the acknowledgment of their decisions by independent companies. In any case, the experience shows that contextual investigations lose their significance as the advancement program develops.

How much data is bundled, what message it presents, and how and who conveys it, is basically essential to its positive effect. The key area explicit components influencing the decision and execution of special apparatuses incorporate the accompanying:

- The level of consistency in size and the board practices of the business-the more prominent the variety, the more noteworthy the need to create various methodologies and instruments for various sub-classes of organizations;
- The level of mechanical refinement in the business, which may decide the requirement for definite direction;
- The presence of an efficient industry affiliation addressing the area, which influences the method of correspondence with singular organizations;
- The public profile of the business, which may decide the degree to which SMEs might be vulnerable to public pressing factor.

The most suitable correspondence channels are probably going to be area explicit, mirroring the distinctive plans of action and exercises inside various areas. Public specialists will in general be most appropriate to conveying "single direction" data, while involved help is better conveyed by business affiliations or private companies. At the point when direction comes from a private area company, it is for the most part seen by independent ventures as dependable, while data from legislative bodies is frequently respected with doubt. Simultaneously, promising however many organizations prudent across all areas to get to midway accessible electronic assets can add to the practical, reliable conveyance of administrative direction.

To ensure the data coordinated at SMEs is significant, working with industry in planning area explicit direction and codes of training is of essential significance. Giving organizations a say in the construction and substance of sustainable direction improves the probability that the material is justifiable and resounds with entrepreneurs. The degree to which SMEs will partake in the plan of data devices and different motivations to a great extent relies upon the presence of set up business companies. It could be hard to convince SMEs to follow up on environment data, in any event, when it is clearly in their own monetary interest. Data, for the most part affects organizations which as of now have a sustainable interest yet regularly don´t arrive at the individuals who are not inspired by green practices. Proof from the writing proposes that raising business mindfulness by furnishing them with more data on their environmental impact will not sustainably prompt changes in conduct (Defra, 2011b). Different contemplations are at any rate as basic, basically the need to fortify market impetuses for sustainable upgrades by straightforwardly (inventory network pressure, green public acquisition) and in a roundabout way (green affirmations and eco-labels) expanding the interest for harmless to the ecosystem products and administrations.

6.12. PROACTIVE DATA DISPERSAL

The least difficult device to spread administrative data is an "administrative watch"-a (paid or free) membership administration sending standard email or cell phone reports on important authoritative turns of events and new relevant administrative necessities. One illustration of such a help, normally settled by profession or business uphold companies, is Enviroveille in France, overseen by the Assembly of French Chambers of Commerce and Industry.

A few environment specialists put together support work areas reacting to consistent inquiries from organizations and different partners. The Swedish EPA works an alleged "lawful help administration" accessible by phone for two hours each working day, which offers exhortation and translation on legitimate issues. The US EPA's Asbestos and Small Business Ombudsman addresses specialized and administrative inquiries coming from private companies on a complimentary hotline, notwithstanding creating other consistent help instruments. A few organizations in OECD nations are investigating the chance of taking advantage of informal communities to give consistent help.

Numerous controllers find giving direct consistence help to administrators during investigation visits to be a viable methodology for managing specific kinds of directed elements, especially SMEs that are by and large willing to consent however who do not know about the administrative necessities or who come up short on the authoritative ability to go along (SNIFFER, 2011). The point is for administrators to consider to be as a "acceptable police officer" yet as a "great guide" and to save money on expenses of working out what they should do and how. Such "prompt and help" visits can be officially recognized from consistent investigations in an implementation office's arrangement of exercises. In Finland, overseers have customary conversations with administrators on existing and potential consistency issues and potential arrangements; and the consequences of such conversations are recorded in the electronic consistency checking framework (OECD, 2009). Notwithstanding, this instrument has a related danger of "catch," as monitors may begin to see the world through the eyes of the organizations they are prompting. Such warning visits are additionally very asset concentrated.

Industry magazines, bulletins, and business or local area occasions are believed to be useful strategies for publicizing administrative prerequisites and implementation cases, especially to some little or country organizations which might not approach the web. Workshops, preparing classes and industry fairs (especially those coordinated in terms of professional career companies and other business researches) can likewise be successful in passing on data or conventional counsel on the best way to follow the prerequisites. They can encourage positive relations among controllers and managed organizations, help share great practices and cultivate agreeable ways to deal with tending to environment issues.

Non-legislative companies, for example, Cleaner Production Centers can likewise give data on green practices, directed at explicit crowds-industry just as public and nearby governments. Different devices that the Centers can utilize incorporate classes, workshops, and researches zeroing in on data dispersal and trade. Nonetheless, most SME administrators are probably not going to be capable or slanted to set aside the effort to go to such meetings, as they ordinarily do not have a committed environment work force. Also, these occasions are not really accommodating in looking for significant criticism on the substance of sustainable direction.

Then again, directed, succinct, easy to understand aides can be helpful in conveying a message that sticking to harmless measures for the ecosystem rehearses (and subsequently agreeing with the law) is a savvy approach to work together. Such aides ought to represent the "business benefits first" way to deal with advancing great sustainable conduct.

The scattering of consistence help data to the managed local area is best accomplished in company with numerous partners. For instance, the pocket-size "Little Environmental Guide for Construction Workers" arranged mutually by the Scottish EPA and the Construction Industry Research and

Information Company targets proficient workers for hire chipping away at a wide range of building locales. It advocates that "working in a 'harmless to the ecosystem' way can assist with improving business execution and set aside you cash all the while. "Hitting the nail on the head [...] causes you to remain in business." There are additionally instances of cross-sectoral guides for SMEs, including the "Climate and Energy Guide for SMEs" gave by the Assembly of French Chambers of Commerce and Industry (ACFCI, 2010).

6.13. WEB-BASED DIRECTION INSTRUMENTS

The critical component of complete data-based help programs is that ventures can get exhortation, enlightening, and methodological materials in a single spot. Throughout the most recent decade, in numerous OECD nations there has been fast multiplication of government-supported business warning sites, particularly focusing on SMEs. Government specialists are keen on using online tools and platforms since they offer administrative consistency of counsel, time, and cost investment encouraging correspondence and communication flow with the controlled local area.

Sustainable direction can be conveyed through environment controllers' own sites, particular destinations subsidized by administrative specialists (those could likewise be services of economies, industry, or agribusiness) and conventional business entryways which direct clients to data on sustainable consistence and great practices. In any case, the turn of events and activity of such projects require critical financing, for the most part from public sources.

The US EPA's online National Compliance Assistance Centers (www.assistancecenters.net, made in 1998) convey data through sites for 16 assembling and administrations areas, bureaucratic offices, and neighborhood governments. The EPA additionally maintains a Small Business Gateway (www.epa.gov/smallbusiness) which, among others, gives data on sustainable help and specialized assistance accessible from the Agency. What is more, the US Small Business Environmental Home Page (www.smallbiz-enviroweb.org) is expected to be a "all-inclusive resource" for independent ventures and help suppliers who look for data on a wide scope of environment points. It guides clients to consistence data (counting connects to state sites), truth sheets on sustainable best administration rehearses in 10 SME areas (pastry kitchens, administration stations, retail locations, and so forth), key private company distributions, data on impending occasions, and so on.

NetRegs, an online device made by the UK environment controllers (for England and Wales, Scotland, and Northern Ireland), gave during 2002–2011 free sustainable direction to small and medium-sized organizations (SMEs) all through the country. Since 2012, this help has been run in Scotland and Northern Ireland simply by the SEPA and the Northern Ireland Environment Agency (NIEA). Area rules are custom-fitted to give explicit direction on environment enactment and great practices appropriate to the cycles in every area, except recognizing the two. A library of sustainable themes contains pragmatic clarifications of issues like bundling, waste, clean air, and emanating the board, which are applicable to all organizations paying little mind to their industry area. Ordinary studies of client organizations added to the unmistakable client assistance focal point of this instrument. A Business Advisory Group involving business agents guarantees that client needs are met.

As a component of the UK Transformational Government Agenda, England's Environment Agency needed to pull out from the NetRegs company just as move its own site to a solitary gov.uk entry. The thought was to encourage client route to various kinds of business-related guidance and to save government assets. Be that as it may, a large part of the environment substance has been taken out simultaneously.

Environment help to European SMEs is additionally accessible from the European Commission (EC). A SME entryway established on its DG Environment site (ec.europa.eu/climate/sme) gives admittance to significant enactment, data, apparatuses, and accessible preparing. The Environmental Compliance Assistance Program (ECAP) set up in 2007 keeps a site which offers an online best practice data set which assists organizations with actualizing European sustainable enactment and limit the environmental impact of their exercises. The EC likewise bolsters the as of late made GreenEcoNet green practice data stage Designing and dispatching an online direction instrument is not sufficient: there should be a successful correspondence methodology to guarantee that organizations proceed to utilize and profit by it. Online devices ought to be enhanced by different instruments (like mailings, leaflets, workshops) which can add critical value. Simultaneously, while mail and one-on-one contact may keep on being a significant course for effort to independent ventures for the time being, improving admittance to, and utilization of, the web among private companies is probably going to be a more practical and savvy type of correspondence in the more drawn-out term.

6.13.1. Direct Limit Building

A new survey of SME upholds activities on asset efficiency in EU part states (EC, 2014a) recognized around 230 specialized help programs supporting organizations in the ID and execution of asset productivity measures. Over portion of those projects give general admittance to data, self-evaluation apparatuses, contextual investigations. Others offer customized, up close, and personal management services to singular organizations. While general projects additionally furnish help with asset efficiency reviews and setting up EMS, these will in general work for the most part if assisted with general methodologies and procedures as opposed to manage singular organizations. For instance, through workshops or preparing occasions.

The job of government experts in giving specialized help to organizations is not pretty much as broad as in the execution of other approach instruments. The down to earth execution of these exercises is for the most part completed by exceptional business uphold companies set up by the public authority. NGOs, for example, Cleaner Production Centers just as counseling organizations may likewise assume this part, while the public authority may furnish them with monetary help.

Involved, direct asset efficiency upholds programs try to overcome any issues between giving general information and applying it to explicit conditions of individual organizations by helping organizations to recognize the two chances and means for executing asset effectiveness measures, just as their possible expenses and advantages.

Non-government organizations, for example, National Cleaner Production Centers can give eye to eye guidance to organizations through reviews of various parts of their sustainable administration, performance projects and their development. Limit building and backing for undertakings may likewise cover exercises, for example, advancement, and spread of methodological materials and contextual analyzes, just as the execution of preparing programs.

To guarantee manageable use of asset effectiveness and other green practices, there is a need to instruct organization troughs. Long haul hands on preparing, joined with train-the-coach courses, is the best method to fabricate proficient limit among private companies. Ranking directors might be focused through short meetings zeroing in on the fundamentals of environment administration and its advantages and difficulties, empowering them to spur their staff. A general point of Such preparing projects ought to be to coordinate environment worries into the standard business system.

A creative method of prompting private companies has been created by the Green Business Partnership (Scotland), whose mainstream Bright Green Placements program has been sorting out for effectively more than 15 years two-multi month understudy arrangements in SMEs to circle back to sustainable reviews and work with the organization's administration to execute the suggested gauges (and accomplish related reserve funds). A comparative activity was to offer an "impromptu sustainable chief" for one day out of each month to a private company that cannot bear the cost of a committed environment supervisor to assist it with environment administration exercises. The quantity of firms liable to participate in executing great practices because of direct, involved limit building exercises, just as the potential monetary and sustainable advantages that may emerge from these projects are probably going to be impacted by the accompanying elements:

- Involving different public area companies and industry relationship in program plan, usage, and vital oversight can give a more extensive point of view and better coordinated backing to SMEs. For instance, the Danish Green Network is run mutually by open and private area agents. The local performance Bretagne environment plus (PBE+) program in France is supported together by the Regional Council, the local government, the neighborhood businesses' company and the Chamber of Commerce and Industry.
- Affordability of the help administrations affects their take-up by SMEs. The administrations ought to be given for nothing out of pocket or at decreased expense rates.
- Programs that give long haul uphold permit tweaking of their administrations and have a more extended enduring effect.
- Consideration of monetary effects of green practices (on organizations' benefit, business, intensity, and so on) can be required to expand the take-up of the program.
- Promoting the program's accomplishments, including by publicizing accomplishment as contextual investigations, can urge different organizations to execute green practices.
- Using nearby conveyance partners empowers limit building projects to acquire neighborhood information, believability, and responsibility.
- Regular, autonomous, and unbiased assessment of the program in general and the advantage to singular organizations can prompt nonstop improvement.

6.14. RECOGNITION OF GREEN PRACTICES

6.14.1. Simplified Environment Administration Frameworks

A new EU-wide examination (Calogirou et al., 2010) has shown that regardless of government motivating forces just 0.4% of European SMEs have an officially ensured EMS. As indicated by a British review (NetRegs, 2009), just 4% of the SMEs studied expressed that they had an EMS set up. Around a 4th of all organizations had an environment approach, and the probability of this expanded with the size of the business. Pretty much one-10th of independent ventures looked at that as an EMS would be "very valuable" or "extremely helpful," and the fewer workers they had, the less well they saw the advantages of such a framework. In spite of the fact that store network pressure in certain areas is an incredible driver for some SMEs to receive an EMS, private ventures face genuine obstructions, including an absence of assets, information, and specialized limit, the way that most EMS-related expenses are forthright and benefits are medium-term, just as low open perceivability.

The key point is to tailor EMSs, both regarding their content and scope, to the particularities of SMEs. The key, in any event for more modest organizations, is to zero in on basic, open enhancements in administration rehearses, as opposed to the presentation of a formal, officially complex EMS.

There are activities in a few OECD nations, for the most part coming from the private area, to configuration improved on EMSs appropriate for independent companies. Econcertive is an Irish organization which offers environment help to organizations and companies on the whole areas, essentially by methods for the EcoCert plot (www.ecocert.ie). The prerequisites for accomplishing the EcoCert certificate are a similar center necessity concerning any perceived EMS standard, however the administrative work is negligible. What is more, the affirmation cycle incorporates the distinguishing proof of energy, waste, and water-related reserve funds.

The Association of French Chambers of Commerce and Industry (ACFCI) drives two activities on "EMS-light," with considerable specialized, methodological, and monetary help from the public Environment and Energy Management Agency (ADEME). The "1.2.3 Environment" program is intended to encourage bit by bit ISO 14001 confirmation. EnVol is an exceptional sustainable administration program for private companies (with under 50 workers) that do not aim completely fledged ISO 14001 certificate however might want to get acknowledgment for their essential EMS, which generally relates to the principal level of "1.2.3 Environment" (ACFCI, 2010).

The "green tick" logo dispatched by Scotland's Green Business Partnership in February 2011 is another illustration of making corporate environment administration open to SMEs. One tick shows that the organization has an environment approach, surveyed its lawful consistence, and is focused on making constant sustainable upgrades. The accreditation with two ticks implies that the business, moreover, deals with its consistency and has a sustainable activity plan. Three ticks imply the presence of a completely fledged environment administration framework.

There are additionally instances of SME-centered public environment certificate programs directed with dynamic company of neighborhood governments, for example, the Eco-Lighthouse Program in Norway.

Improved sustainable administration is additionally in accordance with the idea of corporate social responsibility (CSR), which is characterized by the EC as "the obligation of ventures for their effects on society." To completely meet their CSR, endeavors ought to have set up a cycle to coordinate social, sustainable, moral, common freedoms and shopper worries into their business tasks and center technique in close cooperation with their partners. CSR rules are essential for the ISO 26000 norm, which was distributed in 2010.

SMEs may have lower business motivators to take part in CSR, essentially on the grounds that there are commonly more modest reputational hazards for SMEs than for enormous organizations. All things considered; SMEs have a significant number of the same purposes behind participating in CSR that huge organizations have. The CSR interaction for SMEs will rely upon the size of the endeavor and the idea of its tasks and is probably going to be casual.

6.14.2. Sector-Explicit Green Certifications

The essential objective of green certificate programs is to expand the efforts of the overall industry from their individuals. To make environment administration qualifications more applicable to explicit monetary areas, business relationship in numerous OECD nations work together with sustainable specialists to create green accreditation brands, a significant number of which target SMEs. The environment controller (and, some of the time, neighborhood specialists) work mutually with accreditation bodies to create "green norms" for the area just as rules on how organizations may "acquire" the option to show suitable signs (stickers, banners, and so on) to feature their sustainable practices to their clients. Instances of such projects can be found in an exceptionally wide scope of economic areas, the majority of which are described by direct interface among business and retail clients, permitting SMEs to profit straightforwardly from their improved sustainable picture.

For instance, Ireland's Green Hospitality Program (under the National Waste Prevention Program) has been created to go about as an umbrella brand for friendliness related sustainable activities, including the Green Hospitality Award, Green Restaurants, Green Festivals, and so forth Formal asset productivity reviews, asset utilization benchmarks, workshops, preparing, and direction are given to each taking an interest to empower them to build up their own environment program and plan for the various degrees of grant. Companies pay for enrollment; however, the expense is incompletely financed by the public authority.

A comparable program for print shops has been very famous in France. Made in 1998 by a local Chamber of Trade and Crafts and since turned out from one side of the country to the other, the Imprim'Vert name has been granted to more than 1,800 print shops that hold fast to a bunch of good sustainable practices, for example, not utilizing harmful products and secure stockpiling and suitable removal of waste. Be that as it may, environment consistency is not among the mark the grant measures.

A "green norm" can likewise be essential for a bigger self-administrative business activity. One such activity, the Red Tractor Assurance plot in England and Wales, is directed by Assured Food Standards-an organization possessed by the UK ranch companies and a few agroindustry exchanges bodies. Initially centered around the sanitation issue, Red Tractor Assurance has been stretched out to cover numerous environmental parts of food creation (the executives of pesticides, composts, excrement spillover, and so forth) across around 80,000 taking part cultivates. Under the "sustainable consistency module" for pig and poultry producers, certificate bodies gather information on consistence with environment licenses when completing reviews for the Red Tractor plot. This assists with diminishing the quantity of Environment Office visits to ranches (to simply once at regular intervals) and to cut yearly allow charges for ranchers.

6.14.3. Eco-Labels

Though green confirmations apply to organizations, eco-labels have similar capacity regarding products. Eco-naming plans try to empower makers to tackle customer interest for harmless merchandise by showing a lawfully secured image or logo. On the off chance that the name has this impact, different makers may react by improving the sustainable execution of their products to get a name trying to recover the piece of the pie. This outcomes in a decreased environmental impact from the products inside the product gathering. The effect of reputational motivating forces among SMEs is regularly lower than among bigger endeavors, however they can be successful on the off chance that they are pertinent to nearby stock chains or clients.

Eco-labeling plans are for the most part intentional: a firm that desires to have a sustainable label granted to its product may apply to the labeling plan, and the mark will be granted if the product meets the significant standards. Eco-label measures can be founded on a solitary boundary or on examinations that dissect the sustainable effect of a product or administration for the duration of its life cycle.

As a component of its ISO 14000 arrangement of sustainable norms, the International Standards Organization has drawn up a gathering of guidelines explicitly administering environment marking. The ISO 14020 family covers three kinds of naming plans: Type I is a multi-quality name created by an outsider; Type II is a solitary characteristic mark created by the maker; and Type III is an eco-label dependent on a full life-cycle evaluation. Environment product declaration (EPD) giving quantitative data about a product in a normalized structure may likewise be viewed as a type of eco-labeling. EPD frameworks are generally exorbitant to set up and work, making SMEs' cooperation in them far-fetched.

Single-quality names address a sustainable statement by an undertaking about a specific environment trait of a product, which in certain plans must be checked by an outsider. Such eco-labels can be identified with energy efficiency (for instance, the US "Energy Star"), economical administration of a specific characteristic asset (for example ranger service eco-labels), the level of reused material in a product, and so forth. The effortlessness of single-quality eco-labels makes them especially alluring to SMEs.

A vital component of lifecycle eco-labels is that a free outsider is engaged with allocating the eco-label. Since a product is surveyed against various affirmed rules, the maker is compelled to gather and break down a ton of data that could be utilized to improve product qualities through the whole life cycle. The EU Ecolabel, the Scandinavian "Nordic Swan" and the German "Blue Angel" are instances of lifecycle eco-labels.

The adequacy of eco-labels in rousing undertakings to improve sustainable execution relies upon rules characterized for a specific product gathering. The environment measures should be refreshed and made more severe routinely so that solitary best products can meet them, subsequently guaranteeing that the eco-label stays a sign of greatness inside a product gathering. Marking plans should battle misdirecting claims by makers about their products.

The expansion of green marks may make disarray among firms and purchasers, especially since the check of cases of environment cordiality is troublesome. In some cases, ventures make eco-labeling plans basically to offer themselves to clients, which prompts huge "greenwashing." Consequently, the standards and interaction for deciding if a product justifies an eco-label or green confirmation ought to be straightforward. It is important to guarantee that marks are not granted too effectively, without a thorough examination of each organization's practices.

Eco-labeling plans are typically run by non-benefit companies (counting governments) without business interests. To take care of their expenses, conspire administrators usually an application charge just as a yearly charge, contingent upon the turnover of the marked product. The EU Ecolabel plot, overseen by the EC since 1992, gives particular treatment to SMEs, with significantly diminished application and yearly expenses.

Public eco-label plans may, nonetheless, be expensive for SMEs to partake in. In Korea, for instance, the quantity of eco-ensured products is huge and keeps on developing, however the development of the quantity of organizations creating such products is much slower, which exhibits the overwhelming portion of bigger firms and not of SMEs in the green products market (Figure 6.2). A SME ought to consider applying for an eco-label in the event that it feels that the normal advantages of doing as such (keeping up or expanding its piece of the pie) exceed the expenses (those of meeting the eco-label models and the plan charges).

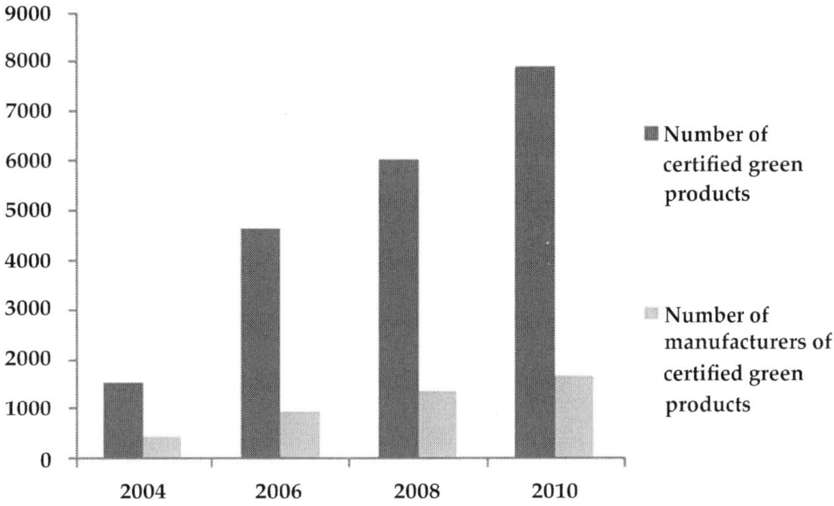

Figure 6.2. Manufacturing of certified green products in Korea.

Source: OECD (2012).

Another point that ought to be taken into considerations is that the foundation of public eco-label plans in little nations regularly does not pay off in view of a restricted market and moderately significant expense for organizations. In any case, it very well may be monetarily and for all intents and purposes doable to set up an improved public product certificate plot for specific products broadly created in the country.

6.14.4. Environmental Acknowledgment Grants

Governments can likewise utilize positive advertising impetuses to advance harmless to the ecosystem business conduct. Environment honors are helping to raise sustainable mindfulness through organizations and the local area and help organizations acquire acknowledgment for their great sustainable performance. For instance, the "Vision in Business for the Environment of Scotland" (VIBES) activity perceives organizations, all things considered, and areas utilizing sustainable prescribed procedures in their day-by-day exercises. The honor program is upheld by the SEPA and run-in organization with other government bodies. It is upheld monetarily through private sponsorship and has in-kind help from various business affiliations. There are a few honor classifications, including Best Environmental Management, Best Environmental Product or Service, Best Co-activity for the Environment, and Best Micro-business Award. A contextual investigation is created for each triumphant business and distributed on the VIBES site. The VIBES grants are likewise utilized as an instrument for giving direct exhortation to candidates through site visits, and further environment enhancements are empowered by means of input and wide data spread.

To be powerful, sustainable honors should be broadly advanced in business and industry media. Be that as it may, some SMEs might not have the monetary or work assets to empower them to finish the application cycle, which may prevent them from entering sustainable honors.

Environment honors can likewise perceive the job of various partners in greening private ventures. The US National Steering Committee for the Small Business Ombudsman/Small Business Environmental Assistance Programs has set up four Small Business Recognition Awards. Among them, the Trade Company Environmental Leadership Award promotes price value execution and authority by an industry exchange company because it improves individuals' consistency with sustainable guidelines. There is additionally an honor for a private venture sustainable help program. The European Enterprise Promotion Awards perceive public bodies and public-private companies that help the improvement of green business sectors and asset efficiency (EC, 2014b).

Chapter 7

Good Business Practice Checklist

CONTENTS

7.1. WHAT ARE THE ADVANTAGES OF GOOD BUSINESS PRACTICE?

Great business practice enhances a business, in all sorts of challenges. A business that follows great practice benefits from multiple points of view, for example:

- The business is bound to be beneficial, have better income, and work with lower environment and monetary risks;
- The business is bound to practice with higher performance and efficiency rates;
- The business is better ready to draw in, hold, and propel staff, in this way improving the company's flexibility and spryness in the worldwide commercial center;
- The business can possibly separate itself and be compensated as a favored seller in a developing green store network;
- The business will have the option to separate itself in a wide-open market, making it simpler to sell the business later on, and potentially at a superior cost;
- The business might have the option to acquire environment risk protection, and potentially at a favored rate; and
- The business may think that its simpler to get to outside money, including bank loans, if necessary.

7.2. WHAT IS THE MANAGERS PART IN GUARANTEEING GREAT BUSINESS PRACTICE?

Executing great business practice includes recognizing the basic undertakings that should be done to keep a business fit as a fiddle, and having the control to guarantee that those errands are completed reliably and consistently. Great business practice requires a yearly survey at any rate; better business practice will enable you to check on regions quarterly, or even month to month. Great business practice is not just about getting your home all together; it is tied in with setting up your business for the difficulties and opportunities it will face later on.

Managers can help their customers execute and keep up great strategic approaches as they are frequently ready to offer autonomous and master guidance. The IFAC SMP Committee has built up this agenda for use by managers, particularly professionals who work in small and medium sized practices (SMPs), to assist them with figuring out what kind of help their private company customers may require.

An agenda like this cannot be complete. In any case, this agenda is planned to begin you pondering the particular activities your customers should take to put their business progressing nicely and keep it there.

7.3. IN WHAT MANNER CAN THIS AGENDA HELP WITH GREAT BUSINESS PRACTICE?

The agenda features great strategic approaches that private ventures ought to take a stab at consistently. In this manner, notwithstanding assisting SMPs with prompting their customers on great business practice, it can likewise be utilized by managers to guarantee their own practices are working in accordance with great strategic policies. On the off chance that you attempt the assignments in this agenda consistently, the finish of the monetary year ought not make unnecessary weight for your business, and you will be bound to have the quality data you need to oversee and develop your business, whatever conditions you face.

7.3.1. Agenda

The following are a few different ways to incorporate significant parts of this agenda into your strategic policies:

- Use the agenda as a feature of the plan in your standard workforce researches and distribute assignments so everybody understands what component of the agenda every individual is responsible for. Request standard reports on each undertaking.
- Write the agenda assignments into your schedule with the goal that you are helped to remember prerequisites at the fitting occasions.
- Build errands from the agenda into the sets of responsibilities of applicable staff.
- The agenda contains six areas as demonstrated as follows. Spaces are given, where proper, in the agenda for you to embed data pertinent to your business (Table 7.1).

1. ***Financial Tasks:*** Errands important to plan budget summaries should be performed routinely. Holding up until the finish of the

monetary year to attempt a considerable lot of these errands will put you under tension, as various returns and structures must be finished not long after the end of the monetary year, which may endanger the quality, and hence handiness, of monetary information. Postponing monetary assignments can likewise deny you ordinary admittance to monetary data, for example, income articulations, which can be basic to assisting you with dealing with the regular rhythmic movement of your business. Monetary undertakings are important to create budget reports, for example, an assertion of economic performance (pay/benefit and misfortune proclamation) and monetary position (asset report), which give data that encourages you to see how your business is performing and to distinguish potential territories for development.

2. ***Strategic Financial Tasks:*** Monetary undertakings do not end with bank compromises or asset reports. There are other monetary errands known as vital monetary undertakings that are basic deciding the future way of your business.
3. ***Strategic Management Tasks:*** Occasionally, ideally at the finish of each monetary year, you should refresh your arranging, planning, and operational techniques. This way your business will be solid and steady for the new monetary year. On the off chance that there are huge changes in your business, it is proposed that these essential administration assignments be embraced all the more routinely.
4. ***Environmental Management Tasks:*** There is mounting proof demonstrating that organizations that set up better control of their relationship with the climate by expanding the custom of their administration exercises profit by increments in efficiency. Thusly, there are enhancements in productivity and thriving.

Better administration control can likewise upgrade consistence with legitimate necessities. Improved sustainable administration is turning into a prerequisite in inventory chains as worldwide organizations are propelled to oversee hazard and their standing, particularly when under tension from non-legislative companies (NGOs), or to meet desires for shoppers. It can assist a business withholding and draw in new clients or access abroad business sectors. Better sustainable administration is required to turn into a factor that can separate one organization from the following in a leave technique or to improve achievement in intergenerational move; it should be a thought in any progression plan. An administration frameworks approach can both upgrade sustainable execution, for example, strength in reacting to bizarre conditions, for example, outrageous climate occasions, and offer the upper hand. See The IFAC Sustainability Framework for more data.

5. ***Regulatory Requirements: Lodging Returns and Forms:*** Staying up with the latest with the lodgment and installment of your legal commitments is viewed as a significant pointer of the monetary danger, wellbeing, and steadiness of your business by banks and different leasers. Consequently, recording the lodgment and installment due dates for every one of the prerequisites underneath is suggested.
6. ***Individual Affairs of Business Owner:*** The finish of the monetary year is likewise a significant opportunity to ensure your own issues are all together.

Table 7.1. Good Practice Checklist

1. Financial Tasks				
√	**Activity**	**Person Responsible**	**Due Date/ Regularity**	**Some Actions to Consider**
	Install financial software.		With new updates	• Ask the software vendor to list what financial statements and reports the software can produce.
				• Use the financial software to produce regular financial statements and reports.
	Enter all data promptly, and with accurate transaction dates.		Ongoing	• Regularly check data entry for quality. • If possible, separate "cash handling" from "data entry" to minimize the potential for fraud.
	Regularly review working capital products, including: • Stock/inventory balances and reconcile to physical		At least quarterly	• Recycle or dispose of old/slow-moving stock/ inventory. • Write-off deadstock/ inventory. • Review purchasing policies to prevent overspending on stock/inventory. • Post materials on a waste, scrap, or materials exchange.
	• Work-in-progress (for construction firms, professional practices, etc.)		At least quarterly	• Bill clients regularly or at milestones.
	• Debtors		At least quarterly	• Invoice as soon as your goods or services are delivered. • Refer bad debts to collection agents. • Review credit screening. • Renegotiate trading terms with consistently slow payers. • Contact slow payers early.

	Reconcile major accounts in balance sheet, including: • Bank and investment accounts		At least monthly	• Have two people undertake the reconciliation. These people should not be the same people who handle cash. • For high volume cash businesses, reconcile daily.
	• Accounts receivable/ debtors' ledger		At least monthly	• Identify customers with large outstanding amounts and follow up.
	• Accounts payable/creditors' ledger		At least monthly	• Reconcile suppliers owed money with a list of approved suppliers.
	• Property and equipment		At least quarterly	• Do an asset stock-take to ensure you still have the assets that are recorded in your accounts. • Identify obsolete, unusable, or written-off assets. Ask your accountant to adjust balances and/or see if such assets can be turned into cash. • Do not over-invest in new capital equipment without an appropriate payback.
	• Sales/Value Added Tax (VAT)		At least quarterly	• Make adjustments quickly through the next activity statement.
	• Equity accounts (especially in partnerships) and shareholder/stockholder loans		At least quarterly	• Operate equity accounts in accordance with the partnership agreement. Try to avoid large imbalances in the amounts contributed by or retained by each partner.
	Review payroll system, including: • Annual leave entitlements		Quarterly	• Encourage staff to take leave regularly-avoid a large build-up of entitlements. • Consider a reserve to fund leave liability.
	•Pension/superannuation		Quarterly	• Comply with legislation regarding frequency of payment, choice of fund and reporting to staff.

	• Income tax withholding		Monthly	• If you have an employee who is about to give birth or has given birth, visit your government's website for information on any obligations
	• Fringe benefits tax		Monthly	
	• Payroll tax		Monthly	
	• Paid parental/maternity leave		Quarterly	
	Translate foreign exchange gains/losses.		Year-end	• Use foreign exchange rates from an official source, such as the tax authority. • Speak to your accountant about how you can manage your foreign exchange risk.
	Market valuation of certain assets.		Year-end	Involve your accountant, or a specialist valuer, as required.
	Review forward orders.		Quarterly	Review forward orders as it will help you plan for any short-term need to expand or contract your business.
	Prepare a statement of financial performance (income/profit and loss statement).		Monthly or quarterly	The profit and loss statement, balance sheet, and cash flow statement can help identify any emerging problems in time for corrective action to be taken. Your accountant can assist in their preparation.
	Prepare a statement of financial position (balance sheet).		Monthly or quarterly	
	Prepare a cash flow statement.		Monthly or quarterly	

2. Strategic Financial Tasks				
√	**Activity**	**Person Responsible**	**Due Date/ Regularity**	**Some Actions to Consider**
	Set targets for financial performance.		At least annually	• Ask your accountant to help you set targets relevant to your industry and your business. • Incorporate set targets into your budgets and strategic plan.

	Review and analyze financial statements.		At least annually; preferably quarterly or monthly	• Compare key ratios from your financial statements, such as working capital ratio, stock/inventory turnover ratio or profit per employee, to averages in your industry. Your accountant may be able to help you get access to such industry averages and assist with calculating and analyzing the ratios. • Compare performance against financial targets and past performance.
	Review actual performance against budget.		Monthly	Undertake variance analysis (ask yourself: What may have caused any gap between budget and actual? How can we overcome unfavorable variances?).
	Undertake sensitivity analysis.		Annually	Ask yourself: What if sales dropped 15 or 20%? Or you lost a major customer? Or a major supplier stopped selling to you? What if your chief sales staff resigned? What if your power source or water supplies were unavailable after an extreme weather event-how long could your business endure this loss? Factor answers to such questions into your forecasts.
	Set sales or production targets.		Ongoing	Undertake a break-even analysis to determine what you need to sell before you make a profit. Ask your accountant to help you with a break-even analysis if you are uncertain.
	Prepare income/profit and loss budget.		Annually	• Make sure your budget reflects your strategic and financial targets. • Incorporate any findings from the variance analysis of the last budget, sensitivity analysis, and the break-even analysis.

	Prepare cash flow forecast.		At least annually	• Have your cash flow forecast show the projected cash flows for each month in the 12-month period. Such forecasts should be updated at least monthly. • Address any future cash shortages, for example, more cash sales, reduced expenses or external finance (such as an overdraft facility). • If you decide to seek external finance for any purpose, go to your lender as soon as possible.
	Review cash flow forecast in light of actual results.		Monthly	Update cash flow forecast to reflect actual events and monitor ongoing cash positions.
	Review bank loans, leases, credit cards or other finance, ensuring you:			
	• Evaluate interest rates on your loans.		Annually	• Look at what other lenders are offering and consider whether you should switch lenders.
	• Provide historic and budgeted information to lenders.		Annually	• Provide information on profit and loss, balance sheet, cash flow statement and budgets.
	• Comply with repayment schedules.		Ongoing	
	• Check compliance with debt covenants.		Ongoing	• Notify your bank immediately if you are in breach of a covenant. If you are uncertain of your covenants, ask your bank.

3. Strategic Management Tasks				
√	**Activity**	**Person Responsible**	**Due Date/ Regularity**	**Some Actions to Consider**
	Create or update your strategic plan.	Owner and key staff	3–5-year horizon, updated annually	• Have a strategic plan for the owners, as well as for the business. This ensures the business complements the owners' needs. • Take time to review lessons learned from the current year and incorporate those lessons into your strategic plan.

	Review employment arrangements, ensuring you: • Conduct performance reviews.	Team leaders	At least annually	• Do not wait until the formal feedback process. Provide regular informal feedback to staff.
	• Consider incentive systems or commission-based pay.	Owner and key staff	At least annually	• Make incentive systems simple, pay promptly, and link the incentives to the controllable success factors for each role. • Consider only paying commission when you have received cash from the sale and paying higher commissions for sales of higher-margin products and services.
	• Get staff to sign an employment agreement (including provisions for confidentiality obligations and ownership of intellectual property).	Owner	Commencement of employment	• Obtain legal advice to ensure employment agreements comply with the law.
	Consider if "restraint of trade" contracts is needed for key staff.		Commencement of employment	• Obtain legal advice to ensure applicable contracts are enforceable and advisable.
	Review sales contracts and customer's payment terms.		Annually	Determine whether your sales contracts protect your business. For example, in a difficult economic environment, you could protect your business by: shortening the payment terms; implementing credit limits; and seeking personal guarantees and security.
	Review suppliers' contracts or payment terms.		Annually	• Negotiate a lengthening of your payment terms of trade. • Review how goods are supplied to you (so that it better meets your needs). • See if you can reduce the minimum quantity you can order. • Look at payment discounts. • As a risk management measure, check alternative suppliers of critical products.
	Review financial commitments, such as: • Office leases		Annually	• Exercise options to renew your lease if premises meet your needs, if they do not, begin planning a move.
	• Equipment leases		Annually	• Understand ownership/payout arrangements at end-of-lease.

	• Securities over assets		Annually	• Check which of your assets is security for which loan and that, where a loan no longer exists, the security is removed.
	• Hedging contracts		Annually	
	• Other		Annually	• Speak to your accountant about what other forms of financing, not outlined within, that might be relevant to your business.
	Establish, update, or review your "Policies Manual," ensuring you: • Document your processes.		Annually	• A good policy manual has the potential to make your business more valuable and easier to run in your absence.
				• Use your process document as a training and quality manual.
	• Allocate specific tasks.		Annually	• Separate record-keeping duties from duties involving the handling of cash and other assets to minimize the risk of fraud or theft by employees.
	• Consider fraud risk.		Annually	• Speak to your accountant about establishing appropriate internal controls.
	• Review staff authority to spend money.		Annually	• Consider authorizing all payments yourself for a short period as part of a cost reduction and quality assurance exercise.
	• Inform and educate staff about your policies		Annually	• Conduct random spot checks to ensure both compliance with your policies and to reduce the risk of fraud.
	Review and update IT systems, ensuring: • You have the licenses you need to use your software.		Annually	• Ensure current versions of software are being used, there are no unauthorized copies, and the number of users your license covers is sufficient for your needs.
	• Back-ups are performed frequently and held offsite.		Daily/weekly	• Test whether your staff knows how to restore the back-ups and that the back-ups work.
	• Staff training needs are met.		Annually	• Appoint a "champion" for each software product to enhance internal transfer of practical knowledge.
	• Disaster recovery plan documentation has been reviewed.		Annually	

	Review your intellectual property by: • Documenting procedures on how your intellectual property is used in your business		Annually	
	• Renewing trading names (including trademarks and business names) and domain names		Annually	Speak to your lawyer to see if your intellectual property is adequately covered.
	Review your insurances, including: • Types of policy required		Annually	• Does your insurance cover match your needs, for instance, insurance covering assets, business interruption, loss of attraction, life insurance, income replacement, etc.?
	• The amount of cover in place		Annually	• Avoid under- and over-insurance.
	Seek ways of reducing resource use in the business. Consider: • The use of water, electricity, gas, petrol/diesel • The use of other resources • Using local suppliers if possible •Eliminating unproductive steps or processes		Annually	• Resource consideration should be part of a cost reduction strategy. • Consider how to operate your business if there was a disruption to the supply of electricity, gas, or water.
	Review any outstanding legal disputes.	Owner and solicitor	At least quarterly	• Keep disputes moving along. • Consider viable ways to settle disputes promptly.
	Determine whether you undertake activities (such as exporting) that may be eligible for a government grant/subsidy.		Annually	Speak to your accountant about what grants/subsidies, if any, you may be eligible for and the eligibility requirements.

4. Environmental Management Tasks				
√	**Activity**	**Person Responsible**	**Due Date/ Regularity**	**Some Actions to Consider**

	Plan to achieve better environmental management and performance, using a systems framework in which you will:	Owner and key personnel	Ongoing	Refer to ISO 14001:2004 for the framework upon which a robust, credible, and reliable environmental management system can be established.
	• Define the scope of your business that will be included.		Initially, and reviewed when changes occur to location or organizational boundaries	• Ensure scope includes your facilities and covers the organization that resides under your control.
	• Identify the significant environmental aspects of your plans, activities, products, and services.		Initially, or with changes to plans, activities, products, and services	• Identify what it is you have or do that causes environmental impacts that add to or subtract from the company's environmental footprint, and can add to or reduce costs and risks, including reputation. As 80% of environmental impacts tend to be location-based, a map can help quickly identify where opportunities are situated.
	• Identify applicable legal and other requirements related to your environmental aspects.		At least annually	• Consult services that provide access to lists of environmental laws. Speak to an environmental lawyer if your need is more acute.
	• Develop an environmental policy.		Initially, and then review annually.	• Ensure it reflects the culture and nature of your business. Make sure all personnel understand it. Post it or be ready to share it upon request.
	• Set environmental objectives and targets.		At least annually	• Make sure your objectives and targets support your policy.
	• Identify the resources needed to set up, maintain, and improve the management system to realize performance improvements.		Annually	• Take into account legal and other requirements, your significant environmental aspects, technical options, financial, and business needs, and the views of interested parties when setting these. • Ask your accountant to assist in costing out objectives and targets to set priorities. • Establish a budget to ensure that you have the resources to meet your objectives and targets. Consult with your accountant for a more detailed analysis if needed.

	• Identify the education and experience needs of personnel.		Annually	• Assign duties to others as required to meet your needs and any milestones. • Conduct a needs analysis to determine what training is needed to educate staff to enable the behavioral changes needed. • Determine the competencies and technical expertise required to ensure personnel can deliver on the policy and reduce the company's environmental footprint.
	• Determine the need to communicate with external stakeholders (see also activity 5 below).		Annually	• Identify the concerns of interested parties (customers, your community, investors, etc.), who are affected by your environmental performance.
				• Determine what information you will share and how you will communicate.
				• Establish procedures to inform appropriate community and regulatory agencies on matters related to emergencies and situations related to the impact of your products and services on the market.
	• Maintain sufficient documentation to ensure efficiency and effectiveness of the EMS.		Ongoing	• Document the key elements of your management activity such as your environmental policy, objectives, and targets to ensure you reduce your environmental footprint.
	• Develop procedures to prevent and respond to emergencies.		Initially, and update as appropriate	• Make sure that you and your staff understand what to do in emergencies.
				• Run periodic tests to make sure your emergency plan works.
	Do, by taking action to: •Establish procedures to prevent significant environmental impact from operations.	Owner or assigned staff	Ongoing	• Ensure that the most critical aspects of your business, which could cause significant environmental impact, are managed to avoid, or control risks like spills or air emissions. Document where there is a low to zero tolerance for failure due to absenteeism or human error.

	Check your progress, ensuring you:			
	• Establish procedures to test the tools used to determine whether indicators of your success are working.	Owner and key personnel	Annually	• Monitor and measure your performance to ensure optimum outcomes.
	• Evaluate status of compliance with legal and other requirements.		Annually	• Check to make sure you are in compliance with laws and other requirements.
	• Maintain records for easy crosschecks on work performed and progress.		Ongoing	• Keep records on your progress up to date, legible, and easily accessible.
	• Conduct an internal audit to ensure that the EMS is working well.		Annually	• Periodically test your system to make sure it is delivering on the value you need.
	• Review the audit results and ensure other key elements of the EMS are suitable, adequate, and efficient to realize value from the environmental management system.		Annually	• Consider the results of your audit to make sure that you take advantage of the opportunity to improve and enhance your position in the market, whether it is with your customers and the supply chain in which they operate, your community, to differentiate yourself in a buyer's market if you are trying to sell the business, or simply for your own internal benefit.
	Act to:	Owner and assigned staff	Ongoing	Identify opportunities to improve your environmental performance, reduce costs,
	Ensure that you are staying current, improving, avoiding problems, resolving mistakes, and reducing impact on the environment.			lower risk, and minimize your environmental footprint.

	Assess the business risk of environmental factors that may affect your business.		Annually	• Ask your accountant to help identify and quantify these factors. • Considerations may include climate change, extreme weather, biodiversity, carbon taxes/prices, or other environmental risks. • Opportunities to be explored could include carbon trading, carbon offsetting, or district heating (whereby a local central plant producing steam, hot water, or chilled water eliminates the need for businesses to have their own boilers or furnaces, chillers, or air conditioners).
	Monitor innovation in environmental technology and reporting.	Owner or assigned staff	At least annually	• Scan reports that provide free updates. • Subscribe to online news services that post highlights. • Read environmental or corporate social responsibility (CSR) reports posted by customers or industry leaders.
	Monitor trends in enforcement.	Owner or assigned staff	Quarterly	Subscribe to news services provided by environmental lawyers on fines and court rulings on environmental offenses.
	Evaluate your succession plan and exit strategy to determine how better environmental management can differentiate your business in a buyer's market.	Owner	Annually	Involve your accountant, or a specialist adviser, as required.
	Determine the need, and value, in reporting on your company's environmental progress.	Owner	Annually, after the tasks above have been addressed	• Ensure that you report on measurable and verifiable progress. Unsubstantiated or incorrectly worded claims can cause reputational risk, lead to your reporting being labeled "greenwash," and even give rise to lawsuits. • Some form of assurance on what is reported may lend credibility to what you report. • Consult a specialist advisor or involve your accountant or lawyer to avoid misinterpretation.

5. Regulatory Requirements: Lodging Returns and Forms				
√	**Requirement**	**Person Responsible**	**Due/Payment Dates**	**Some Actions to Consider**
	Income tax return			Provide information, including financial statements, to your accountant for review; highlight large or unusual transactions.
	Corporate/business tax returns			If you have difficulties with your BAS or IAS, ask your accountant to complete it or engage a bookkeeper recommended by your accountant.
	Securities regulator annual report/return/filing (listed companies only)			Ask your accountant to prepare these.
	Income tax withholding annual payment summary			Perform test reconciliation in the month before year-end to highlight any processing problems.
	Income tax statements (group certificate) for employees			Reconcile totals to your ledgers first.
	Payroll tax			Speak to your accountant if you are unsure of the rates and any thresholds.
	Workers' compensation insurance			• Determine your projected wages and salaries for the year. • Find out if there are any exclusions and, if so, whether they are adequately covered in another way.
	Pension/superannuation payments			Pay monthly; produce notices for staff regularly.
	Fringe benefits tax return			
	Solvency declaration—for companies only			
	Staff salaries and conditions			Review staff salaries and conditions to ensure compliance with awards (where appropriate) and legal requirements.
	Government grants			If you are in receipt of government grants, ensure you meet your obligations under the grant.
	Others (list)			

6. Personal Affairs of Business Owner				
√	**Activity**	**Person Responsible**	**Due Date/ Regularity**	**Some Actions to Consider**
	Ensure trust distributions are properly made.		At least annually	The tax treatment of trusts can be complex and is subject to change: any could expose you to large unforeseen tax bills. Speak to your adviser about your trust.
	Undertake tax and personal financial planning.		Annually (before year-end)	• Year-end presents a number of tax planning opportunities and risks. Speak to your accountant about tax and personal financial planning. • Do not invest in any year-end tax planning schemes until you speak to your accountant.
	Review any loan agreements with your business.		Annually	
	Review personal insurances.		Annually	Disability, life, and trauma
	Ensure Power of Attorney is current.		Annually	
	Review your succession/ retirement plan.	Your accountant and lawyer	Annually	Remember that your will does not take effect until you are dead, so you need a succession plan for the handing over of the business or its management if you prematurely die, as well as a will.
	Review your will, particularly if there has been a change in your circumstances.	Your accountant and lawyer	Annually	
	Review the structures you have in place to protect your personal assets.	Your accountant and lawyer	Annually	This area of law is constantly evolving. Therefore, to be safe, you should review the effectiveness of your business structures and your asset protection strategies.

Great strategic approaches will help guarantee your business is very much run. An all-around run business will help place your business in the most ideal situation to react to whatever exchanging conditions you face and help you move your business toward the path you need it to go.

In the event that your business is developing firmly, at that point, be careful about expanding fixed overheads too soon (it is prescribed you attempt to help additional outstanding task at hand through extra time or with easygoing staff until you are certain about the strength of your recuperation).

Abstain from over-purchasing stock things or over-putting resources into capital hardware.

On the off chance that your business is encountering powerless or moderate development, screen intently markers of future deals action and remain zeroed in on controlling expenses.

On the off chance that your business is attempting to develop, search for methods of expanding each selling opportunity—frequently it is as straightforward as "requesting the request" or inquiring as to whether the client "might want something different with that." A keen deals procedure does not need extreme and unsafe limited time exercises: basic deals strategies can be okay and minimal effort but profoundly powerful.

Whatever the condition of your business, search for administrations or products that are not creating a decent return—low deals or continuous issues with product backing may be helpful pointers. Your monetary framework should have the option to reveal to you whether there is next to zero gross benefit/edge from a product, or the product may tie up an excess of working capital comparative with its benefit level. When you know the wellspring of the issue, see whether it tends to be amended or whether you ought to consider done selling that product or administration.

Primary changes are regularly best made during great occasions since faculty can without much of a stretch be redeployed somewhere else for more noteworthy benefit. Notwithstanding, in the event that you need to roll out underlying improvements in less vigorous occasions, at that point, discuss transparently with the influenced individuals and ensure you treat them decently.

Regardless of whether your business is solid, powerless, or inconsistent, this agenda will help you take advantage of any circumstance and feel more in charge of your business.

Chapter 8

Challenges and Opportunities for the MSME Sector: Women Entrepreneurship

CONTENTS

8.1. INTRODUCTION

MSMEs While micro, small, and medium-sized ventures (MSMEs) are consistently "little," there can be numerous approaches to classify them, and small is relative. There is no worldwide acknowledged meaning of what firms establish the MSME area. All in all, MSMEs are regularly characterized dependent on numerous rules like representative headcount, capital contributed, and deals volume. Measurable information utilized by worldwide companies like the International Finance Corporation (IFC) and the European Commission (EC) recognize MSMEs by the quantity of representatives. Tables 8.1 and 8.2 exhibit the various meanings of MSME classes by the IFC and EC, individually.

Table 8.1. Micro-, Small-, and Medium-Sized Enterprises, as Defined by the International Finance Corporation

Indicators	Micro	Small	Medium
Employee count	<10	<50	<300
Total assets	<$100,000	<$3,000,000	<$15,000,000
Total annual sales	<$100,000	<$3,000,000	<$15,000,000

Source: IFC (2012).

Table 8.2. Micro-, Small-, and Medium-Sized Enterprises, as defined by the European Commission

Indicators	Micro	Small	Medium
Employee count	<10	<50	<250
Annual turnover	≤€2,000,000	≤€10,000,000	≤€50,000,000
Annual balance sheet total	≤€2,000,000	≤€10,000,000	≤€43,000,000

Source: EC (2015).

In this research, the MSME area is extensively characterized utilizing the EC's definition. The contextual analyzes, nonetheless, will follow the country-explicit definitions. In many nations, MSMEs represent 90% of ventures; micro and small undertakings, along with sole ownerships, represent a stunning 70% of work around the world (ILO, 2020). The

MSME area produces around 40% of GDP in developing economies; in developed economies, 7 out of 10 positions are made by the MSME area (WBG, 2020). MSMEs have high potential for employment creation, and the sector is viewed as basic to financial improvement in many nations. In its Small Matters Report, the ILO (2019) has recorded a positive connection between country pay levels and the split among formal and informal work. They found that nations with higher pay levels have a higher portion of work in the formal MSME area. Figure 8.1 shows that developing economies have a bigger portion of the casual MSME area. The discoveries from the report likewise recommend that woman have a lower portion of work in the informal area contrasted with men, as it opens them to weak circumstances.

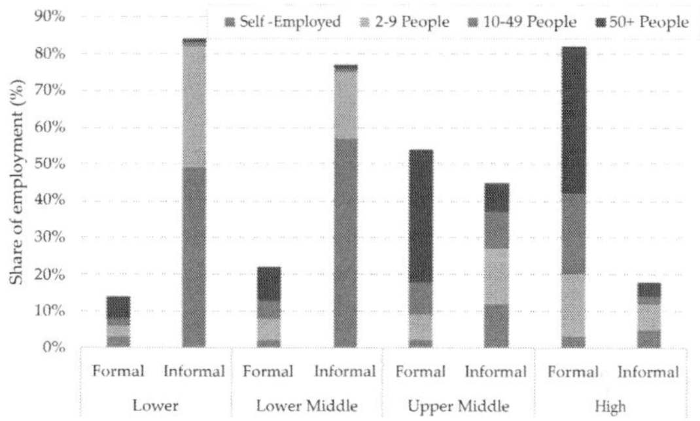

Figure 8.1. Distribution of employment by sector (formal vs. informal) and economic unit size, across country income groups.

Source: ILO (2019).

Figure 8.2 shows the conveyance of MSME work in the three total areas of agribusiness, industry, and administrations across six distinct districts (EAP: East Asia and Pacific; ECA: Europe and Central Asia; LAC: Latin America and the Caribbean; MENA: Middle East and North Africa; SA: South Asia; SSA: sub-Saharan Africa). The portion of work in industry (26%) in the Europe and Central Asia (ECA), is second just toward the East Asia and the Pacific (EAP) district at 36%. The two areas additionally have the most minimal work share in farming (5%). In developed nations (ECA), under 5% of absolute business is in horticulture, with 70% in administrations. The business portions of horticulture and administrations are generally identified with a country's pay level. A high portion of farming raises concerns in regards to sectoral efficiency, and whether an enormous portion of horticulture work is monetarily reasonable because of its low commitment to GDP. The developed nations have effectively made the change towards the administrations area. The job of the administrations area has additionally gotten progressively significant in developing economies over the most recent 20 years, contrasted with different areas, like manufacturing and farming. The expanding share in the worldwide monetary development of the assistance area has expanded work opportunities in many nations.

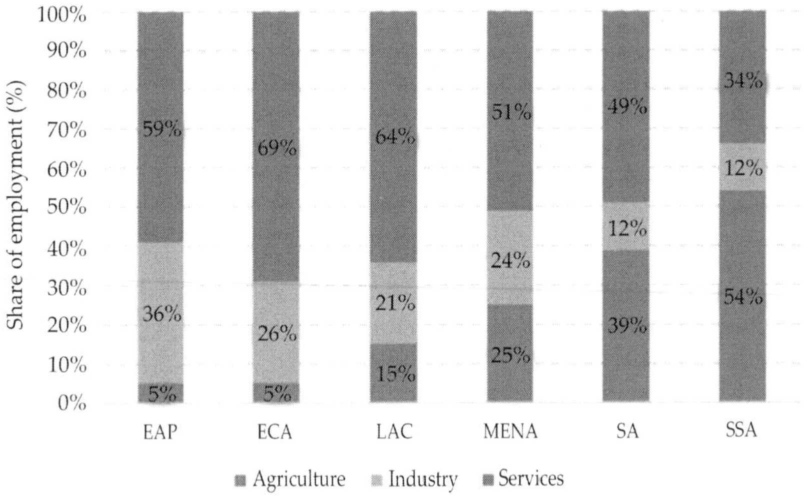

Figure 8.2. Employment distribution by sector and region, measuring the share of MSMEs.

Source: ILO (2019).

In 2017, 70% of work business was in the administrations area in OECD nations, including government and private administrations. Woman in the MSME Sector the Global Entrepreneurship Monitor 2016/2017 report (GEM, 2017) assessed that 163 million women began new organizations in 74 nations, notwithstanding 111 million running set up organizations in 2016, mirroring an expansion in female business visionaries by 16% from 2014 to 2016. Around the world, about 60% of overview respondents rate business venture as a profession—this is valid for the two sexes; this gender equality understanding is steady across both area and pay level (GEM, 2019).

Why at that point do woman have a lower propensity to be business visionaries? Hidden most endeavors and structures to energize business is the supposition that the odds of progress, just as admittance to assets, interest, and backing are totally merit-based. A decent strategy in the opportune time and ideal spot is key for success. Notwithstanding, it is frequently the situation that territorial culture and monetary setting might be significant variables. They may affect woman' discernments, expectations, inspirations, business interests, and development yearnings uniquely in contrast to men.

These elements may help clarify the noticed contrasts. Nonetheless, woman managing MSMEs shows various attributes that are normal to MSMEs: woman announced having lower certainty levels than men in their abilities to begin a business, and there is no area wherein woman rank higher than men. The gender equality gap is narrowing yet woman actually will in general be risk-averse, restricting their business decisions. MSMEs managed by woman are ordinarily situated in conventional businesses like manufacturing. Notwithstanding by and large having advanced education levels, woman driven MSMEs are more averse to introduction to non-conventional businesses or export-oriented markets.

8.2. CORONAVIRUS SITUATION AND IMPACT ON MSMES

The COVID-19 pandemic has made a worldwide monetary stun across all economies and vigorously upset cross-line exchange, supply chains, ventures, and the travel industry. The ensuing downturn is not normal for that of any previous pandemics, on the grounds that the present world is considerably more interconnected, permitting effects on spread universally.

The pandemic has influenced all aspects of the world, with the size differing, contingent upon the spread of the contamination and financial construction/development. The synchronized idea of COVID-19 has affected progress and changed economies in an unexpected way. Nations are experiencing the aggravation in supply chains, social limitations, and exacting lockdown measures; nations that depend on basic necessity products import/trade have been seriously influenced by the spread of COVID-19. In any case, the most noticeably terribly influenced nations are the developing economies, which need general medical care administrations, depend on casual work, need appropriate disinfection, and have a feeble public monetary area.

The dubious effect of COVID-19, with improvement of an antibody as yet progressing, is seriously harming economies, and there is no clearness on the span of a procedure with downturn. Policymakers are wrestling with the interruption brought about by COVID-19, the impacts of which are as yet unfurling. With no reference point for policymakers to comprehend the bleak reality and future vulnerabilities from COVID-19 and its drawn-out sway on the general public and economy, policymakers are confronting exceptional macroeconomic difficulties. Pretty much every area has been contrarily affected by COVID-19, except for a couple of areas which have a bullish viewpoint. Monetary areas that have been most adversely influenced incorporate administrations and basic products extraction.

The administrations area saw a significant breakdown because of lockdown limitations being executed to control the spread of the infection. Specifically, the food, retail, and diversion subsectors have endured substantial financial misfortunes. Regular asset extraction businesses-like oil and gaseous petrol and mining (minerals and metals)—have likewise been hit hard. For instance, the interest for oil-based goods has been seriously affected. Confinement made mandatory worldwide has prompted diminished stream of fuel utilization, influencing oil sends out. The sharp decrease in numerous industry supply chains has amplified the effect, bringing about additional decreases in oil interest. For instance, oil costs in 2020 encountered their most exceedingly terrible decrease in late history.

At some center areas in the United States, the cost of a barrel of oil even entered the negative rate. Diminished interest for oil-based commodities has added to joblessness among oil and petroleum gas laborers. Worldwide inventory network disturbances have likewise influenced the renewables area, particularly in energy stockpiling and electric vehicles (EV). While these ventures are beginning to recuperate, with creation of sequential construction systems for EVs restarting, the decrease in buyer spending is causing a gradually expanding influence and affecting the extractives business (digging for lithium utilized for batteries in EVs, and so on). The solitary characteristic assets area that has recuperated hitherto is farming. Agribusiness at first confronted a minor decrease because of store network disturbance, the transient idea of the labor force (casual work), and cross-line transport limitations, undermining food security. Notwithstanding, without hardly lifting a finger of lockdown limitations and with an increment in neighborhood food creation and restored supply chains, the area has transcendently bobbed back. The pandemic has amplified a few real factors of the world; especially, the worldwide interdependency which exists today between organizations.

The interruption of key information supply chains is compromising the worldwide value chain. As demonstrated in Figure 8.3, the intricacy of worldwide stockpile chains implies a lockdown in one nation can have expanding influences across the globe. Going ahead, nations may progress to depending more on creating nearby inventory chains to restart their economies.

Be that as it may, this may have the ensuing impact of causing bankruptcy for some, ventures depending on the worldwide inventory network. Considering the breakdown of worldwide inventory anchors because of the pandemic, and the more extensive effect on the worldwide economy, recuperation may require a worldwide upgrade bundle (United Nations, 2020).

Worldwide improvement supporting organizations in managing rent, contracts, and compensation. Such improvement would help support SMEs in supply chains, in addition to families. To completely uphold MSMEs, support bundles ought to be intended to target informal businesses, which are for the most part not upheld by open approaches. As well as conceivably helping 80% of undertakings, this could help formalize them (United Nations, 2020). A multilateral economic accord can relieve this impact by making worldwide cooperation and perhaps lead to the improvement of new guidelines and guidelines for cross-line exchanging, expanding upon the recently procured learning. Models could remember logical cooperation in the search of the COVID-19 antibody, restricting the untamed life exchange because of its effect on wellbeing, and setting global environment guidelines to secure characteristic territories.

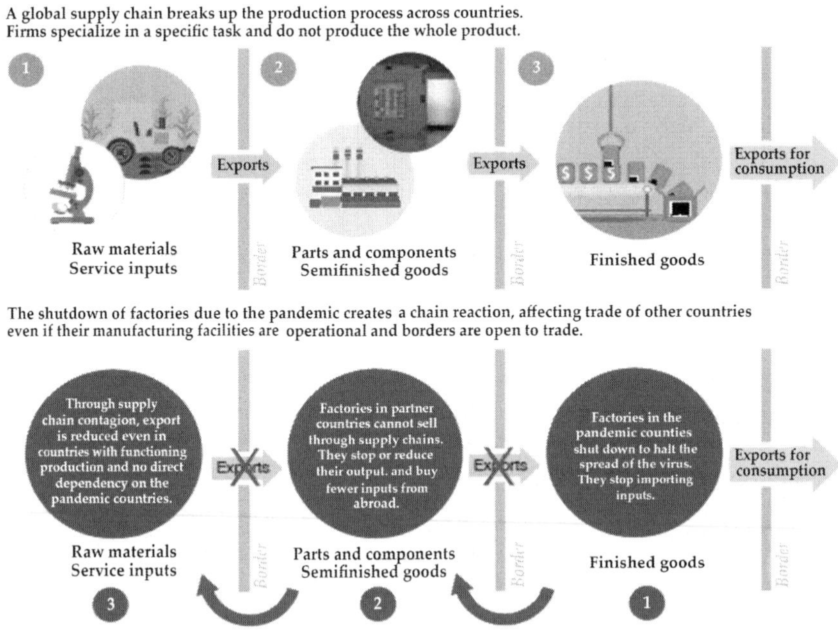

Figure 8.3. Impact of COVID-19 on supply chains.

Source: World Bank (2019).

MSMEs are a profoundly weak segment of the worldwide inventory network that are totally reliant on others, and the effect of COVID-19 on MSMEs has been lopsidedly grave. It was expected that, when the vast majority of the world's economies shut down for about a month and a half, the income of MSMEs declined steeply, compromising their monetary endurance and occupation misfortunes. Further, many could not acquire monetary help from governments and banks to endure the troublesome times and needed to close activities. Numerous nations are expecting a second influx of COVID-19 diseases and dangers of a subsequent lockdown. Working with lawful and social imperatives (like social separating) is pushing the profitability of MSMEs really close to fall. Control strategies and measures embraced by certain nations to secure their residents' prosperity have likewise caused extreme interruptions across worldwide stock chains. A valid example in the characteristic assets area is the food production network.

Food supply chains have been fundamentally disturbed, not due to the deficiency of production in exporting nations, however because of control approaches (Røynesdal, 2020). The seriousness of interruption influenced food security issues and affected the overall government assistance of individuals all throughout the planet. The present circumstance called for global bodies like the WTO, the WHO, also, the FAO to urge nations to show fortitude by opening exchange hindrances, on the side of significant food-importing nations. Without such help, many would have to put pressure on nearby assets and develop food unreasonably to address neighborhood issues, contrarily affecting the environment (FAO, 2020).

It is essential presently to screen and support the MSMEs to restart their tasks as economies to a great extent rely upon them. The SME Competitiveness Outlook 2020 (ITC, 2020) is an investigation embraced by the Worldwide Trade Center (ITC), which studied MSMEs across 85 nations to survey the effect of MSMEs in Sustainable and Integrated Management of Sustainable Resources COVID-19 on business exercises. Figure 8.4 shows that more modest organizations endured more critical effects because of COVID-19, when contrasted with enormous organizations.

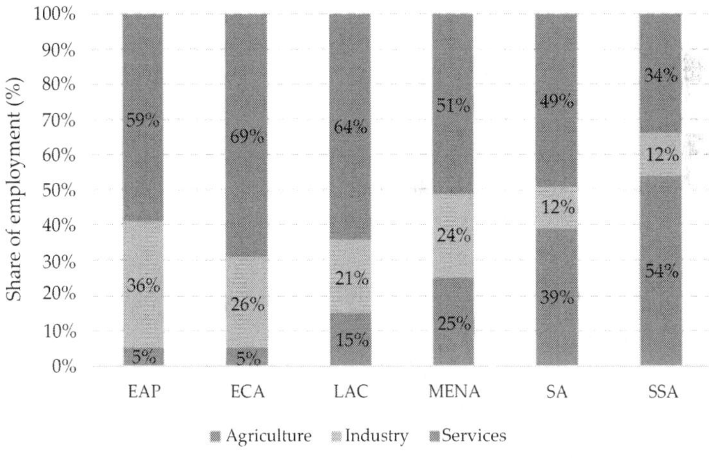

Figure 8.4. COVID-19 impact on business operations categorized by severity and size of firm.

Source: ITC (2020).

MSMEs have been hit the hardest as they are to a great extent addressed in the administrations area (food, convenience, and so on), which encountered the most extreme declines. Following the administrations area, the most influenced areas were manufacturing, retail, and transport sectors. Figure 8.5 shows how the seriousness of effect shifts by area.

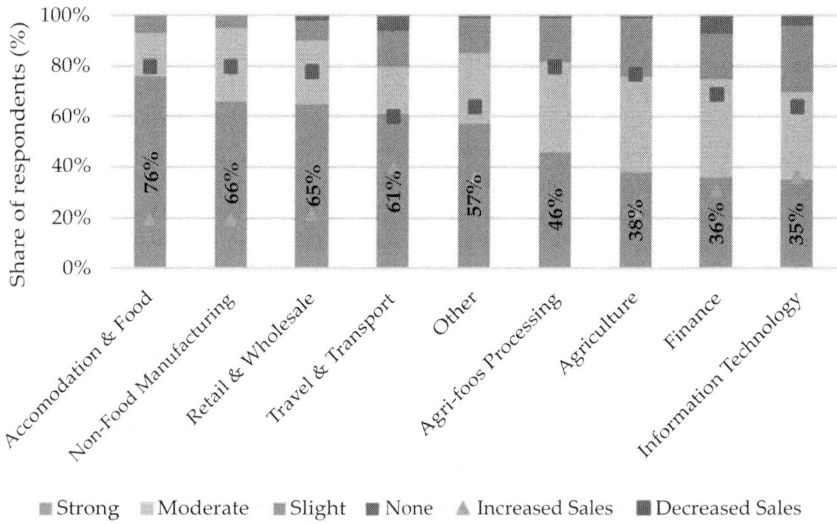

Figure 8.5. COVID-19 impact on business operations categorized by severity and economic sector.

Source: ITC (2020).

The oil and gas, petroleum, mining, agriculture, officer administration, fishing, water, and renewables subsectors make the natural resources management (NRM) sectors. Our reliance on ordinary resources to meet fundamental perseverance necessities (food, cover, clothing, and water) and other material prerequisites creates significant challenges, similar to negative sustainable externalities, normal resource utilization, shakiness in product costs, and assorted complexity of dangers.

The overall oil gas industry is a real representation of eccentrics and the incredible idea of risks which has expanded as a result of the COVID-19, influencing the regular resources industry encountering huge change. Surely, petrol gas was going through four changes simultaneously (Tsafos, 2020). First thing, petrol gas was by then experiencing oversupply and the ensuing low expenses, as a component of the market cycle. Disregarding such a great deal of weakness about the destiny of non-sustainable power sources, interests in oil gas were particularly high. Additionally, the set-up game plan of long stretch agreements with costs requested to oil was in the midst of a change to more versatile, flitting contracting. Third, the business was going through global change, with four nations getting huger with an unbalanced impact on the overall oil gas markets-the United States, the Russian Federation, Qatar, and China. Finally, petrol gas expects a particularly huge part in the energy mix of countries under change and is being squeezed: some industry individuals support combustible gas as being useful to improve spasmodic sources, for instance, wind, and sun-based PV, while others should see the consuming of all non-environmentally friendly power sources stopped immediately.

As open spending plans are being pushed by COVID-19, and plans supporting economic force experience brutal analysis, a couple of governments may move more assistance to petrol gas for financial affectation (Tsafos, 2020). Despite how the situation progresses, the COVID-19 pandemic is influencing a petrol gas industry beforehand going through a colossal change and under strong pressure. Examples of the impact of the COVID-19 crisis on the petrol gas industry, which may resemble the impact on other basic resources, fuse (Tsafos, 2020):

1. ***Demand:*** Some factors are positive and some are negative; these vary impressively by region and area; an overall net lessening is likely.
2. ***Production:*** With existing oversupply, low expenses, and lower interest, production ought to be diminished.
3. ***Operational/Improvement Possibilities:*** Worker commitment flows are diminishing and timing plans changing to restrict travel and individual area to limit the spread of the contamination.
4. ***Investment:*** Tighter capital spending plans and crediting stores will reduce adventure, yet government enhancements may support theories; interest markets may be changing their point of view on rudiments.
5. ***Structural Changes:*** These are unavoidable, with long stretch arrangements and oil-requesting likely ending. Combustible gas customers and suppliers have a similar need towards operational flexibility to bear the staggers COVID-19 is giving the petrol gas market. Nevertheless, the NRM territory makes liberal pay for trademark resource-based economies. Figure 8.6 ponders overall extraction volumes of ordinary resources organized by type for 2010 and 2017 (UNEP, 2019). With an augmentation in per capita demand, especially in made economies, materials use created by 17.4% in this period, by, and large controlled by non-metallic materials.

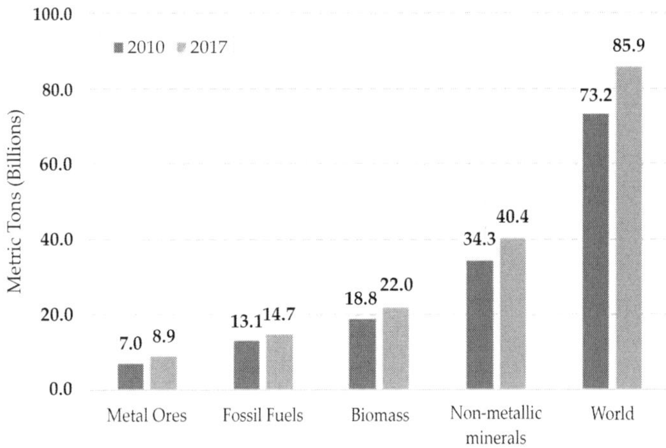

Figure 8.6. Global extraction volumes by type of material and year.

Source: UNEP (2019).

This fast development has made the need to direly diminish natural resources utilization. By reusing and reusing crude materials previously separated, as well as easing back the exhaustion of natural resources, nations can decrease the carbon impression of their extractive enterprises. Driving this change in regular resource sector can turn into a monetary chance for investigation by the MSMEs.

Furthermore, the mining area makes crude materials that feed into most different areas, especially transportation (streets) and media communications. Reuse and reusing of crude materials can likewise diminish these areas' carbon impressions. It is fundamental to dissect the monetary connections occurring between different areas, and if these circuitous commitments are considered, the mining and other basic resource sector can assume a vital part in building up a sustainable and green economy. With the expanding effect of extractive businesses on the climate, nations are confronting a test to make an interpretation of basic products abundance into feasible improvement results with an emphasis on long haul financial turn of events. The danger of environmental change and the limited accessibility of resources has acquired another period of improvement in the common area, explicitly in mining, for example, resource productivity. The straightway followed by nations in the regular assets area-the worldview of "take, make, arrange"-is advancing into building up a coordinated framework way to deal with increment resource productivity and lessen waste for a sustainable and green future. The sustainable resources sector straightforwardly integrates with each of the 17 UN sustainable development goals (SDGs). MSMEs in the sustainable resources sector possibly investigate and accomplish the SDGs while making financial value, particularly in the lower-to center pay economies. Figure 8.7 shows a few jobs MSMEs can play and contribute towards accomplishing the SDGs in the sustainable resources sector.

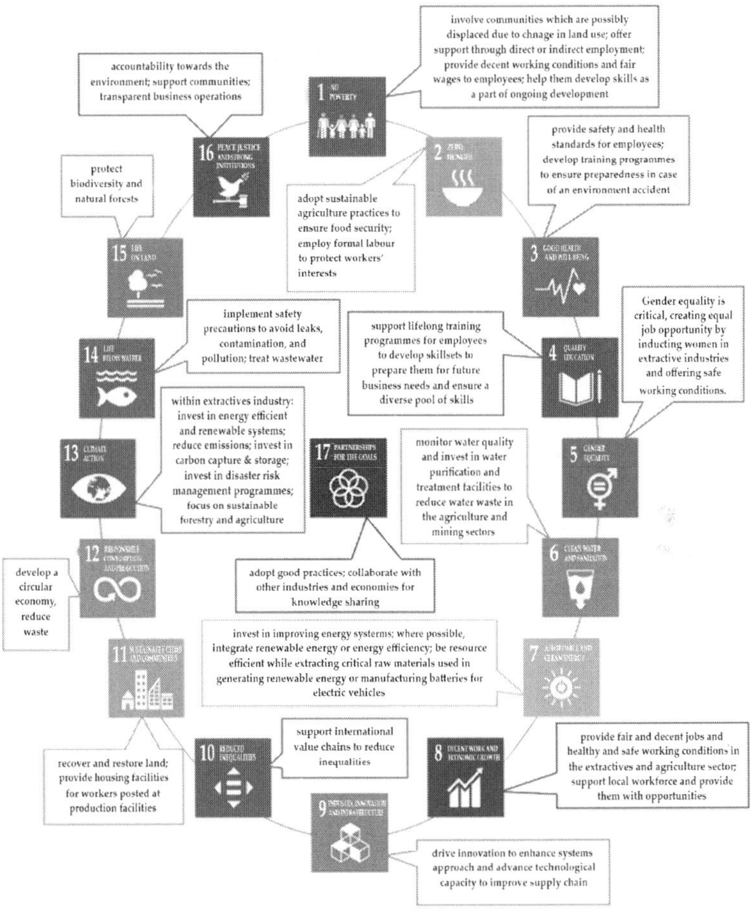

Figure 8.7. Some roles SMEs can play in the sustainable resources sector, supporting UN SDGs.

The United Nations is building up a willful worldwide norm to incorporate resource management, called the United Nations Resource Management System (UNRMS), to speed up the turn of events and selection of sustainable resources within the board arrangements. This framework depends on the United Nations Framework Classification (UNFC) for resources, which has been arranging and investigating minerals and other natural resources of nations since 1997 (UNECE, 2020a). The objective of the include networks which are perhaps uprooted because of progress in land use; offer help through immediate or roundabout business:

- Give respectable working conditions and reasonable wages to representatives;
- Assist them with creating abilities as a piece of continuous improvement embrace sustainable farming practices to guarantee food security;
- Utilize formal work to ensure laborers' inclinations give wellbeing and wellbeing principles to workers;
- Create preparing projects to guarantee readiness if there should arise an occurrence of a climate mishap support deep-rooted preparing programs for representatives to create ranges of abilities to set them up for future business needs and guarantee an assorted pool of abilities. Gender fairness is basic, setting out equivalent occupation freedom by enlisting woman in extractive ventures and offering safe working conditions.
- Screen water quality and put resources into water cleaning and treatment offices to diminish water waste in the horticulture and mining areas put resources into improving energy frameworks;
- Where conceivable, coordinate environmentally friendly power or energy effectiveness; be asset proficient while separating basic crude materials utilized in creating sustainable power or assembling batteries for EV give reasonable and respectable positions and solid and safe working conditions in the extractives and farming area;
- Support neighborhood labor force and give them opportunities drive development to upgrade frameworks approach and advance mechanical ability to improve inventory network support global value chains (GVCs) to decrease recuperate and reestablish land;
- Disparities give lodging offices to laborers posted at creation offices build up a roundabout economy, lessen waste receive great practices;

Team up with different enterprises and economies for information sharing inside the extractives industry.

- Put resources into energy productive and inexhaustible frameworks; diminish emanations;
- Put resources into carbon catch and capacity;
- Put resources into catastrophe hazard the executives programs;
- Center around feasible ranger service and agribusiness carry out security insurances to stay away from breaks, defilement, and contamination;
- Treat wastewater ensure biodiversity and normal woodlands responsibility towards the climate; support networks; straightforward business activities.

By incorporating the exercises of the sustainable resource management with different areas, the framework might have the option to feature future patterns that can affect the resource sector (UNECE, 2020b). While the UNRMS was carried out to help the UN Decade of Action (2020–2030) by speeding up the change to feasible regular asset the board, its more extensive objective is to empower accomplishment of all the SDG's, which independently depend upon characteristic asset (UNECE, 2020b). This is the center standard of the UNRMS and why it was assembled to line up with the SDGs from the beginning. The UNRMS is far cutting edge from most resource executives' structures being used; it is planned with frameworks see, utilizing the ideas of numerical intricacy and non-direct cycles. Intended to advance with quick headways in 4th Industrial Revolution innovations, the UNRMS is deliberately focusing on bringing mechanical progressions like AI and large information to the common sectors (UNECE, 2020b).

There are inconsistent advancements across the world in utilizing such innovations, however the area has not yet filled toward this path in many nations. The reception of AI, generally for self-sufficient decision-making, will open freedoms that would somehow be excessively dangerous. In any case, the difficulties that should be confronted incorporate recognizing where to improve, scaling arrangements, and keeping sustainability as a focal fundamental. Joined with other new advances (enormous information, distributed computing, and so forth), AI can possibly help tackle environment issues just as convey groundbreaking arrangements in the sustainable management of the resources sector (UNECE, 2020b). For instance, Figure 8.8 gives a brief look at certain utilization of AI for keeping up the health of oceans (World Economic Forum, 2018).

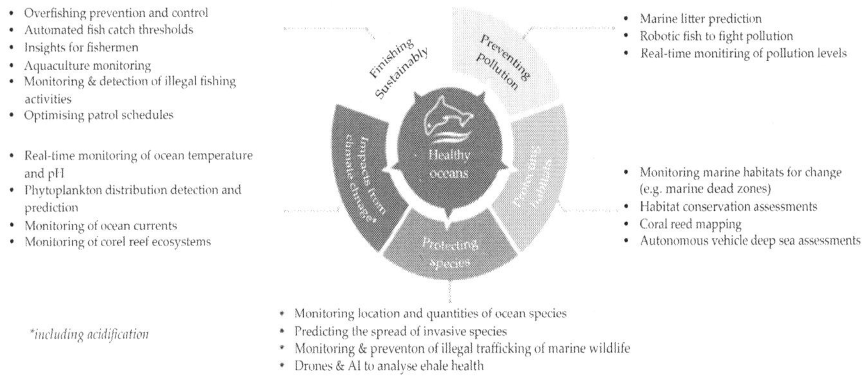

Figure 8.8. AI for maintaining ocean health.

Source: World Economic Forum (2018).

8.3. PART OF WOMEN IN MSME SECTOR IN SUSTAINABLE RESOURCE MANAGEMENT

The sustainable resources sector all in all is right now seeing a decrease of laborers. US work insights show that solitary 1.8% of the United States labor force was occupied with mining and farming in 2018 (United States Bureau of Labor Statistics, 2019). For instance, woman make just 15% out of the United States oil field administrations labor force, 15% of the worldwide metals and mining labor force, and 1 out of 20 CEOs in the mining area (Wood Mackenzie, 2019).

The oil and petroleum gas industry have battled over the course of the years to pull in, hold, and advance woman in the labor force, and it is significant for this area to diminish the sex gap as it is now confronting business challenges. These business challenges are generally because of two factors: the maturing labor force, and the business' diminished appeal to the more youthful populace. As the area endeavors to build up a heartier pool of new ability, it is basic that woman' investment ought to be expanded in growing new expertise zones like man-made consciousness and advanced mechanics (McKinsey, 2019). The natural resources areas are tormented with issues of gender equality imbalance in the labor force; woman is underrepresented in each space of NRM, regardless of their capability to contribute considerably. Maybe this is because of an absence of certainty to voice sentiments (see Figure 8.10), or social/social hindrances impeding them from dynamic jobs. Woman frequently fill jobs that are less obvious and not officially perceived (ADB, 2017). For instance, woman will in general work on the land to which they have no proper rights, performing exercises like gathering water, fuelwood, food, and grub for their family (WWF, 2012). As this is neglected, it is not officially accounted as "work." As another model, woman who fish likewise repair their nets, set up the catch, and sell/market the fish, yet are regularly not considered fishers (WWF, 2012). In numerous places of the world, the support of woman in local area dynamic is restricted, which gives them less authority over the air and the board of common assets. Moreover, woman is frequently obviously missing from administrative or dynamic jobs inside companies advancing MSMEs (ADB, 2017). This could ingrain and maintain any current social inclinations that might be frustrating the investment of woman. Indeed, strategies to explicitly support woman business visionaries in NRM are either non-existent or in beginning phases of improvement.

The oil and petroleum gas area positions the least when contrasted with other science, technology, engineering, and mathematics (STEM) enterprises in woman support. Figure 8.9 shows the overall level of woman working in the business versus different areas ((a) banking; (b) shopper merchandise; (c) buyer tech; (d) food/refreshment dist.; (e) equipment; (f) medical care; (g) IT administrations and telecom; (h) protection; (I) financial backers; (j) assembling; (k) media and entertainment; (l) drugs; (m) force utilities; (n) proficient administrations; (o) eateries; (p) retail; (q) programming; (r) transportation); yellow markers demonstrate STEM businesses, orange markers are non-STEM ventures.

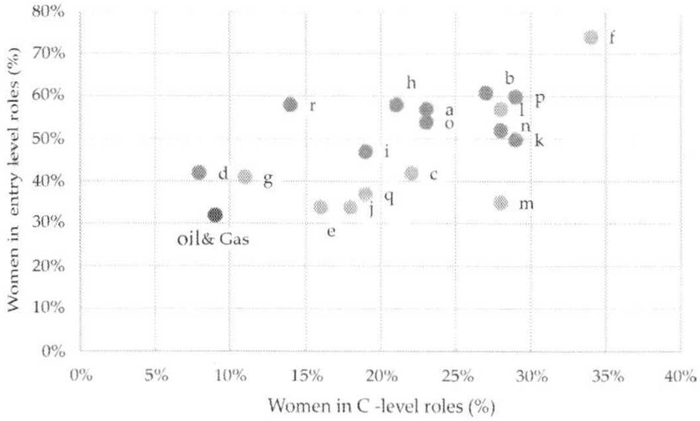

Figure 8.9. Correlation between share of women in entry-level and C-level (CEO, CFO, etc.), roles.

Source: McKinsey and Company (2019).

Empowering the interest of woman in the MSME area can improve the enterprising environment across economies, set out business opportunities, and drive monetary variety. While advanced education assumes a part in sex contrasts in innovative exercises, instructive capabilities do not generally convert into effective results. This examination centers around possible freedoms, which can be abused by woman in the sustainable resources sectors. Figure 8.10 is a guide to show the certified number of women in the STEM area from chose nations in Eastern Europe, the Caucasus, and Central Asia.

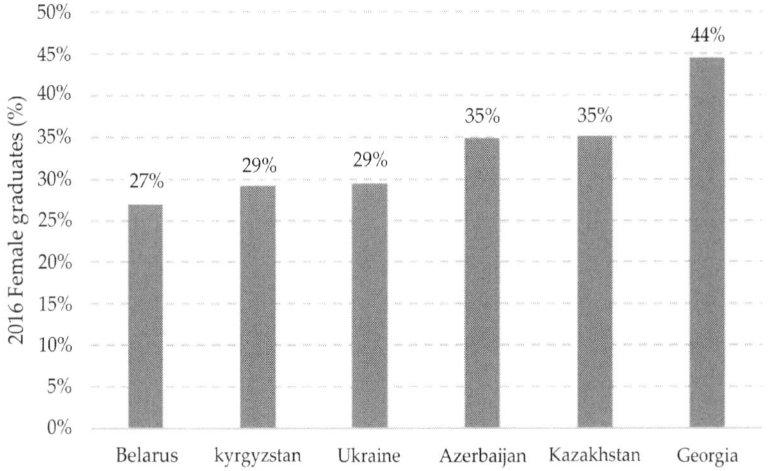

Figure 8.10. Share of female STEM graduates at the tertiary level.

Source: UNSTATS.

Characteristics and abilities like administration capacity, innovativeness, risk management, and dynamism are generally significant for the accomplishment of Ventures- and are apathetic regarding sex. In any case, businesswoman faces efficient inclination in setting up organizations (Dilli and Westerhuis, 2018). This part closes with a couple of difficulties which should be considered to guarantee a fair and level-battleground to advance financial development and work opportunities for the MSME area. These difficulties may require explicit approach mediations in both developed and non-industrial nations to guarantee gender uniformity.

- ***Difficulties 1:*** Admittance to Markets and Finance: According to the IFC, 70% of woman managing SMEs are underfunded, with the setback projected to be up to $285 billion. Businesswoman face boundaries in raising capital. This inclination depends on unwarranted proof; the OECD takes note of that woman will in general have preferable credit reimbursement records over men (IFC, 2014).

Because of cultural standards and oblivious inclinations, male financial backers are less certain about putting resources into woman driven organizations (IFC, 2014). Figure 8.11 shows the sources of start-up finding reported globally in 2018 (OECD, 2019); as indicated by this information, men will in general utilize bank credits more regularly than woman.

- ***Difficulties 2:*** Admittance to Information: Access to data is basic for MSMEs. The absence of data, for example, government activities to design and adjust in questionable occasions, can make disarray. Hazy messages or the shortfall of correspondence from the public authority on strategies and measures can seriously disturb business arranging. For instance, during the COVID-19 pandemic, the data on lockdown measures for organizations was sudden and indistinct, prompting huge monetary misfortunes.
- ***Difficulties 3:*** Acquiring and Skill Development: The memorable gender gap is narrowing, yet sex predisposition stays in certain areas of the world. Sex dissimilarity additionally exists in instruction at the tertiary level. Approaches focusing on the STEM gender gap in tertiary instruction ought to consider sex contrasts arising prior throughout everyday life. Diminishing this gap prior, at the family level (OECD, 2012; Dilli et al., 2015), will be best at affecting socially installed jobs.

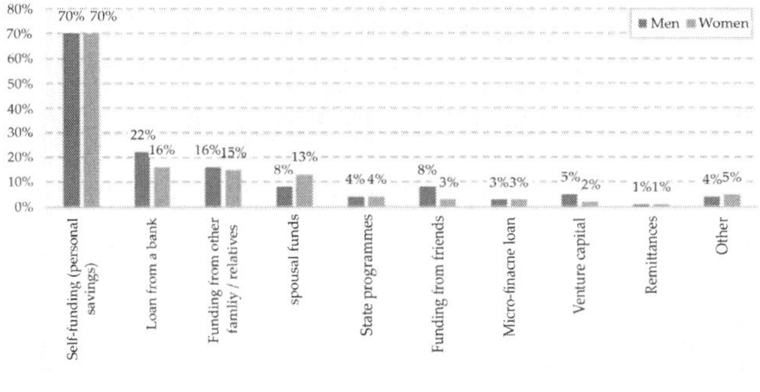

Figure 8.11. Sources of start-up finding reported globally in 2018.

Source: OECD (2019).

8.4. CORONAVIRUS IMPACT ON WOMEN ENTREPRENEURS IN SUSTAINABLE RESOURCE MANAGEMENT

Prior to the pandemic, empowering, and supporting woman business venture was gaining strength across companies and monetary establishments. Social insights, questioning the capacities of woman in high-hazard areas, were gradually developing towards recognizing the significance of female investment.

In any case, with the COVID-19 circumstance, the pace of private speculation and raising capital for new and existing business has moved away from specially supporting woman driven firms, because of the financial decline.

Expanded market unpredictability and monetary lull have been difficulties for woman business visionaries (McKinsey and Company, 2020). In terms of Monetary Risk, women will in general, work more modest and more secure organizations.

While this is likely because of an overall inclination for soundness and security, it could likewise be because of a precise contrast that may exist in the public arena and organizations, debilitating their interest as business visionaries. The gender inequality begins impacting the learning and instructive pathways, prompting scaling down their aspirations (OECD, 2019).

Dread of disappointment keeps woman from starting their business, and in the event that they choose to become business visionaries, they settle on more secure business decisions. Figure 8.12 presents the extent of people reviewed somewhere in the range of 2014 and 2018, who detailed fearing beginning a business. The pandemic has additionally strengthened the difficulties that woman as of now face and dread in beginning their business. As indicated by McKinsey and Company (2020), the extreme disturbance brought about by COVID-19 on worldwide exchange and supply chains probably expanded uneasiness and diminished certainty levels of female business visionaries.

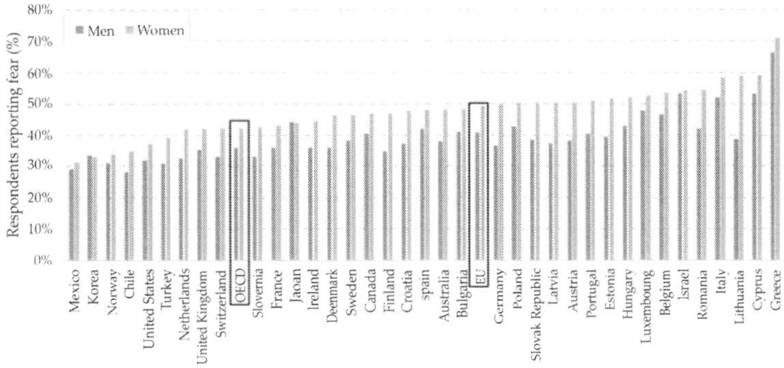

Figure 8.12. Share, by country, of EU and OECD country respondents reporting fear of starting a business.

Source: OECD (2019).

Woman are frequently oppressed in getting credit (OECD, 2019). Government bailouts and support measures ought to be sexually impartial and cover MSMEs in rustic and metropolitan areas. As indicated by the GEM (2015) report, 95% of woman business visionaries self-account their business. Because of the lockdown measures and COVID-19-initiated business decay, woman business visionaries can be at specific danger of monetary difficulty. Social Impact is a topic woman have consistently been the essential guardians of the family, and that job has not changed, regardless of their expanded support in the work labor force. In many nations, woman actually assume the part of the familial guardian by default. Woman attempt the obligation regarding the kids, other relatives, and family (cooking, cleaning, and other related tasks) alongside paid business. During the COVID-19 pandemic, woman' family obligations have increased. With lockdown limitations and schools/day-cares shut, woman is bearing an expanded homegrown responsibility, as well as attempting to keep their organizations above water. During the COVID-19 pandemic, woman driven firms, which are for the most part addressed in the administrations area, endured huge misfortunes. As demonstrated in Figure 8.13, the SME Competitive Outlook (ITC, 2020) reports that 64% of woman driven undertakings showed that their business endured solid misfortunes, when contrasted with 52% of organizations driven by men. When the lockdown measures are facilitated across nations, and economies enter the recuperation stage, woman business visionaries may track down the predisposition gap against interest in woman driven MSMEs has additionally enlarged.

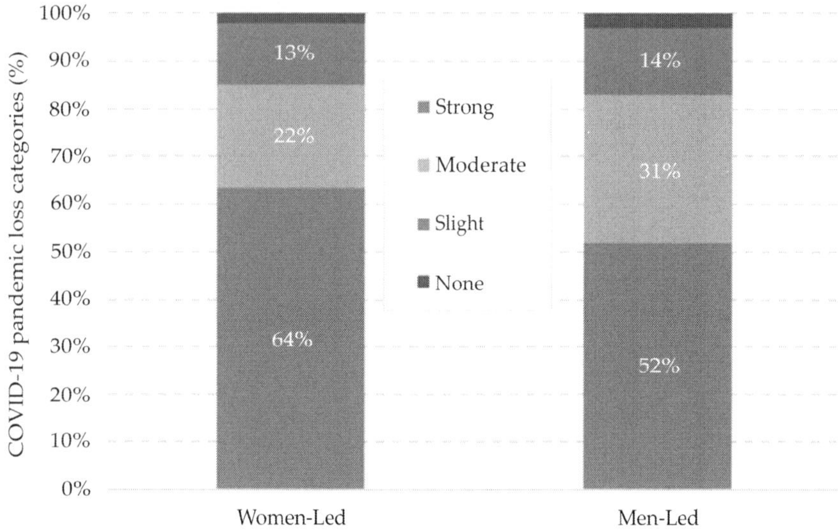

Figure 8.13. Self-reported COVID-19 pandemic loss severities categorized.

Source: ITC (2020).

8.5. NEW OPPORTUNITIES FOR WOMEN ENTREPRENEURS IN SUSTAINABLE RESOURCE MANAGEMENT

The COVID-19 pandemic and its outcomes present a chance for nations to attempt financial change by embracing sustainable strategic policies and empowering the improvement of green and low-carbon economies, bringing about a stronger and vigorous economy. A restored monetary change can possibly make an equivalent and more grounded financial society with nice work approaches to ensure the privileges of the weak labor force-explicitly woman and transient specialists. There lies a chance for advancing MSMEs in assembling and other capital-concentrated organizations which additionally have higher operational expenses, however businesswoman infrequently investigates such freedoms and are known to be hazard unwilling. In any case, a few chances for woman to take part in the regular assets area remain-if not straightforwardly than through auxiliary administrations.

Opportunities in offering of information by administrations, which can uphold the natural resources area, are bountiful. Models incorporate statistical surveying, publicizing, logical investigations, development, and specialized exercises, law, HR, and review and bookkeeping administrations. It is significant for nations to help and advance the correct business freedoms to gain by MSMEs investment. The case underneath features activities of four-woman business visionaries in India, supporting other MSMEs in their organizations across enterprises.

It is normal for oil and flammable gas and mining organizations to subcontract activities to numerous sorts of firms, including global organizations, huge public partnerships, and little neighborhood organizations. Surely, in light of critical advantages that can emerge out of neighborhood MSMEs, numerous as of now focus on little providers in acquisition approaches; these advantages incorporate advancing nearby business and development, empowering rivalry, and supporting nearby economies.

Notwithstanding monetary advantages for the organization, companies with nearby economies cultivates altruism. Depending upon a neighborhood production network can regularly restrict limit and adaptability and require huge capacity building speculations. By expanding variety, the improvement of supply chains, including woman driven little endeavors can build vigor and lessen acquirement and operational expenses. With low cooperation of woman in these businesses, there are numerous chances for woman business visionaries to join NRM supply chains. Figure 8.9 sums up the spaces of intercession, four-woman driven new companies that are assisting SMEs with flourishing offering types of assistance, for example, information investigation, bookkeeping, and working with administrative compliances.

CAXpert gives basic, helpful, and prudent bookkeeping answers for small and medium ventures. The beginning-up offers types of assistance to deal with orders, record deals, costs, and time usage, and furthermore prescribes approaches to enhance business tasks.

Econolytics, an all-inclusive resource for all information related necessities, the beginning up is a curated commercial center of information researchers and designers who can be recruited by organizations on-interest for adaptable spans.

Banka and Banka Services assists SMEs with corporate and legal consistence exercises like direct and circuitous charges, normal assessment filings, corporate administration, and so on.

Aaroh assists SMEs with characterizing their advertising technique and interchanges, whether or not they are hoping to fill in India or grow universally. Business entrepreneurs from SMEs-MSME-and startups use explicit techniques, that have tried to attempt to support the improvement of woman entrepreurship development (WED) (Source: https://yourstory.com/herstory/2020/06/woman) (Figure 8.14).

Figure 8.14. Interventions and strategies for women entrepreneurship development (WED).

Source: ILO (2018).

8.6. CLEANER AND GREENER ECONOMIC OPPORTUNITIES IN NATURAL RESOURCE MANAGEMENT

The NRM area is filling in numerous spaces. This presents a few chances for businesswoman who, because of different reservations, are keener on non-extractive enterprises. Several nations are creating procedures to investigate the expected force of bioscience, which works across all areas-from horticulture to drugs, to assembling and energy. The capability of a bio-based economy offers critical freedom to handle the difficulties of environmental change, increment food utilization, and lessen tension on the indigenous habitat. A manageable bio-economy can possibly make respectable positions, and the initiation of embedding environment in the biotechnology area can assume a significant part in boosting the economy while building a carbon-neutral future. The bio-economy conveys the utilization of bioscience-utilizing sustainable organic assets to improve and develop the way food, materials, and products are delivered and burned-through while keeping a sound biological system. The bio-economy can uphold the progress of economies by decreasing 26 conditions on limited fossil assets in a few ventures, including development, synthetic compounds, ranger service, purchaser products, and so forth.

Exploration and advancement in life sciences and biotechnologies can prompt the creation of new and sustainable biobased products (bio-synthetics and bio-energies) and modernize or make new inventory chains for mechanical exercises. In the European Union (EU)'s 2018 State of the Union Address (European Commission, 2018), the EC underlined their technique on bio-economy for a reasonable Europe, boosting occupations, development, and interests in the EU.

The Commission assessed the potential for bio-economy jobs to be 1 million green positions by 2030; the district's drawn-out arrangement is having the objective of boosting the bio-based areas and modernize the European economy and ventures (European Commission, 2018). Woodland bio-economy is one sub-area of the bio-economy (others recorded in the passages above), acquiring a lot of impact inside the EU and other developed nations. Biomass is an organic material with tremendous potential. For instance, Finland's woods cover is roughly 74% of its territory region, and the nation has been a pioneer in tapping the likely estimation of their trees-particularly the bark (Upton, 2020). Trees are customarily utilized just as a wellspring of wood and kindling, yet it has been tracked down that the bark of a birch tree, for instance, contains against microbial and cell reinforcement intensifies that can be utilized as additives in food, drugs, and beautifiers (Upton, 2020). It likewise has modern applications, for example, for glues and protecting materials. In spite of the potential for some, different applications, birch bark is right now utilized exclusively for burning. Nonetheless, there are difficulties in embracing these new applications. Bark-based products should contend with petrol subordinates that have long periods of accumulated benefits. Contrasted with oil, bark is incredibly mind-boggling, and it will take a significant measure of exploration to completely comprehend and misuse its synthetic segments and cell tissues. This is only one of numerous likely substitutes uses for timberland assets in the bio-economy.

Notwithstanding these difficulties, energy is developing for utilizing reasonable and bio-based products. With expanding mindfulness, common assets can be burned through efficiently and profitably. The effect of COVID-19 on business overall featured the requirement for remaking the economy in a sustainable manner. The bio-economy can lead the path in supporting the improvement of innovations and systems to make privately sourced reasonable food, powers, and customer products, diminishing the reliance on cross-line exchange. Roundabout Economy Sustainable assets-either inexhaustible or non-sustainable-are available in each modern product fabricated or administration (energy, for instance): metal, petrol, plant matter, freshwater, and so forth-Notwithstanding, shopper request is expanding, which can outperform the inventory of assets. Albeit the awkwardness can be overwhelmed by subbing with different products or expanding sources, it is still obvious that there is a restricted measure of natural resources accessible in the world. An innovative bio-based economy can help in building up a hearty round economy, to extricate and use natural resources present in waste. For instance, extricating metals from electronic gadgets has demonstrated to be more productive and financially savvy than digging for new metals. An activity drove by the University of New South Wales has tracked down that 450 g of copper, 227 g of aluminum, and 5.6 g of gold can be removed from a regular TV or PC screen. In 2016, 435,000 tons of cell phones were disposed of, containing €9.4 billion value of crude materials (Woollacott, 2018). Most nations are offering endowments for reusing e-waste, and the measure of e-waste is relied upon to increment.

The International Telecommunications Union assessed that 45 million tons of e-waste were produced in 2016; this figure is required to outperform 50 million tons by 2021 (Woollacott, 2018). An examination by Beijing's Tsinghua University and Macquarie University in Sydney found that mining from metal was multiple times more costly than e-waste mining, when representing costs for waste assortment, work, energy, material, transportation, and capital expenses for reusing focuses and counterbalancing the advantages from appropriations (Zeng et al., 2018). A critical chance exists in the MSME area for metal subject matter experts and specialists to exploit and draw on the sustainable, social, and financial advantages made by e-waste the executives while making occupations. Conventional mining area exercises have been direct and have not utilized sustainable cycles, for example, broadening the product use stage, for example, reuse and reusing of waste from modern and buyer exercises. The business can make new monetary value from mining waste by incorporating the round economy into its business measures. This will not just bring financial interest yet additionally limit the business' social and sustainable effects by lessening mining waste. A roundabout economy approach can assist with decreasing the negative externalities (sustainable corruption, water tainting, and so on) from mining while lessening the requirement for separating and handling new assets. Following the "3R" waste decrease standard (diminish, reuse, reuse) can contribute essentially to lessening costs, just as set out opportunities for development. Notwithstanding, progressing towards building up around economy will require foundation improvement, supporting enactment, and financial impetuses. The COVID-19 pandemic has prompted the selection of new standards and guidelines compromising the round economy framework-in particular the multiplication of single-use things.

In any case, as nations enter the recuperation stage, the reception of savvy mining advancements can wipe out the effect on human wellbeing from the treatment of unsafe mining waste. This change would be relied upon to increment working expenses incidentally, yet then expenses are projected to diminish, predictable with other new innovations (photovoltaic cells, wind turbines, and so forth) (Rumbens and Campbell-Sloan, 2020). Digitalization, Big Data, and Artificial Intelligence The speeding up speed of innovative progression has changed robotization measures in the mining area, empowering people to zero in on the part of chiefs and activity regulators, utilizing machines for actual work. The mining and metals industry has since quite a while ago drove innovation advancement in tasks, however with expanding speculations and diminishing expenses, there is a developing pattern towards digitalization. Similarly, as with most areas, the mining area keeps on getting more worldwide, depending on innovation to interface unique activities through advanced foundation-even to distant areas.

Advanced devices are additionally keeping up labor force security and oversee hazards in hazardous working conditions. These progressions are progressively significant as the current labor force ages, and the area battles to fill the subsequent work gap.

Progressed mechanical technology, augmented reality, intellectual processing, distributed computing, and man-made brainpower are generally advanced innovations that are changing customary plans of action and evolving ventures (see Figure 8.15). For mining, computerization, and mechanical technology are assuming a pivotal part in this change. Digitalization in the mining area is being conveyed to deal with exercises that were generally embraced by people or physically controlled machines. At a more elevated level, there is the degree for examination utilizing AI and computerized reasoning to deal with information to design future tasks.

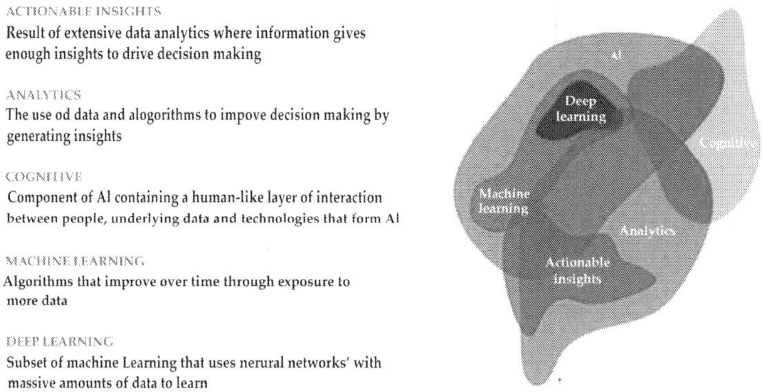

Figure 8.15. Five transformative digital technologies and their intersections.

Source: Deloitte and NORCAT (2018).

A vigorous innovation push is needed for the advancement of low-carbon advances, giving crude materials to photovoltaics, windmills, EV, gadgets, and so forth. The developing part of minerals and metals in the improvement of low-carbon innovation and a net-zero future offers opportunities for MSMEs to broaden in the field of advancement, man-made brainpower, computational displaying, and progressed investigation-digitalization.

The product showcases, especially those for oil-based commodities, have seen a critical decrease during the COVID-19 pandemic. In numerous areas, the abrupt decrease in oil costs has caused oil creation to get uneconomic. Investigation by numerous organizations has slowed down, existing wells are being closed in, and the labor force is in effect significantly diminished. In the United Kingdom's North Sea, for instance, seaward apparatus staffing levels have been sliced almost down the middle since November 2019. Metal costs have likewise endured sharp decreases, adversely affecting incomes. Maybe the most unmistakable chance for MSMEs in mining lies in cost enhancement, with the selection of digitalization and innovation enablement. Far off activities places can be concentrated, giving an offsite climate to tasks faculty to work together while based distantly in charge rooms.

Advances, for example, live video transfers, can empower representatives to screen tasks and utilize constant mine information to decide. The lethargic speed of the COVID-19 recuperation additionally offers a chance to create medium-and long-haul plans for online stages to advance expertise building programs that will guarantee the accessibility of a gifted labor force.

8.7. ADVANCEMENT, RESEARCH, AND DEVELOPMENT

There is a critical chance for woman driven MSMEs to drive advancement. An approach brief named "Does Gender Matter for the Innovativeness of SMEs?" (Akulava, 2015) introduced results dissecting the connection among innovativeness and the gender of MSME administration. Their outcomes recommend, for five distinct proportions of imaginativeness, that advancement is more common in woman driven MSMEs. Along these lines, the support of woman in innovative work to grow low-carbon arrangements in NRM can lead the route for an underlying movement to a greener and sustainable economy.

8.8. ADVANCING NEW OPPORTUNITIES THROUGH TRAINING AND SKILL DEVELOPMENT

The COVID-19 lockdown stage presents a remarkable chance to put resources into upgrading and growing new abilities. Retraining laborers to set them up for changes in business activities because of COVID-19 is a drawn-out speculation that can begin now. Receiving economical strategic approaches and changing to a low-carbon economy can likewise be a huge concentration during these occasions. The ranges of abilities needed in the extractive and natural resources sectors are intricate and require improvement at all levels of the value chain. For MSMEs, it is vital to make a different pool of assets to improve limit preparation. The advancement of an online foundation for conveying preparing programs across the regular assets area for woman laborers and business visionaries could be a solid potential business opportunity for MSMEs. The COVID-19 decline presents an ideal chance to create and alter preparing programs. For instance, "preparing for woman by woman" projects to address neighborhood issues, upgrade commonality and solace, and give extraordinary mentorship opportunities. Preparing and expertise improvement for female business people and representatives presently can help fabricate limit and make woman-driven ventures future-evidence.

8.9. CONCLUSIONS

Micro-, small-, and medium-sized undertakings (MSMEs) fill critical jobs in economies everywhere on the world. MSMEs can frequently advance, turn, and for the most part explore the worldwide financial waters more rapidly than their enormous partners.

Universally, MSMEs represent 90% of business endeavors; miniature and little ventures together record for a stunning 70% of work around the world. The MSME area creates around 40% of gross domestic product (GDP) in developing economies; in created economies, 7 out of 10 positions are made by MSMEs. MSMEs have exceptionally high occupation creation potential, and the area is viewed as basic to financial advancement in many nations. Furthermore, as most economies are progressing towards sustainability, MSMEs are especially very much positioned to drive answers for environmental change.

Notwithstanding, woman are underrepresented in MSMEs in each monetary area. This might be connected to an absence of certainty to voice feelings and social boundaries impeding them from dynamic jobs. While opportunities exist for businesswoman in all areas of the economy, there are not many that can be considered as especially appropriate as MSMEs.

These areas incorporate administrations, the round economy, data innovation, and the executives of natural resources.

Every one of them has in any event one of the accompanying attributes: moderately low capital necessities, dependence on mechanical headways, for example, AI, and huge information, and the need to adjust to rapidly evolving conditions. This report has zeroed in on the natural resource management (NRM) area as remarkably appropriate for MSMEs, in light of the fact that it has each of the three of these qualities. Further, the area presents engaging, different, and long-haul effective freedoms.

As non-inexhaustible resource drain, the regular assets industry is moving away from the worldview of "take, make, arrange" towards coordinated frameworks ways to deal with increment resource efficiency and diminish waste. Advancements, for example, these are information escalated, instead of capital-concentrated, and consequently available to MSMEs. In an industry experiencing significant change, undertakings that adjust rapidly will be the best.

8.9.1. Difficulties for Women-Driven MSMEs in Sustainable Resource Management and the Impact of the COVID-19 Pandemic

Despite the undeniable degree of significance, the potential for monetary development, and different freedoms for MSMEs, woman-driven MSMEs in NRM face numerous difficulties. Because of their size, numerous MSMEs are particularly defenseless and face difficulties brought about by characteristic and man-made calamities.

A critical number of women-driven MSMEs work in the farming area, enlisting casual work who are not ensured reasonable compensation, respectable work conditions, and professional stability. Such MSMEs will in general have lower profitability levels and restricted freedoms to grow tasks or access financing and markets. MSMEs and their labor force are by and large more defenseless against monetary stuns. The continuous COVID-19 pandemic is an ideal illustration of this; it has made difficulties for MSMEs across all financial areas in essentially all economies, including those nations, where regulation measures were not very rigid. At the point when studied about the effect of COVID-19 on their business activities, almost 90% of micro and small endeavors sorted the effect as moderate to extreme, just the same as more than 80% of enormous organizations. Notwithstanding the difficulties looked by all MSMEs, there is proof proposing that woman driven MSMEs should defeat extra hindrances. Woman will in general work more modest and more secure organizations. While this is likely because of an overall inclination for strength and security, it could likewise be because of a methodical predisposition, debilitating their interest as business people. Dread of disappointment keeps woman from beginning their business, and on the off chance that they choose to become business visionaries, they settle on more secure business decisions.

Woman are frequently oppressed in getting to credit; 95% of woman business visionaries reviewed say they self-finance their business. Besides, woman is regularly prominently missing from administrative or dynamic jobs inside companies advancing MSMEs, which could ingrain and maintain any current social predispositions that might be ruining the investment of woman. In NRM, woman is under-addressed in each space. Among the potential reasons are an absence of certainty to voice sentiments, feeling strange in a business talk that is transcendently manly in nature, and social hindrances that block them from dynamic jobs. It is basic to guarantee that foundational gender predisposition does not obstruct the financial improvement of woman driven MSMEs. There is research information that shows that development is more pervasive in woman driven MSMEs. As economies grapple with the COVID-19 emergency while previously attempting to drive environmental change moderation endeavors and progress to a low-carbon economy, development is especially significant. By advancing sustainable mindfulness and supporting a financial progress, woman driven MSMEs can lead the change towards building a greener, gender equivalent, and more feasible economy.

Coming up next are the significant key findings:

1. There is a clear gender variety issue in NRM sectors. For instance, the oil and gaseous petrol industry has battled throughout the years to pull in, hold, and advance women in the labor force, and it is significant for this area to diminish the gender equality gap as it is as of now confronting work difficulties. Most of NRM woman business visionaries are in the agribusiness area.
2. The COVID-19 pandemic at the same time presents remarkable difficulties and novel freedoms to woman-driven MSMEs. MSMEs all in all, and woman driven MSMEs specifically, have been particularly powerless against the effects of the pandemic. Be that as it may, the pandemic has additionally caused an emotional move in the same old thing approach and made ready for advancements, green development, and practical turn of events. Woman driven MSMEs might be best prepared to make the most of these chances.
3. There are not many arrangements to advance business-woman in NRM. To some degree, this could be because of the absence of adequately productized information. The seriously restricted measure of pertinent information obstructs investigation and makes it hard to plan public arrangements to advance the interest of female business visionaries in the area.
4. As of late, the quantity of woman considering science, innovation, designing, and math (STEM) subjects has expanded. An expansion in woman gifted in STEM themes should bring about more woman driven MSMEs making the most of chances introduced by 4th Industrial Revolution advances, for example, AI, distributed computing, and huge information. Proposals Based on the investigation and its key discoveries, coming up next are the

suggestions for need moves those nations can make to energize the support of woman driven MSMEs in regular assets the board.

- ***Recommendation A:*** Enabling business climate: Ensure steady, straightforward enactment and arrangements that help all business visionaries, and businesswoman specifically, remembering simple admittance to freely accessible data for beginning a business.
- ***Recommendation B:*** Pro-development charge frameworks: Ensure that charge frameworks cultivate as opposed to obstruct business venture and development of new companies.
- ***Recommendation C:*** Labor market adaptability: Ensure that work strategy structures support adaptable working methodologies for woman business visionaries and their organizations.
- ***Recommendation D:*** Challenge social and social shame: Empower woman by assisting them with creating abilities to construct certainty to address social standards that may debilitate woman setting up an undertaking.
- ***Recommendation E:*** Information and information dissemination framework: Collect and cycle exceptional, significant information on woman driven MSMEs across all areas that would permit the improvement of legitimate help strategies.
- ***Recommendation F:*** Disaster the board methodology: An organized methodology on arranging rules, charge changes, sponsorships, and different measures to moderate the effect of COVID-19 can be advantageous for recognizing change needs and to execute new guidelines that can be utilized to beat results of future pandemics and different catastrophes.
- ***Recommendation G:*** Non-separation: Ensure that property rights and admittance to fund, including for value speculation, do not segregate by gender.
- ***Recommendation H:*** Networking and coaching: Find approaches to help companies among female and male business visionaries, including through private venture activities and interfacing enormous and independent company.
- ***Recommendation I:*** Affordable childcare and medical care: Access to quality reasonable childcare and medical care is basic for advancing woman business in all areas, including common asset the board.

- ***Recommendation J:*** Capacity development: Provide opportunities for women to access training and education programs that improve entrepreneurship and technical skills, to increase chances for success of women-led MSMEs in sustainable resource management.
- ***Recommendation K:*** Green economic recovery: Financial investments in the sustainable resources sector supporting innovation, green growth, and sustainable development can create multiple opportunities for women entrepreneurs to "build back better" and promote low-carbon solutions during the socioeconomic recovery from the COVID-19 pandemic.
- ***Recommendation L:*** Create a platform for MSMEs, policymakers, and financial institutions to support the resilience of resource supply chains in the ECE region.

Bibliography

1. Abella, D., & Yap, D., (2012). *The Organizational Benefits of Going Green*. Philippine Daily Inquirer, http://business.inquirer.net/100449/the-organizational-benefits-of-going-green (accessed on 14 June 2021).
2. Action Aid, (2016). *Through a Different Lens: Action Aid's Resilience Frame Work, 16*(3), 293–303. Johannesburg: Action Aid International.
3. Adger, W. N., Arnell, N. W., & Tompkins, E. L., (2005). Successful adaptation to climate change across scales. *Global, 16*(3), 293–303.
4. Ahlering, J., (2009). *RE: 2009 Ceres-ACCA Sustainability Reporting Awards*, pp. 10–15.
5. Ahmed, A. L., (2013). *Intellectual Property Rights and Clean Energy Technologies*. International Center for Trade and Sustainable Development, https://sustainabledevelopment.un.org/content/documents/3628latif.pdf (accessed on 14 June 2021).
6. Alcan, (2010). *Alcan Composites: Serving Customers with Multi-Material Solutions*. Retrieved from: http://www.alcancomposites.com/contact.html (accessed on 14 June 2021).
7. Alexander, D. E., (2013). Resilience and disaster risk reduction: An etymological journey. *Sustainable Hazards and Earth System Sciences, 13*(11), 2707–2716.
8. Aloise, P., & Macke, J., (2017). *Eco-innovations in Developing Countries: The Case of Manaus Free Trade Zone (Brazil)*. http://dx.doi.org/10.1016/j.jclepro.2017.08.212 (accessed on 14 June 2021).

9. Aragón-Correa, J. A., & Lopez, E. A. R., (2007). Proactive corporate environmental strategies: Myths and misunderstandings. *Long Range Planning 40*(3), 357–381.
10. Argyris, C., & Schön, D. A., (1978). *Organizational Learning: A Theory of Action Perspective.* Addison-Wesley Series on Organization Development. Addison-Wesley Pub. Co.
11. Argyris, C., (1992). *On Organizational Learning.* Massachusetts: Blackwell.
12. Arnall, A., (2014). A climate of control: Flooding, displacement and planned resettlement in the Lower Zambezi River valley, Mozambique. *The Geographical Journal, 180*(2), 141–150.
13. Arrow, K. J., Chenery, H. B., Minhas, B. C., & Solow, R. M., (1961). Capital-labor substitution and economic efficiency. *The Review of Economics and Statistics, 43*(3), 225–250.
14. Asif, M., Bruijn, E. J. D., Fisscher, O. A. M., & Searcy, C., (2010). Meta-management of integration of management systems. *The TQM Journal, 22*(6), 570–582.
15. Asif, M., Searcy, C., & Fisscher, O. A. M., (2010). Meta-management of corporate social responsibility. In: Lindgreen, A., Sen, S., Maon, F., & Vanhamme, J., (eds.), *Sustainable Value Chain Management: Analyzing, Designing, Implementing, and Monitoring for Social and Environmental Responsibility* (pp. 25–40). Gower Publishing.
16. Autio, E., Sapienza, H. J. and Almeida, J. G. (2000) Effects of age at entry, knowledge intensity, and imitability on international growth, Academy of Management Journal 43, 909-924.
17. Auger, P., & Devinney, T., (2007). Do what consumers say matter? The misalignment of preferences with unconstrained ethical intentions. *Journal of Business Ethics, 76*(4), 361–383.
18. Auger, P., Devinney, T. M., Louviere, J. J., & Burke, P. F., (2008). Do social product features have value to consumers? *International Journal of Research in Marketing, 25*(3), 183–191.
19. Auger, P., Devinney, T. M., Louviere, J. J., & Burke, P. F., (2010). The importance of social product attributes in consumer purchasing decisions: A multi-country comparative study. *International Business Review, 19*(2), 140–159.

20. Aupperle, K. E., (1984). *An Empirical Measure of Corporate Social Orientation*. Research in corporate social policy and performance. Greenwich: JAI Press, Google Scholar.

21. Aupperle, K. E., Carroll, A. B., & Hatfield, J. D., (1985). An empirical examination of the relationships between corporate social responsibility and profitability. *Academy of Management Journal, 28*(2), 446–463. View Article Google Scholar.

22. Autodesk, (2009). *Improving Environmental Performance through Life Cycle Assessment and Digital Prototyping*. Autodesk.com. Retrieved from: http://usa.autodesk.com/company/sustainable-design/articles/improving-environmental-performance-through-life-cycle-assessmentand-digital-prototyping (accessed on 14 June 2021).

23. Autry, W. C., Goldsby, J. T., & Bell, E. J., (2013). *Global Macro Trends and Their Impact on Supply Chain Management*. New Jersey: Pearson Education.

24. Awaysheh, A., & Klassen, R. D., (2010). The impact of supply chain structure on the use of supplier socially responsible practices. *International Journal of Operations and Production Management, 30*(12), 1246–1268.

25. Ayers, J., (2011). Resolving the adaptation paradox: Exploring the potential for deliberative adaptation policy-making in Bangladesh, *Global Environmental Politics, 11*(1), 62–88.

26. Baggio, J. A., Brown, K., & Hellebrandt, D., (2015). Boundary object or bridging concept? A citation network analysis of resilience. *Ecology and Society, 20*(2), 2.

27. Bagozzi, R. P., & Yi, Y., (1988). On the evaluation of structural equation models. *Journal of the Academy of Marketing Science, 16*(1), 74–94.

28. Bagozzi, R. P., Gopinath, M., & Nyer, P. U., (1999). The role of emotions in marketing. *Journal of the Academy of Marketing Science, 27*(2), 184–206.

29. Bahadur, A. V., & Tanner, T. M., (2014). Transformational resilience thinking: Putting people, power and politic sat the heart to urban climate resilience. *Environment and Urbanization, 26*(1), 1–15.

30. Bahadur, A. V., Peters, K., Wilkinson, E., Pichon, F., Gray, K., & Tanner, T., (2015). *The 3 As: Tracking Resilience Across Braced*. Working Paper. London: Overseas Development Institute.

31. Bahadur, A., Ibrahim, M., & Tanner, T. M., (2013). Characterizing resilience: Unpacking the concept for tackling climate change and development. *Climate and Development, 5*(1), 55–65.
32. Bai, C., & Sarkis, J., (2010). Green supplier development: Analytical evaluation using rough set theory. *Journal of Cleaner Production, 18*(12), 1200–1210.
33. Barnett, M. L., (2007). Stakeholder influence capacity and the variability of financial returns to corporate social responsibility. *Academy of Management Review, 32*(3), 794–816.
34. Barrett, C. B., & Constas, M. A., (2014). *Toward a Theory of Resilience for International Development Applications, 26*(1), 1–15.
35. Bavly, D., (1999). *Corporate Governance and Accountability: What Role for the Regulator, Director, and Reviewer?* (pp. 10–25). Quorum Books, Westport, Conn, London.
36. Beck, T., et al., (2004). *SMEs, Growth, and Poverty: Cross-Country Evidence*. 30-270.
37. Becker-Olsen, K. L., Cudmore, B. A., & Hill, R. P., (2006). The impact of perceived corporate social responsibility on consumer behavior. *Journal of Business Research, 59*(1), 46–53.
38. Beijerse, R. P. U., (1999). Questions in knowledge management: Defining and conceptualizing a phenomenon. *Journal of Knowledge Management, 3*(2), 94–109.
39. Bell, S. T., Kuriloff, P. J., & Lottes, I., (1994). Understanding attributions of blame in stranger rape and date rape situations: An examination of gender, race, identification, and students' social perceptions of rape victims. *Journal of Applied Social Psychology, 24*(19), 1719–1734.
40. Bendoly, E., Donohue, K., & Schultz, K. L., (2006). Behavior in operations management: Assessing recent findings and revisiting old assumptions. *Journal of Operations Management, 24*(6), 737–752.
41. Béné, C., (2013). *Towards a Quantifiable Measure of Resilience*. IDS Working Paper 434. Brighton: Institute of Development Studies.
42. Béné, C., Cannon, T. C., Gupte, J., McGranahan, G., Mehta, L., & Tanner, T. M., (2017a). Resilience as a policy narrative: Potentials and limits in the context of urban planning. *Climate and Development.* http://dx.doi.org/10.1080/17565529.2017.1301868.
43. Béné, C., Chowdhury, F. S., Rashid, M., Dhali, S. A., & Jahan, F., (2017b). Squaring the circle: Reconciling the need for rigor with

the reality on the ground in resilience impact assessment. *World Development, 97*, 212–231.

44. Béné, C., Frankenberger, T., & Nelson, S., (2015). *Design, Monitoring and Evaluation of Resilience Interventions: Conceptual and Empirical Considerations*. IDS Working Paper 459. Brighton: Institute of Development Studies.
45. Béné, C., Headey, D., Haddad, L., & Von, G. K., (2016). Is resilience a useful concept in the context of food security and nutrition programs? Some conceptual and practical considerations. *Food Security, 8*(1), 123–138.
46. Béné, C., Newsham, A., Davies, M., Ulrichs, M., & Godfrey-Wood, R., (2014). Review article: Resilience, poverty, and development. *Journal of International Development, 26*(5), 598–623.
47. Béné, C., Wood, R., Newsham, A., & Davies, M., (2012). *Resilience: New Utopia or New Tyranny? Reflection about the Potentials and Limits of the Concept of Resilience in Relation to Vulnerability Reduction Programs*. IDS Working Paper No. 405. Brighton: Institute of Development Studies.
48. Berkes, F., Colding, J., & Folke, C., (2008). *Navigating Social-Environment Systems: Building Resilience for Complexity and Change*. Cambridge: Cambridge University Press.
49. Berkhout, F., (2008). Order in socio-technical systems: The dark side of resilience. In: Leach, M., (ed.), *Re-framing Resilience: A Symposium Report*. STEPS Working Paper 13. Brighton; Institute of Development Studies, STEPS Center.
50. Berman, S. L., Wicks, A. C., Kotha, S., & Jones, T. M., (1999). Does stakeholder orientation matter? The relationship between stakeholder management models and firm financial performance. *Academy of Management Journal, 42*(5), 488–506.
51. Bettencourt, L., Rodriguez, N., & West, G., (2010). A unified theory of urban living. *Nature, 467*, 911–913.
52. Beymer-Farris, B. A., Bassett, T. J., & Bryceson, I., (2012). Promises and pitfalls of adaptive management in resilience thinking: The lens of political ecology. In: Plieningerand, T., & Bieling, C., (eds.), *Resilience in the Cultural Landscape*. Cambridge: Cambridge University Press.
53. Birks, M., & Mills, J., (2015). *Grounded Theory: A Practical Guide*. London: Sage Publications.

54. Blackburn, R., & Ram, M., (2006). Fix or fixation? The contributions and limitations of entrepreneurship and small firms to combating social exclusion. *Entrepreneurship and Regional Development*. http://dx.doi.org/10.1080/08985620500419566.
55. Blackorby, C., & Donaldson, D., (1982). Ratio-scale and translation-scale full interpersonal comparability without domain restrictions: Admissible social-evaluation functions. *International Economic Review, 23*(2), 249–268.
56. Blanchard, D., (2008). *SC Johnson Finds a Greener Way to Load Trucks*. Industry Week. 10-17.
57. Bleicher, K., (1996). *Das Konzept Integriertes Management (The Concept of Integrated Management)*. Campus, Frankfurt/Main. 2833–2850].
58. Boarini, R., Murtin, F., & Schreyer, P., (2015). *Inclusive Growth: The OECD Measurement Framework*. OECD Publishing, Paris. http://dx.doi.org/10.1787/5jrqppxjqhg4-en.
59. Bonanno, G. A., (2004). Loss, trauma, and human resilience: Have we underestimated the human capacity to thrive after extremely aversive events? *American Psychologist, 59*(14), 20–28.
60. Bonn, I., & Fisher, J., (2011). Sustainability: The missing ingredient in strategy. *J. Bus. Strategy, 32*(1), 5–14.
61. Botha, D. F., (2000). A conceptual framework for the management of knowledge in a knowledge-based enterprise. *South African Journal of Business Management, 31*(4), 141–148.
62. Boubaker, S., & Nguyen, D. K., (2012). *Board Directors and Corporate Social Responsibility* (pp. 50–66). Palgrave Macmillan M.U.A., GB.
63. Bounfour, A., (2003). *The Management of Intangibles: The Organization's Most Valuable Assets*. London: Routledge.
64. Bousquet, A., & Simon, C., (2011). Beyond models and metaphors: Complexity theory, systems thinking and international relations. *Cambridge Review of International Affairs, 24*(1), 43–62.
65. Bowen, A., & Kuralbayeva, K., (2015). *Looking for Green Jobs: The Impact of Green Growth on Employment*. http://www.lse.ac.uk/grantham/ (accessed on 14 June 2021).
66. Bowen, H., (1953). *Social Responsibilities of the Business Man*. New York: Harper and Row. Google Scholar.

67. Boyden, J., & Cooper, E., (2006). *Questioning the Power of Resilience: Are Children up to the Task of Disrupting the Transmission of Poverty?* Chronic Poverty Research Center (CPRC) Working Paper 73. Oxford: Young Lives.

68. Bozza, A., Asprone, D., & Manfredi, G., (2015). Developing an integrated framework to quantify resilience of urban systems against disasters. *Sustainable Hazards, 78*, 1729–1748.

69. Brand, F. S., & Jax, K., (2007). Focusing the meaning(s) of resilience: Resilience as a descriptive concept and a boundary object. *Ecology and Society, 12*(1), 23.

70. Braunsberger, K., & Buckler, B., (2011). What motivates consumers to participate in boycotts: Lessons from the ongoing Canadian seafood boycott? *Journal of Business Research, 64*(1), 96–102.

71. Briguglio, L., Cordina, G., Farrugia, N., & Vella, S., (2009). Economic vulnerability and resilience: Concepts and measurements. *Oxford Development Studies, 37*(3), 229–247.

72. Brod, M., Laura, E. T., & Torsten, L. C., (2009). Qualitative research and content validity: Developing best practices based on science and experience. *Quality of Life Research, 18*(9), 1263–1278.

73. Broman, G. I., & Karl-Henrik, R., (2015). A framework for strategic sustainable development. *Journal of Cleaner Production,* 1–15.

74. Broman, G., John, H., & Karl-Henrik, R., (2000). Simplicity without reduction: Thinking upstream towards the sustainable society. *Interfaces, 30*(3), 13–25.

75. Brown, K. A., Willis, P. G., & Prussia, G. E., (2000). Predicting safe employee behavior in the steel industry: Development and test of a socio technical model. *Journal of Operations Management, 18*(4), 445–465.

76. Brown, K., (2012). Policy discourses of resilience. In: Pelling, M., Manuel-Navarrete, D., & Redclift, M., (eds.), *Climate Change and the Crisis of Capitalism*. Abingdon: Routledge.

77. Brunsson, N., (2002). *The Organization of Hypocrisy.* Oslo: Abstrakt Liber Copenhagen Business School Press. Second edition with a new introduction.

78. Bryman, A., & Bell, E., (2011). *Business Research Methods* (3rd edn.). Oxford: Oxford University Press.

79. Bryman, A., (2008). *Social Research Methods* (3rd edn.). New York: Oxford University Press.
80. Bunn, & Simon, (2009). Greenhouse gas reduction as an additional benefit of optimal pump scheduling for water utilities. *IBM Journal of Research and Development*. 180-250.
81. Burke, L., & Logsdon, J., (1996). How corporate social responsibility pays off. *Long Range Planning, 29*(4), 495–502.
82. Burton, B. K., & Hegarty, W. H., (1999). Some determinants of student corporate social responsibility orientation. *Business and Society, 38*(2), 188–2005. (View Article Google Scholar).
83. Burton, I., & Van, A. M., (2004). *Look Before You Leap: A Risk Management Approach for Incorporating Climate Change Adaptation in World Bank Operations*. Washington DC: World Bank.
84. Campbell, J. L., (2007). Why would corporations behave in socially responsible ways? An institutional theory of corporate social responsibility. *Academy of Management Journal, 32*(3), 946–967.
85. Cannon, T., & Müller-Mahn, D., (2010). Vulnerability, resilience, and development discourses in the context of climate change. *Sustainable Hazards, 55*(3), 621–635.
86. Carpenter, S. R., Westley, F., & Turner, G., (2005). Surrogates for resilience of social-environment systems. *Ecosystems.*
87. Carroll, A. B., & Buchholtz, A. K., (2015). *Business and Society: Ethics, Sustainability and Stakeholder Management* (9th edn., pp. 25–30). Stamford: Cengage Learning. Google Scholar.
88. Carroll, A. B., & Shabana, K. M., (2010). The business cases for corporate social responsibility: A review of concepts, research, and practice. *International Journal of Management Reviews, 12*(1), 85–105. (View Article Google Scholar).
89. Carroll, A. B., (1979). A three-dimensional conceptual model of corporate social performance. *Academy of Management Review, 4*, 497–505. (Google Scholar).
90. Carroll, A. B., (1979). A three-dimensional conceptual model of corporate performance. *Academy of Management Review, 4*(4), 497–505.
91. Carroll, A. B., (1991). The pyramid of corporate social responsibility: Toward the moral management of organizational stakeholders. *Business Horizons, 34*(4), 39–48. (View Article Google Scholar).

92. Carroll, A. B., (1999). Corporate social responsibility: Evolution of a definitional construct. *Business and Society, 38*, 268–295. (View Article Google Scholar).

93. Carroll, A. B., (2015a). Corporate social responsibility: The centerpiece of competing and complementary frameworks. *Organizational Dynamics, 44*, 87–96. (View Article Google Scholar).

94. Carroll, A. B., (2015b). The state of CSR in 2015 and beyond. *Global Compact International Yearbook* (pp. 10–13). Macondo Publishers, Global Logistics Partner, Deutsche Post DHL Group.

95. Carroll, A. B., Lipartito, K. J., Post, J. E., Werhane, P. H., & Goodpaster, K. E., (2012). *Corporate Responsibility: The American Experience*. Cambridge: Cambridge University Press. Google Scholar.

96. Carter, C. R., (2000). Ethical issues in international buyer-supplier relationships. *International Journal of Physical Distribution & Logistics Management*, *45*, 140–160.

97. Carter, C., & Jennings, M., (2004). The role of purchasing in corporate social responsibility: A structural equation analysis. *Journal of Business Logistics, 25*, 145–186.

98. Cassidy, M., (2014). *Assessing Gaps in Indicator Availability and Coverage* (pp. 100–150). SDSN working paper. New York: Sustainable development solutions Network Conservation international, 2015. Ocean Health Index. Washington, DC: Conservation International.

99. Castka, P., Bamber, C. J., Bamber, D. J., & Sharp, J. M., (2004). Integrating corporate social responsibility (CSR) into ISO management systems in search of a feasible CSR management system framework. *The TQM Magazine, 16*(3), 216–224.

100. Ceres, (2017). *Gap, eBay, and Symantec Join Business Coalition Calling for Action on Clean Energy and Climate Change*. Ceres.com. Boston, MA. Retrieved from: http://www.ceres.org/Page.aspx?pid=1060 (accessed on 14 June 2021).

101. Ceres, (2017). *Identifying Stakeholders*. Diagram. Boston, MA: 2009.

102. Ceres, (2017). *Sustainability Shareholder Resolution Trends 2000–2009*. Graph. Boston, MA: 2009.

103. Ceres, Bloomberg L. P., *(2017). Joins the Ceres Network*. Ceres.com. http://www.ceres.org/Page.aspx?pid=1067 (accessed on 14 June 2021).

104. Chandler, D., (2014). Beyond neoliberalism: Resilience, the new art of governing complexity. *Resilience: International Policies, Practices and Discourses, 2*(1), 47–63.

105. Chelleri, L., Waters, J. J., Olazabal, M., & Minucci, G., (2015). Resilience trade-offs: Addressing multiple scales and temporal aspects of urban resilience. *Environment & Urbanization, 27*(1), 181–198.

106. Chen, L., & Patrick, S. W. F., (2015). Evaluation of knowledge management performance: An organic approach. *Information & Management, 52*(4), 431–453 Elsevier B.V.

107. Chie-Min, C., (2011). A framework for aligning strategic positioning and knowledge management system. *Information Technology Journal, 10*(8), 1594–1600.

108. Chiva, R., Antonio, G., & Joaquín, A., (2010). Adaptive and generative learning: Implications from complexity theories. *International Journal of Management Reviews, 12*(2), 114–129.

109. Cho, C. H., Matias, L., Robin, W. R., & Michelle, R., (2015). Organized hypocrisy, organizational façades, and sustainability reporting. *Accounting, Organizations and Society, 40*, 78–94. Elsevier Ltd.

110. Chrisman, J. J., & Carroll, A. B., (1984). SMR forum: Corporate responsibility-reconciling economic and social goals. *Sloan Management Review* (pp. 59–65). Winter.

111. Ciliberti, F., Pontrandolfo, P., & Scozzi, B., (2008). Investigating corporate social responsibility in supply chains: A SME perspective. *Journal of Cleaner Production, 16*(15), 1579–1588.

112. Cisco, (2017). *Cisco Study Finds Telecommuting Significantly Increases Employee Productivity, Work-Life Flexibility, and Job Satisfaction.* cisco.com. San Jose, California. Retrieved from: http://newsroom.cisco.com/dlls/2009/prod_062609.html (accessed on 14 June 2021).

113. Clarkson, M. B. E., (1995). A stakeholder framework for analyzing and evaluating corporate social performance. *Academy of Management Review, 20*, 92–117. (Google Scholar).

114. Claver, E., Patrocinio, Z., & Diego, Q., (2007). Practical experiences in knowledge management processes by multinational firms: A multiple case study. *Int. J. Knowledge Management Studies, 1*(3, 4), 261–275.

115. Cochran, I., et al., (2014). *Public Financial Institutions and the Low-Carbon Transition: Five Case Studies on Low-Carbon Infrastructure*

and Project Investment. OECD Publishing, Paris, http://dx.doi.org/10.1787/5jxt3rhpgn9t-en.

116. Colloff, M. J., Martín-López, B., Lavorel, S., Locatelli, B., Gorddard, R., Longaretti, P. Y., Walters, G., et al., (2017). An integrative research framework for enabling transformative adaptation. *Environmental Science & Policy, 68,* 87–96.
117. Cone, (2009). *Consumer Environmental Survey Fact Sheet, 18,* 47–63.
118. Constas, M., Frankenberger, T., Hoddinott, J., Mock, N., Romano, D., Béné, C., & Maxwell, D., (2014). *A proposed Common Analytical Model for Resilience Measurement: A General Causal Framework and Some Methodological Options*. Published by the Food and Agriculture Organization and the World Food Program under the Food Security and Information Network.
119. Conway, D., (2012). *Sustainable Procurement Policies and Practices at the State and Local Government Level.* in Greening Local Government.
120. Cornett, M. M., Marcus, A. J., Saunders, A., & Tehranian, H., (2007). The impact of institutional ownership on corporate operating performance. *Journal of Banking and Finance, 31*(6), 1771–1794.
121. Cottrell, J., et al., (2016). *Environmental Tax Reform in Developing, Emerging and Transition Economies.*
122. Craig, R. C., Dale, S. R., (2008). A framework of sustainable supply chain management: Moving toward new theory. *International Journal of Physical Distribution & Logistics Management, 38*(*5*), *360–387*.
123. Cramer, J., (2008). Organizing corporate social responsibility in international product chains. *Journal of Cleaner Production, 16*(3), 395–400.
124. Crane, A., & Matten, D., (2007). *Business Ethics: Managing Corporate Citizenship and Sustainability in the Age of Globalization* (2nd edn.). Oxford University Press.
125. Crane, A., Matten, D., & Spence, L., (2008). *Corporate Social Responsibility: Readings and Cases in a Global Context* (2nd edn., pp. 3–26). New York: Routledge (Google Scholar).
126. Creech, H., et al., (2014). Small-scale social-environmental enterprises in the green economy: Supporting grassroots innovation. *Development in Practice*, http://dx.doi.org/10.1080/09614524.2014.899561.

127. Cretney, R., & Bond, S., (2014). Bouncing back to capitalism? Grass-root autonomous activism in shaping discourses of resilience and transformation following disaster. *Resilience, 2*(1), 18–31.

128. Crossley, C. D., (2009). Emotional and behavioral reactions to social undermining: A closer look at perceived offender motives. *Organizational Behavior and Human*, 48–60.

129. Crowne, D. P., & Marlowe, D., (1960). A new scale of social desirability independent of psychopathology. *Journal of Consulting Psychology, 24*(4), 349–354.

130. Da Silva, J., & Morera, B., (2014). *City Resilience Framework: City Resilience Index*. Arupand The Rocke Feller Foundation.

131. Dadush, S., (2015). *Regulating Social Finance-Can Social Stock Exchanges Meet the Challenge*. Penn Law: Legal Scholarship Repository, https://scholarship.law.upenn.edu/cgi/viewcontent.cgi?article=1906&context=jil (accessed on 14 June 2021).

132. Daft, R. L., (2008). *The New Era of Management*. Thomson: South-Western, Mason: OH.

133. Dahlsrud, A., (2006). How corporate social responsibility is defined: An analysis of 37 definitions. *Corporate Social Responsibility and Environmental Management, 15*, 1–13. (View Article Google Scholar).

134. Dahlsrud, A., (2008). How corporate social responsibility is defined: An analysis of 37 definitions. *Corporate Social Responsibility and Environmental Management, 15*(1), 1–13.

135. Dale, B. G., (2003). *Managing Quality* (pp. 1–40). Blackwell Publishing, Oxford.

136. Dam, L., & Bert, S., (2012). The curse of the haven: The impact of multinational enterprise on environmental regulation. *Environment Economics, 78*, 148–456. Elsevier B.V.

137. Davenport, K., (2000). Corporate citizenship: A stakeholder approach for defining corporate social performance and identifying measures for assessing it. *Business and Society, 20*(2), 210–219.

138. Davenport, T. H., Jarvenpaa, S. L., & Beers, M. C., (1996). Improving knowledge work processes. *Sloan Management Review, 37*(4), 53–65.

139. Davies, M., Béné, C., Arnall, A., Tanner, T., Newsham, A., & Coirolo, C., (2013). Promoting resilient livelihoods through adaptive social protection: Lessons from 124 programs in South Asia, *Development Policy Review, 31*(1), 27–58.

140. Davis, K., (1975). Blamestorm. *Business and Society: Environment and Responsibility* (3rd edn.). New York: McGraw-Hill Book Company. (Google Scholar).

141. Davis, S. C., Susan, W. D., & Robert, G. B., (2009). *Transportation Energy Data Book* (28th edn.). U.S. Department of Energy. Retrieved at: http://www-cta.ornl.gov/data/index.shtml (accessed on 14 June 2021).

142. Davoudi, S., (2012). Resilience: A bridging concept or a dead end? *Planning Theory & Practice, 13*(2), 299–307.

143. Dawar, N., & Pillutla, M. M., (2000). Impact of product-harm crises on brand equity: The moderating role of consumer expectations. *Journal of Marketing Research, 37*, 27–59.

144. De Colle, S., & Gonella, C., (2002). The social and ethical alchemy: An integrative approach to social and ethical accountability. *Business Ethics: A European Review, 11*(1), 86–96.

145. De Colle, S., & Gonella, C., (2003). Corporate social responsibility: The need for an integrated management framework. *International Journal of Business Performance Management, 5*(2, 3), 199–212.

146. De Joy, D. M., (1994). Managing safety in the workplace: An attribution. *Theory Analysis*, 100–150.

147. Delmas, M., & Montiel, I., (2009). *Greening the Supply Chain: When is Customer Pressure*, 35–80.

148. Deming, W. E., (1994). *The New Economics for Industry, Government, Education*. MIT Press, Cambridge, MA.

149. Dercon, S., (2005). Risk, poverty, and vulnerability in Africa. *Journal of African Economies, 14*(4), 483–488.

150. Deutsch, C., (2017). *Companies Giving Green an Office*. The New York Times. Retrieved from: http://www.nytimes.com/2007/07/03/business/03sustain.html (accessed on 14 June 2021).

151. Dittrich, R., Wreford, A., & Moran, D., (2016). A survey of decision-making approaches for climate change adaptation: Are robust methods the way forward? *Environment Economics, 122*, 79–89.

152. Doerr, J., (2017). Green beat 2009: Intro and opening keynote. *In Green Beat 2009: The Conference on the Smart Grid.* 265-275.

153. Doppelt, B., (2003). Overcoming the seven sustainability blunders. *Systems Thinker, 14*(5), 2–6.

154. Dunford, R., (2000). Key challenges in the search for the effective management of knowledge in management consulting firms. *Journal of Knowledge Management, 4*(4), 295–302.

155. Dyllick, T., & Kai, H., (2002). Beyond the business case for corporate sustainability. *Business Strategy and the Environment, 11*(2), 130–141.

156. Earl, M., (2001). Knowledge management strategies: Toward a taxonomy. *Journal of Management Information Systems, 18*(1), 215–233.

157. Eaton, J., Czyznielewski, A., & Dupuis, R., (2005). Judging up the corporate ladder: Understanding the social conduct of workers. *Journal of Applied Social,* 10–35.

158. Eckerd, S., Hill, J., Boyer, K. K., Donohue, K., & Ward, P. T., (2013). The relative impact of attribute, severity, and timing of psychological contract breach on behavioral and attitudinal outcomes. *Journal of Operations Management, 31*(7, 8), 567–578.

159. Economist Intelligence Unit, (2006). *Doing Good: Business and the Sustainability Challenge*. EIU.com. Retrieved from: http://www.eiu.com/site_info.asp?info_name=corporate_sustainability (accessed on 14 June 2021).

160. Economist, (2008). Corporate social responsibility-the next question. *The Economist Special Report, 386*(17), 8–10.

161. Economy, E., (2013). *China's Water Pollution Crisis*. http://thediplomat.com/2013/01/ (accessed on 14 June 2021).

162. Edgeman, R. L., & Hensler, D. A., (2001). The AO chronicle: Earth@omega or sustainability@alpha? *The TQM Magazine, 13*(2), 83–90.

163. Edmondson, V. C., & Carroll, A. B., (1999). Giving back: An examination of the philanthropic motivations, orientations, and activities of large black-owned businesses. *Journal of Business Ethics, 19*, 171–179. (View Article Google Scholar).

164. Elkington, J., (1999). *Cannibals with Forks: The Triple Bottom Line of 21st Century Business* (pp. 120–140). Capstone Publishing Ltd, Oxford.

165. Elkington, J., (2004). *Enter the Triple Bottom Line*. http://www.johnelkington.com/archive/TBL-elkington-chapter.pdf (accessed on 14 June 2021).

166. Ellen, P. S., Webb, D. J., & Mohr, L. A., (2006). Building corporate businesses: Consumer attributions for corporate socially responsible programs. *Journal of the Academy,* 30–70.

167. Elsevier Journals, (2017). *Most Downloaded Business Horizons Articles*. http://www.journals.elsevier.com/business-horizons/most-downloaded-articles/ (accessed on 14 June 2021).

168. Engert, S., Romana, R., & Rupert, J. B., (2015). Exploring the integration of corporate sustainability into strategic management: A literature review. *Journal of Cleaner Production, 112*, 2833–2850. Elsevier Ltd.

169. Ernst, & Young, L. L. P., (2017). *Role of HR in Driving Sustainable Business Practices* (pp. 1–40). Published in India.

170. Ernstson, H., Van, D. L. S., Redman, C., Meffert, D., Davis, G., Alfsen, C., & Elmqvist, T., (2010). Urban transitions: On urban resilience and human-dominated ecosystems. *Ambio: A Journal of the Human Environment, 39*, 531–545.

171. European Commission, (2016). *Green and Sustainable Public Procurement*. http://ec.europa.eu/environment/gpp/versus_en.htm (accessed on 14 June 2021).

172. European Commission, (2017). *The SME Test*. 0-78.

173. European Commission, (2018). *What is EMAS?* http://ec.europa.eu/environment/emas/index_en.htm (accessed on 14 June 2021).

174. Federation of Small Businesses, (2012). *Making Sense of Going Green 50-150.*

175. Field, A., & Hole, G., (2003). *How to Design and Report Experiments?* (pp. 38–80). Sage, London, UK.

176. Fincham, F., & Jaspars, J. M., (1980). *Attribution of Responsibility: From Man the Scientist to Man as Lawyer*. 10.1016/S0065-2601(08)60131-8.

177. Fitzpatrick, K., (2017). *CalPERS Boosts Corporate Governance Strategy*. Pensions Gym. Retrieved from: http://www.pensionsgym.com/pensions-news/archive/more.asp?article=2926 (accessed on 14 June 2021).

178. Fleet, D., Palladino, M., & Da Costa, S., (2015). *Assessing the Potential Cost Savings and Resource Savings of Investments in 4 SME Sectors*.

179. Fletcher, D., & Sarkar, M., (2013). *Psychological Resilience: A Review and Critique of Definitions. Concepts, and Theory 28-40.*

180. Foerstl, K., Reuter, C., Hartmann, E., & Blome, C., (2010). *Managing Supplier Sustainability*, 15–45.

181. Foley, K. J., (2005). *Meta Management: A Stakeholder/Quality Management Approach to Whole-of-Enterprise Management* (pp. 59–140). Standards Australia Ltd, Sydney.

182. Folke, C., (2006). Resilience: The emergence of a perspective for social-environment systems analyses. *Global Environmental Change, 16*(3), 253–267.

183. Folke, C., Carpenter, S., Walker, B., Scheffer, M., Chapin, T., & Rockstrom, J., (2010). Resilience thinking: Integrating resilience, adaptability, and transformability. *Ecology and Society, 15*(4), 20.

184. Folkes, V. S., (1984). Consumer reactions to product failure: An attributional approach. *Journal of Consumer Research, 10*(4), 398–409.

185. Fombrun, C., Gardberg, N., & Barnett, M., (2000). Opportunity platforms and safety nets: Corporate citizenship and reputational risk. *Business and Society Review, 105*(1), 85–106.

186. Fragale, A. R., Rosen, B., Xu, C., & Merideth, I., (2009). The higher they are, the harder they fall: The effects of wrongdoer status on observer punishment recommendations and intentionality attributions. *Organizational Behavior and Human Decision Processes, 108*(1), 53–65.

187. Frantz, P., & Instefjord, N., (2007). Socially and privately optimal shareholder activism. *Journal of Management and Governance, 11*(1), 23–43.

188. Freeman, R. E., (1984). *Strategic Management: A Stakeholder Approach* (pp. 100–140). Pitman, Boston.

189. Frey, C. H., (2017). *Identification and Evaluation of Potential Best Practices for Greenhouse Gas Reductions in Freight Transportation.* California air resources board chair's air pollution seminar series. 37-49.

190. Friedman, M., (1962). *Capitalism and Freedom.* Chicago: University of Chicago Press. (Google Scholar).

191. Friedman, M., (1985). Consumer boycotts in the United States, 1970–1980: Contemporary events in historical perspective. *Journal of Consumer Affairs, 19*(1), 96.

192. Friend, R., & Moench, M., (2013). What is the purpose of urban climate resilience? Implications for addressing poverty and vulnerability. *Urban Climate, 6*, 98–113.

193. Friend, R., & Moench, M., (2015). Rights to urban climate resilience: Moving beyond poverty and vulnerability. *Wiley Interdisciplinary Reviews: Climate Change, 6*(6), 643–651.

194. Frooman, J., (1999). Stakeholder influence strategies. *Academy of Management Review, 24*(2), 191–205.

195. Frynas, J. G., (1998). Political instability and business: Focus on shell in Nigeria. *Third World Quarterly 19*(3), 357–478.

196. Gaillard, J., (2007). Resilience of traditional societies in facing sustainable hazards. *Disaster Prevention and Management.*

197. Gallopín, G. C., (2006). Linkages between vulnerability, resilience, and adaptive capacity. *Global Environmental Change.*

198. Gallup, (2015). *Gallup World Poll* (pp. 25–35). Washington, DC: Gallup.

199. Gao, H., Knight, J. G., Zhang, H., Mather, D., & Tan, L. P., (2012). Consumer scapegoating during a systemic product-harm crisis. *Journal Marketing Management, 28*(11, 12), 1270–1290.

200. Gao, J., & Bansal, P., (2013). Instrumental and integrative logics in business sustainability. *Journal of Business Ethics, 112*(2), 241–255.

201. Gap, (2017). *Supply Chain: Our Program in Action*. Gap, Inc. 2007–2008, Social responsibility report 2009. 450-490.

202. García-Morales, V. J., Verdú-Jover, A. J., & Francisco, J. L., (2009). The influence of CEO perceptions on the level of organizational learning. Single-loop and double-loop learning. *International Journal of Manpower, 30*(6), 567–590.

203. García-Rodríguez, F. J., García-Rodríguez, J. L., Castilla-Gutiérrez, C., & Silvério, A. M., (2013). Corporate social responsibility of oil companies in developing countries: From altruism to business strategy. *Corporate Social Responsibility and Environmental Management, 20*(6), 371–384.

204. Garret-Peltier, H., James, H., & Robert, P., (2017). *The Economic Benefits of Investing in Clean Energy: How the Economic Stimulus Program and New Legislation can Boost U.S. Economic Growth and Employment*. Amherst, Massachusetts. 270-340.

205. Gassert, F., Reig, P., Luo, T., & Maddocks, A., (2013). *Aqueduct Country and River Basin Rankings: A Weighted Aggregation of Spatially Distinct Hydrological Indicators*. Working paper. Washington, DC: World Resources Institute.

206. Gavronski, I., Klassen, R. D., Vachon, S., & Nascimento, L. F. M. D., (2011). A resource-based view of green supply management. *Transportation Research Part E: Logistics and Transportation Review, 47*(6), 872–885.

207. Geels, F., (2018). *Socio-Technical Transitions to Sustainability*. Oxford Research Encyclopedia of Environmental Science, http://environmentalscience.oxfordre.com/view/10.1093/acrefore/9780199389414.001.0001/acrefore-9780199389414-e-587 (accessed on 14 June 2021).

208. GIB, (2016). S*uRe*® The Standard for Sustainable and Resilient Infrastructure v 0.3. Basel: Global Infrastructure Basel.

209. Gibbs, D., & O'Neill, K., (2014). Rethinking sociotechnical transitions and green entrepreneurship: The potential for transformative change in the green building sector. *Environment and Planning A*. http://dx.doi.org/10.1068/a46259.

210. Gibson, T., (2008). *Defining SMEs: A Less Imperfect Way of Defining Small and Medium Enterprises in Developing Countries*. 9-70.

211. Gillard, R., (2016). Questioning the diffusion of resilience discourses in pursuit of transformational change. *Global. 190-200.*

212. Giuliani, E., & Chiara, M., (2014). Multinational corporations' economic and human rights impact on developing countries: A review and research agenda. *Cambridge Journal of Economics, 38*(2), 479–517.

213. GIZ, (2015). *Inclusive Business Toolbox: Promoting Inclusive Business Models in Development Cooperation Programs*. 170-180.

214. GIZ, (2017). *Green and Inclusive Business Toolbox-Promoting Green and Inclusive Business Models in Development Cooperation Programs*. 280-310.

215. Global Reporting Initiative, (2015). *Sustainability Disclosure Database*. http://database.globalreporting.org/ (accessed on 14 June 2021).

216. Godfrey, P. C., Merrill, C. B., & Hansen, J., (2009). The relationship between corporate social responsibility and shareholder value: An empirical test of the risk management hypothesis. *Strategic Management Journal, 30*(4), 425–445.

217. Goel, R., (2005). *Guide to Instruments of Corporate Responsibility: An*

Overview of 16 Key Tools for Labor Fund Trustees. Schulich Business School, York University, Toronto.

218. Goleman, & Daniel, (2017). *Winning in an Age of Radical Transparency*. Harvard Business Publishing blog. Retrieved from: http://blogs.harvardbusiness.org/leadinggreen/2009/05/radicaltransparency.html (accessed on 14 June 2021).
219. Government of Malaysia, (2018). *Overview of the FiT System in Malaysia*. 15-27.
220. Grant, R. M., (1996). Prospering in dynamically competitive environment: Organizational capability as knowledge integration. *Organization Science, 7*(4), 375–387. Quoted in: Kim,
221. Grant, R. M., (1996). Toward a knowledge-based theory of the firm. *Strategic Management Journal, 17*, 109–122.
222. Greenpeace, (2009). *Playing Dirty: How Factories Hide Their Pollution in China,* 1–10.
223. Gregorowski, R., Dorgan, A., & Hutchings, C., (2017). *Resilience Measurement-MEL Approaches in Practice. 56-78.*
224. Greiner, M. E., Tilo, B., & Helmut, K., (2007). A strategy for knowledge management. *Journal of Knowledge Management, 11*(6), 3–15.
225. GRI, (2006). *Sustainability Reporting Guidelines: Version 3.0* (pp. 20–45). GRI, Amsterdam, the Netherlands.
226. Griffin, P. A., & Yuan, S., (2013). Going green: Market reaction to CSR wire news releases. *Journal of Accounting and Public Policy, 32*(2), 93–113. doi: 10.1016/j.jaccpubpol.2013.02.002.
227. Gunderson, L. H., & Holling, C. S., (2002). *Panarchy: Understanding Transformations in Human and Sustainable Systems*. 120-170.
228. Gunningham, N., & Sinclair, D., (1999). *Designing Smart Regulation*. 180-190.
229. Hahn, T., & Frank, F., (2011). Beyond the Bounded instrumentality in current corporate sustainability research: Toward an inclusive notion of profitability. *Journal of Business Ethics, 104*(3), 325–345.
230. Hair, J. F., Black, W. C., Rabin, B. J., Anderson, R. E., & Tatham, R. L., (2006). *Multivariate Data*, 40–60.
231. Hallegatte, S., Bangalore, M., & Vogt-Schilb, A. C., (2016). *Assessing Socioeconomic Resilience to Floods in 90 Countries*. 210-340.

232. Hamilton, V. L., (1978). Obedience and responsibility: A jury simulation. *Journal of Personality and Social Psychology, 36*(2), 126–146.

233. Handfield, R., Straube, F., Pfohl, H. C., & Wieland, A., (2013). *Trends and Strategies in Logistics and Supply Chain Management,* 65–80.

234. Hansen, M. C., et al., (2013). High-resolution global maps of 21st-century forest cover change. *Science, 342*(6160), 850–853.

235. Hansen, M. T., Nohria, N., & Tierney, T., (1999). What is your strategy for managing knowledge? *Harvard Business Review, 77*(2), 106–116.

236. Hariharan, A., (2015). *The Strategic Knowledge Management Handbook: Driving Business Results by Making Tacit Knowledge Explicit*. Milwaukee: American Society for Quality, Quality Press.

237. Harrison, J. S., Bosse, D. A., & Phillips, R. A., (2010). Managing for stakeholders. *Stakeholder*, 49–70.

238. Hedenus, F., Martin, P., & Frances, S., (2016). *Sustainable Development. History, Definition & The Role of the Engineer*. Göteborg: Chalmers University of Technology.

239. Helliwell, J. F., Layard, R., & Sachs, J., (2015). *World Happiness Report 2015*. New York: Sustainable development solutions network.

240. Helm, R., Stephanie, K., & Martin, S., (2014). Conceptualization and integration of marketing intelligence: The case of an industrial manufacturer. *Journal of Business-to-Business Marketing, 21*(4), 237–255.

241. Herman Miller, Inc., (2009). *Our Journey Toward a Better World Around You: A Report from Herman Miller, Inc. 2009* (pp. 39–52). Zeeland, Michigan.

242. Hillman, A. J., & Keim, G. D., (2001). Shareholder value, stakeholder management, and social issues: What is the bottom line? *Strategic Management Journal, 22*, 125–139.

243. Hitt, M. A., Ireland, R. D., & Hoskisson, R. E., (2003). *Strategic Management: Competitiveness and Globalization* (pp. 108–120). Thomson South-Western, Mason, Ohio.

244. Holder-Webb, L., Cohen, J. R., Nath, L., & Wood, D., (2009). The supply of corporate social responsibility disclosures among U.S. firms. *Journal of Business Ethics, 84*, 497–527.

245. Holdsvalue, R., (2003). Practical applications approach to design, development, and implementation of an integrated management system. *Journal of Hazardous Materials, 104*(1), 193–205.

246. Holling, C. S., & Gunderson, L. H., (2002). In: Gunderson, L. H., & Holling, C. S., (eds.), *Resilience and Adaptive Cycles*.

247. Holling, C. S., (1996). Engineering resilience versus environment resilience. In: Schulze, P. C., (ed.), *Engineering within Environment Constraints*. Washington DC: National Academy Press.

248. Holling, C., (1973). Resilience and stability of ecological systems. *Annual Review of Ecology and Systematics, 4,* 1–23.

249. Holmberg, J., & Robert, K. H., (2000). Backcasting: A framework for Strategic planning. *International Journal of Sustainable Development & World Ecology, 7*(4), 291–308.

250. Homer-Dixon, T., (2011). Complexity science. *Oxford Leadership Journal, 2*(1), 1–15.

251. Hoon, S. J., Uhm, D., & Won, Y. S., (2011). Organizational knowledge creation practice: Comprehensive and systematic processes for scale development. *Leadership & Organization Development Journal, 32*(3), 243–259.

252. Hora, M., & Klassen, R., (2013). Learning from others misfortune: Factors influencing knowledge acquisition to reduce operational risk. *Journal of Operations Management, 31*, 52–61.

253. Hora, M., Bapuji, H., & Roth, A. V., (2011). *Safety Hazard and Time to Recall: The Role of Recall*, 47–90.

254. Horibe, F., (1999). Building a learning organization. *Harvard Business Review, 71*(4), 78–91.

255. Huff, A. S., Floyd, S. W., Sherman, H. D., & Terjesen, S., (2009). *Strategic Management: Logic and Action* (pp. 10–45). John Wiley and Sons, Hoboken: NJ.

256. Hye, M., & Md. Zabid, I. A., (2009). *Skills for Green Jobs in Bangladesh*. http://www.ilo.org/publns (accessed on 14 June 2021).

257. Idemudia, U., (2009). Oil extraction and poverty reduction in the Niger Delta: A critical examination of partnership initiatives. *Journal of Business Ethics, 90*, 91–116.

258. IEA, (2016). *Uttar Pradesh Mini-Grid Policy 2016*. https://www.iea.org/policiesandmeasures/pams/india/name-165001_(accessed on 14 June 2021).

259. ILO, (2018). *World Employment Social Outlook 2018: Greening with Jobs*. 270-350.

260. IMF, (2015). *IMF Survey: Counting the Cost of Energy Subsidies, IMF.* https://www.imf.org/en/News/Articles/2015/09/28/04/53/sonew070215a (accessed on 14 June 2021).

261. IMF, (2015). *World Economic Outlook Database* (pp. 48–59). Washington, DC: International Monetary Fund.

262. Immelt, J., (2009). *Chairman's Presentation to the General Electric Shareholders*. General electric annual shareholders meeting. 26-79.

263. Institute for Fiscal Studies, (2015). *Fiscal Incentives to Eligible Companies: A Right Step in Encouraging Investors in the Renewable Energy Market*. 60-78.

264. Intergovernmental Panel on Climate Change (IPCC), (2012). In: Field, C. B., Barros, V., Stocker, T. F., Qin, D., Dokken, D. J., Ebi, K. L., Mastrandrea, M. D., et al., (eds), *Managing the Risks of Extreme Events and Disasters to Advance Climate Change Adaptation*. A special report of working groups I and II of the intergovernmental panel on climate change. Cambridge and New York: Cambridge University Press.

265. International Finance Corporation, (2017). *MSME Finance Gap: Assessment of the Shortfalls and Opportunities in Financing Micro, Small and Medium Enterprises in Emerging Markets*. 36-91.

266. ITU, (2015). *World Telecommunication/ICT Indicators Database*. Geneva: International Telecommunication Union.

267. Iveco, (2009). *Iveco-FedEx Express: First Results of the Daily Hybrid Evaluation*. Iveco.com. http://www.iveco.com/enus/PressRoom/PressRelease/Pages/FedEx-apr09.aspx (accessed on 14 June 2021).

268. Jamali, D., (2008). A stakeholder approach to corporate social responsibility: A fresh perspective into theory and practice. *Journal of Business Ethics, 82*(1), 213–231.

269. Jan, O. A., & Mattias, L., (2001). Environmentally unsustainable trade. *Environment Economics, 37*(1), 113–122.

270. Jayaraman, V., Linton, J., & Klassen, R., (2005). Sustainable supply chains: An introduction. *Journal of Operations Management, 2007*, 40–160.

271. Jeans, H., Thomas, S., & Castillo, G., (2016). *The Future is a Choice: The Oxfam Framework and Guidance for Resilient Development*. Oxford: Oxfam International.

272. Jennings, M. M., (2004). The role of purchasing in corporate social responsibility: A structural equation analysis. *Journal of Business Logistics, 25*(1), 145–186.

273. Jiang, B., (2009). Implementing supplier codes of conduct in global supply chains: Process explanations from theoretic and empirical perspectives. *Journal of Business*, 65–90.

274. Jones, L., & Tanner, T. M., (2017). Subjective resilience: Using perceptions to quantify household resilience to climate extremes and disasters, *Regional Environmental Change, 17*, 229–243.

275. Jonker, J., & Karapetrovic, S., (2004). Systems thinking for integration of management systems. *Business Process Management Journal, 10*(06), 608–615.

276. Jørgensen, T. H., (2008). Towards more sustainable management systems: Through life cycle management and integration. *Journal of Cleaner Production, 16*(10), 1071–1080.

277. Jørgensen, T. H., Remmen, A., & Mellado, M. D., (2006). Integrated management systems three different levels of integration. *Journal of Cleaner Production, 14*(8), 713–722.

278. Joseph, J., (2013). Resilience as embedded neoliberalism: A governmentality approach. *Resilience: International Policies, Practices and Discourses, 1*(1), 38–52.

279. Kalamas, M., Cleveland, M., & Laroche, M., (2014). *Pro-Environmental Behaviors for Thee*, 38–61.

280. Karapetrovic, S., & Jonker, J., (2003). Integration of standardized management systems: Searching for a recipe and ingredients. *Total Quality Management, 14*(4), 451–459.

281. Karapetrovic, S., & Willborn, W., (2001). Review and self-assessment in quality management: Comparison and compatibility. *Managerial Reviewing Journal, 16*(6), 366–377.

282. Karapetrovic, S., (2002). Strategies for the integration of management systems and standards. *The TQM Magazine, 14*(1), 61–67.

283. Karapetrovic, S., (2003). Musings on integrated management systems. *Measuring Business Excellence, 7*(1), 4–13.

284. Karl-Henrik, R., (2000). Tools and concepts for sustainable development, how do they relate to a general framework for sustainable development, and to each other? *Journal of Cleaner Production, 8*, 243–254.

285. Karl-henrik, R., (2009). Real change through backcasting from sustainability principles: Presentation of an international research program built on a unifying framework for strategic sustainable development (FSSD). *Progress in Industrial Ecology: An International Journal,* 6(3), 207–215.

286. Karl-Henrik, R., Göran, B., David, W., Henrik, N., Sophie, B., David, C., Lena, J., et al., (2015). *Strategic Leadership Towards Sustainability* (9th edn.). Karlskrona: Blekinge Institute of Technology.

287. Kates, R. W., Travis, W. R., & Wilbanks, T. J., (2012). Transformational adaptation when incremental adaptations to climate change are insufficient. *Proceedings of the National Academy of Sciences, 109*(19), 7156–7161.

288. Keeble, J., Topiol, S., & Berkeley, S., (2003). Using indicators to measure sustainability performance at a corporate and project level. *Journal of Business Ethics, 44*, 149–158.

289. Keeley, J., & Scoones, I., (2014). *Understanding Environmental Policy Processes: Cases from Africa*. London: Routledge.

290. Kelman, I., (2008). Relocalizing disaster risk reduction for urban resilience. *Urban and Design Planning 161*(4), 197–204.

291. Kelman, I., Gaillard, J. C., & Lewis, J., (2016). Learning from the history of disaster vulnerability and resilience research and practice for climate change. *Sustainable Hazards, 82*, S129–S143.

292. Kelman, I., Gaillard, J. C., & Mercer, J., (2015). Climate change's role in disaster risk reduction's future: Beyond vulnerability and resilience. *International Journal of Disaster Risk Science, 6*(1), 21–27.

293. Kemp, R., (1994). Technology and the transition to environmental sustainability: The problem of technological regime shifts. *Futures, 26*(10), 1023–1046.

294. Key, S., & Popkin, S. J., (1998). Integrating ethics into the strategic management process: Doing well by doing good. *Management Decision, 36*(5), 331–338.

295. Kim, E. H., & Lyon, T. P., (2011). Strategic environmental disclosure: Evidence from the DOE's voluntary greenhouse gas registry. *Journal of Environmental Economics and Management, Elsevier, 61*(3), 311–326.

296. Kim, Y. J., Seokwoo, S., Sambamurthy, V., & Young, L. L., (2012). Entrepreneurship, Knowledge integration capability, and firm

performance: An empirical study. *Information Systems Frontiers 14*(5), 1047–1060.

297. Klassen, & Vereecke, (2012). Social issues in supply chains: Capabilities link responsibility, risk (opportunity), and performance. *International Journal of Production Economics, 140*(1), 103–115.
298. Klein, J., & Dawar, N., (2004). Corporate social responsibility and consumers attributions and brand evaluations in a product-harm crisis. *International Journal of Research in Marketing, 21*, 203–217.
299. Klein, R. J., Nicholls, R. J., & Thomalla, F., (2003). Resilience to sustainable hazards: How useful is this concept? *Global Environmental Change Part B: Environmental Hazards, 5*(1, 2), 35–45.
300. Kleine, A., & Hauff, M. V., (2009). Sustainability-driven implementation of corporate social responsibility: Application of the integrative sustainability triangle. *Journal of Business Ethics, 85*(3), 517–533.
301. Kleine, A., & Von, H. M., (2009). Sustainability-driven implementation of corporate social responsibility: Application for the integrative sustainability triangle. *J. Bus. Ethics, 85*, 517–533.
302. Kostopoulos, K. C., Dimitrios, A. B., Sophia, S. P., & Ioannis, N. K., (2010). Knowledge-based approaches in strategic management: A review of the literature. *International Journal of Applied Systemic Studies, 3*(4), 389–403.
303. Kouabenan, D. R., Medina, M., Gilibert, D., & Bouzon, F., (2001). Hierarchical position, gender, accident severity, and causal attribution. *Journal of Applied Social Psychology*, 120–140.
304. Kovács, G., (2008). Corporate environmental responsibility in the supply chain. *Journal of Cleaner Production, 16*(15), 1571–1578.
305. Kroll, C., (2015). Sustainable development goals: Are the rich countries ready? *Gutersloh: Bertelsmann Foundation*, 37–90.
306. Kudłak, R., & Kathleen, Y. J. L., (2015). Special issues dedicated to CSR and corporate sustainability: A review and commentary. *Long Range Planning, 48*(3), 215–227.
307. Kuhlicke, C., (2013). Resilience: A capacity and a myth: Findings from an in-depth case study in disaster management research. *Sustainable Hazards, 67*(1), 61–76.
308. Kurucz, E., Colbert, B., & Wheeler, D., (2008). The business case for corporate social responsibility. In: Crane, A., McWilliams, A., Matten,

D., Moon, J., & Siegel, D., (eds.), *The Oxford Handbook of Corporate Social Responsibility* (pp. 83–112). Oxford: Oxford University Press (Google Scholar).

309. Law, M. S., Peter, H., & Billy, C. H. H., (2015). Engaging employees in sustainable development: A case study of environmental education and awareness training in Hong Kong. *Business Strategy and the Environment*.
310. Leach, M., (2008). *Re-Framing Resilience: A Symposium Report*. Brighton: Institute of Development Studies, STEPS Center.
311. Lee, K. C., Sangjae, L., & In Won, K., (2005). KMPI: Measuring knowledge management performance. *Information and Management, 42*(3), 469–482.
312. Lee, M. D. P., (2008). A review of the theories of corporate social responsibility: Its evolutionary path and the road ahead. *International Journal of Management Reviews, 10*(1), 53–73. (View Article Google Scholar).
313. Lee, S. Y., & Klassen, R. D., (2008). *Drivers and Enablers That Foster Environmental Management Capabilities in Small- and Medium-Sized Suppliers in Supply Chains*, 25–67.
314. Leichenko, R., (2011). Climate change and urban resilience. *Current Opinion in Environmental Sustainability, 3*(3), 164–168.
315. Levitt, T., (1958). *The Dangers of Social Responsibility* (pp. 41–50). Harvard Business Review.
316. Li, M., Choi, T. Y., Rabinovich, E., & Crawford, A., (2013). *Self-Service Operations at Retail*, 12–32.
317. Lohman, C., Fortuin, L., & Wouters, M., (2004). Designing a performance measurement system: A case study. *European Journal of Operational Research, 156*(2), 267–286.
318. Lovell, E., Bahadur, A., Tanner, T., & Morsi, H., (2016). *Resilience: The Big Picture*. London: Overseas Development Institute.
319. Lozano, R., (2012). Orchestrating organizational changes for corporate sustainability. *Greener Management International, 57,* 43–64.
320. MacClune, K., Allan, C., Venkateswaran, K., & Sabbag, L., (2014). *Floods in Boulder: A Study of Resilience*. Boulder.
321. Macey, J. R., (1997). Institutional investors and corporate monitoring: A demand-side perspective: Introduction. *Managerial and Decision Economics (1986–1998), 18*(7, 8), 601.

322. MacKenzie, S. B., & Podsakoff, P. M., (2012). *Common Method Bias in Marketing: Causes*, 56–90.

323. Madden, J., (2012). Operational activism hits the boardroom: One of the most important trends in governance is the increasing activity of shareholders pressuring boards not on classic governance subjects but on the actual strategic direction or management of the business of the corporation. *Directors and Boards, 37*(1), 37.

324. Makni, R., Francoeur, C., & Bellavance, F., (2009). Causality between corporate social performance and financial performance: Evidence from Canadian firms. *Journal of Business Ethics, 89*, 409–422.

325. Malik, O., (2013). *Global Database of Toil Wastewater Treatment* (pp. 56–71). New Haven, CT: Yale Center for Environmental Law and Policy.

326. Maon, F., Lindgreen, A., & Swaen, V., (2009). Designing and implementing corporate social responsibility: An integrative framework grounded in theory and practice. *Journal of Business Ethics, 87*(1), 71–89.

327. Maon, F., Lindgreen, A., & Swaen, V., (2010). Organizational stages and cultural phases: A critical review and a consolidative model of corporate social responsibility development. *International Journal of Management Review, 12*(1), 20–38.

328. Margolis, J., & Walsh, J., (2003). Misery loves companies: Rethinking social initiatives by business. *Administrative Science Quarterly, 48*(2), 268–305.

329. Martin, A., (2007). *In Eco-Friendly Factory, Low-Guilt Potato Chips*. NYTimes.com. Retrieved from: http://www.nytimes.com/2007/11/15/business/15plant.html (accessed on 14 June 2021).

330. Matos, S., & Hall, J., (2007). *Integrating Sustainable Development in the Supply Chain*, pp. 43–90.

331. Matyas, D., & Pelling, M., (2015). Positioning resilience for 2015: The role of resistance, incremental adjustment, and transformation in disaster risk management policy. *Disasters, 39*, s1–s18.

332. Maxwell, D., Constas, M., Frankenberger, T., Klaus, D., & Mock, M., (2016). *Qualitative Data and Subjective Indicators for Resilience Measurement*. Rome: Food Security Information Network.

333. McDonald, M., Mors, T. A., & Phillips, A., (2003). Management system integration: Can it be done? *Quality Progress, 36*(10), 67–74.

334. McDonough, W., & Michael, B., (2002). *Cradle to Cradle* (pp. 1–15). North Point Press.
335. McGee, J., & Howard, T., (2007). Knowledge as a lens on the jigsaw puzzle of strategy. Reflections and conjectures on the contribution of a knowledge-based view to analytic models of strategic management. *Management Decision, 45*(3), 539–563.
336. McGiboney, M., (2009). *Twitter's Tweet Smell of Success*. Nielsen wire. 50-87.
337. McGraw Hill Construction and Siemens, (2009). *Greening of Corporate America: The Pathway to Sustainability*. Retrieved from: http://construction.com/market_research/FreeReport/GreeningCorpAmerica/GreeningCorporateAmerica.asp (accessed on 14 June 2021).
338. McKinsey and Company, (2008). *McKinsey Global Survey Results: Valuing Corporate Social Responsibility*. McKinsey Quarterly. 60-72.
339. Mechler, R., (2016). Reviewing estimates of the economic efficiency of disaster risk management: Opportunities and limitations of using risk-based cost-benefit analysis. *Sustainable Hazards, 81*(3), 2121–2147.
340. Melnyk, S. A., Sroufe, R. P., & Calantone, R., (2003). Assessing the impact of environmental management systems on corporate and environmental performance. *Journal of Operations Management, 21*(3), 329–351.
341. Mena, C., Humphries, A., & Choi, T., (2013). Toward a theory of multi-tier supply chain management. *Journal of Supply Chain Management, 49*(2), 58–77.
342. Metcalf, L., & Benn, S., (2012). The corporation is ailing social technology: Creating a 'fit for purpose' design for sustainability. *J. Bus. Ethics, 111*, 195–210.
343. Methmann, C., & Oels, A., (2015). From fearing to empowering climate refugees: Governing climate-induced migration in the name of resilience. *Security Dialogue, 46*(1), 51–68.
344. Meyer, & Tobias, A., (2009). *Energy Efficient Supply Chains*. McKinsey Quarterly. 12-19.
345. Millon, D., (2015). Corporate social responsibility and environmental sustainability. *Company Law and Sustainability: Legal Barriers and Opportunities*, 35–78.

346. Mishra, R. K., & Jhunjhunwala, (2013). *SBooks24x7, I Diversity and the Effective Corporate Board* (1st edn.), Academic Press, US.

347. Mitchell, R. K., Agle, B. R., & Wood, D. J., (1997). Towards a theory of stakeholder identification and salience: Defining the principle of who and what really counts. *Academy of Management Review, 22*(4), 853–886.

348. Mochizuki, J., Keating, A., Mechler, R., Egan, C., & Hochrainer-Stigler, S., (2016). If numbers can speak, who listens? Creating engagement and learning for effective uptake of DRR investment in developing countries. *PLoS Currents, 8*.

349. Moench, M., Norton, R., & Venkateswaran, K., (2015). *Refining the Resilience Narrative: A Critical Reflective Review of the Current Discourse*. Boulder: The Institute for Social and Environmental Transition (ISET)-International.

350. Mohamed, M., Michael, S., & Mona, M., (2009). An empirical assessment of knowledge management criticality for sustainable development. *Journal of Knowledge Management, 13*(5), 271–286.

351. Moneva, J. M., Archel, P., & Correa, C., (2006). GRI and the camouflaging of corporate unsustainability. *Accounting Forum, 30*(2), 121–137.

352. Monks, R. A. G., & Minow, N., (2012). *Corporate Governance* (5th edn., 12–45). John Wiley and Sons.

353. Montiel, I., (2008). Corporate social responsibility and corporate sustainability. *Organization & Environment, 21*, 245–569.

354. Muthén, L. K., & Muthén, B. O., (2010). Mplus. *Statistical Analysis with Latent Variables* (6th edn.). User's Guide, Muthén and Muthén, Los Angeles, CA.

355. Muthén, L. K., & Muthén, B. O., (2013). *Chi-Square Difference Testing Using the Santora-Bentler Scaled Chi-Square*. http://www.statmodel.com/chidiff.shtml (accessed on 14 June 2021).

356. NALGEP and Smart Growth Leadership Institute, (2004). *Smart Growth is Smart Business*. Washington, DC.

357. Narasimhan, R., & Talluri, S., (2009). Perspectives on risk management in supply chains. *Journal of Operations Management, 27*(2), 114–118.

358. New, S., (2004). The ethical supply chain. In: New, S., & Westbrook, R., (eds.), *Understanding Supply Chains: Concepts, Critiques, and Futures* (pp. 253–280). Oxford University Press, Oxford, UK.

359. Newton, A., (2015). Biodiversity risks of adopting resilience as a policy goal. *Conservation Letters, 9*(5), 369–376.

360. Nicolai, S., Hoy, C., Berliner, T., & Thomas, A., (2015). *Projecting Progress: Reaching the SDGs by, 2030* (pp. 35–62). London: Overseas Development Institute.

361. Nielsen, B. B., & Snejina, M., (2007). Knowledge management systems in multinational corporations: Typology and transitional dynamics. *Long Range Planning, 40*(3), 314–340.

362. Nijhof, A., Bruijn, T. D., Fisscher, O. A. M., Jonker, J., Karssing, E., & Schoemaker, M., (2005). Learning to be responsible: Developing competencies organization-widen wide CSR. In: Jonker, J., & Cramer, J., (eds.), *Making a Difference: Dutch National Research* (pp. 45–78).

363. Noe, T. H., (2002). Investor activism and financial market structure. *The Review of Financial Studies, 15*(1), 289–318.

364. Nonaka, I., & Takeuchi, H., (1995). *The Knowledge-creating Company: How Japanese Companies Create the Dynamics of Innovation.* Oxford University Press, New York, NY.

365. Nonaka, I., (1991). The knowledge-creating company. *Harvard Business Review* (pp. 96–104).

366. Nonaka, I., Toyama, R., & Konno, N., (2000a). SECI, Ba and leadership: A unified model of dynamic knowledge creation. *Long Range Planning, 33*, 5–34.

367. Nye, J. S., (1974). Multinational corporations in world politics. *Foreign Affairs, 53*(1), 153–175.

368. O'Brien, K. L., & Wolf, J., (2010). A values-based approach to vulnerability and adaptation to climate change. *WIREs Climate Change, 1*(2), 232–242.

369. O'Brien, K., (2012). Global environmental change II: From adaptation to deliberate transformation, *Progress in Human Geography. 36*(5), 667–676.

370. O'Hare, P., & White, I., (2013). Deconstructing Resilience: Lessons from planning practice. *Planning Practice & Research.*

371. O'Rourke, A., (2003). A new politics of engagement: Shareholder activism for corporate social responsibility. *Business Strategy and the Environment, 12*(4), 227.

372. O'Dell, C., & Grayson, C. J. Jr., (1997). *If Only We Knew What We Know: The Transfer of Internal Knowledge and Best Practice*. New York, NY: The Free Press.

373. ODI/MEL-COP, (2016). *Analysis of Resilience Measurement Frameworks and Approaches*. Washington, DC: Winward Fund. www.fsnnetwork.org/sites/default/files/analysis_of_resilience_measurement_frameworks_and_approaches.pdf (accessed on 14 June 2021).

374. OECD, (2004). OECD principles of corporate governance. *Journal of Economic Literature, 42*(4), 1199.

375. OECD, (2016). OECD stat. *Paris: Organization for Economic Co-Operation and Development*, pp. 24–28.

376. Olsson, L., Jerneck, A., Thoren, H., Persson, J., & O'Byrne, D., (2015). Why resilience is unappealing to social science: Theoretical and empirical investigations of the scientific use of resilience. *Science Advances, 1*(4), e1400217.

377. Orlitzky, M., Schmidt, F., & Rynes, S., (2003). Corporate social and financial performance: A meta-analysis. *Organization Studies, 24*(03), 403–441.

378. Orogun, P. S., (2010). Resource control, revenue allocation and petroleum politics in Nigeria: The Niger delta question. *Geo Journal, 75*(5), 459–507.

379. Oskarsson, K., & Malmborg, F. V., (2005). Integrated management systems as a corporate response to sustainable development. *Corporate Social Responsibility and Environmental Management, 12*(3), 121–128.

380. Oyebisi, O. I., & Dominic, P. D. D., (2013). Knowledge management systems use and competency development among knowledge workers. *VINE: The Journal of Information and Knowledge Management Systems, 43*(4), 482–500.

381. Paraschiv, D. M., Estera, L. N., Claudia, A. L., & Tünde, S., (2012). Eco-innovation, responsible leadership, and organizational change for corporate sustainability. *Amfiteatru Economic, 14*(32), 404–419.

382. Park, A., (2011). Beware paradigm creep and buzzword mutation. *The Forestry Chronicle, 87*(3), 337–344.

383. Park, J., Seager, T., Rao, P., Convertino, M., & Linkov, I., (2013). Integrating risk and resilience approaches to catastrophe management in engineering systems. *Risk Analysis, 33*(3), 356–367.

384. Parmigiani, A., Klassen, R. D., & Russo, M. V., (2011). Efficiency meets accountability: Performance implications of supply chain configuration, control, and capabilities. *Journal of Operations Management, 29*(3), 212–223.

385. Patel, S. S., Rogers, M. B., Amlôt, R., & Rubin, G. J., (2017). What do we mean by community resilience? A systematic literature review of how it is defined in the literature. *PLOS Currents Disasters.*

386. Pedersen, E. P., (2006). Making corporate social responsibility (CSR) operable: How companies translate stakeholder dialogue into practice. *Business and Society Review, 111*(2), 137–163.

387. Pelling, M., (2011). *Adaptation to Climate Change: From Resilience to Transformation.* Abingdon: Routledge.

388. Pemberton, J. D., & George, H. S., (2000). Organizational learning and knowledge assets: An essential partnership. *The Learning Organization, 7*(4), 184–194.

389. Peters, K., Langston, L., Tanner, T., & Bahadur, A., (2016). *Resilience Across the Post-2015 Frameworks: Towards Coherence?* ODI Working Paper. London: Overseas Development Institute.

390. Phares, E. J., & Wilson, K. G., (1972). Responsibility attribution: Role of outcome severity, situational ambiguity internal-external control. *Journal of Personality*, *40*(3), 392–406.

391. Phillips, R., & Caldwell, C. B., (2005). Value chain responsibility: A farewell to arm's length. *Business and Society Review, 110*(4), 345–370.

392. Pinkston, T. S., & Carroll, A. B., (1996). A retrospective examination of CSR orientations: Have they changed? *Journal of Business Ethics, 15*(2), 199–206. (View Article Google Scholar).

393. Podsakoff, P. M., MacKenzie, S. B., Lee, J. Y., & Podsakoff, N. P., (2003). Common method biases in behavioral research: A critical review of the literature and recommended remedies. *Journal of Applied Psychology, 88*(5), 879–904.

394. Program on Corporate Social Responsibilities, (2000). *Ministry of Economic Affairs* (p. 57e84). The Hague.

395. Rahman, M. A., Alaniz, R., King, K., McNamara, K., Nadiruzzaman, M., Henly-Shepard, S., & Thomalla, F., (2015). Livelihood resilience in the face of climate change. *Nature Climate Change, 5,* 23–26.

396. Reghezza-Zitt, M., Rufat, S., Djament-Tran, G., Le Blanc, A., & Lhomme, S., (2012). What resilience is not: Uses and abuses? *Cybergeo: European Journal of Geography.*

397. Rehbein, K., Waddock, S., & Graves, S. B., (2004). Understanding shareholder activism: Which corporations are targeted? *Business and Society, 43*(3), 239.

398. Renewable Energy World.com. (2009). *Installed US Wind Energy Capacity Grows by Record 8,300 MW*. Washington, DC. Retrieved from: http:/www.renewableenergyworld.com/rea/news/article/2009/01/installed-us-wind-energy-capacity-grows-by-record–8300-mw–54619 (accessed on 14 June 2021).

399. Reuter, C., Foerstl, K., Hartmann, E., & Blome, C., (2010). Sustainable global supplier management: The role of dynamic capabilities in achieving competitive advantage. *Journal of Supply Chain Management: A Global Review of Purchasing and Supply, 46*(2), 45–63.

400. Rickels, W., Quaas, M. F., & Visbeck, M., (2014). How healthy is the human-ocean system? *Environmental Research Letters*, 9. doi: 10.1088/1748-9326/9/4/044013.

401. Rinne, P., & Nygren, A., (2015). *From Resistance to Resilience: Media Discourses on Urban Flood Governance in Mexico*. 45-80.

402. Robèrt, K. H., Basile, G., Broman, G., Byggeth, S., Cook, D., Haraldsson, H., Johansson, L., et al., (2004). *Strategic Leadership towards Sustainability*. Course Book at the Department for Mechanical Engineering, Blekinge Institute of Technology, printed by Psilanders Grafiska in Karlskrona.

403. Robèrt, K. H., Göran, I. B., & George, B., (2013). Analyzing the concept of planetary boundaries from a strategic sustainability perspective: How does humanity avoid tipping the planet? *Ecology and Society, 18*(2).

404. Robèrt, K. H., Schmidt-Bleek, B., Aloisi, D. L. J., Basile, G., Jansen, J. L., Kuehr, R., Price, T. P., et al., (2002). Strategic sustainable development: Selection, design, and synergies of applied tools. *Journal of Cleaner Production, 10*, 197–214.

405. Roblek, V., Maja, M., Mirjana, P. B., & Andrej, B., (2014). Impact of knowledge management on sustainable development in the innovative economy. *Paper Presented at the 2nd International Symposium "Systems Thinking for a Sustainable Economy. Advancements in Economic and Managerial Theory and Practice."* Rome, Italy.

406. Rocha, M., Searcy, C., & Karapetrovic, S., (2007). Integrating sustainable development into existing management systems. *Total Quality Management and Business Excellence, 18*(1, 2), 83–92.

407. Rodin, J., (2014). *The Resilience Dividend: Being Strong in a World Where Things Go Wrong*. Washington DC: Public Affairs.

408. Rodrigues, A. S., Brooks, T. M., Butchart, S. H., Chanson, J., Cox, N., Hoffmann, M., & Stuart, S. N., (2014). Spatially explicit trends in the global conservation status of vertebrates. *Plus One, 9*(11), e113934.

409. Roehm, M. L., & Tybout, A. M., (2006). When will a brand scandal spillover, and how should competitors respond? *Journal of Marketing Research, 43*(3), 366–373.

410. Rose, A., (2007). Economic resilience to sustainable and man-made disasters: Multidisciplinary origins and contextual dimensions. *Environmental Hazards, 7*(4), 383–398.

411. Roth, A. V., Tsay, A. A., Pullman, M. E., & Gray, J. V., (2008). Unraveling the food supply chain: Strategic insights from China and the 2007 recalls. *Journal of Supply Chain Management, 44*(1), 22–39.

412. Rowley, T. I., & Moldoveanu, M., (2003). When will stakeholder groups act? An interest-based model of stakeholder group mobilization. *Academy of Management Review, 28*(2), 204–219.

413. Russell, D. A. M., & Shiang, D. L., (2013). Dawn thinking about more sustainable products: Using an efficient tool for sustainability education, innovation, and project management to encourage sustainability thinking in a multinational corporation. *ACS Sustainable Chem. Eng. 1*(1), 2–7.

414. Salomone, R., (2008). Integrated management systems: Experiences in Italian organizations. *Journal of Cleaner Production, 16*(16), 1786–1806.

415. Salzmann, O., Iones, A., & Steger, U., (2005). The business case for corporate sustainability: Literature review and research options. *European Management Journal, 23*(1), 27–36.

416. San Diego Company of Governments (SANDAG), (2006). *Smart Growth Definition, Principles, and Designations*.39-61.

417. Sapountzaki, K., (2007). Social resilience to environmental risks: A mechanism of vulnerability transfer? *Management of Environmental Quality: An International Journal, 18*(3), 274–297.

418. Sarkis, J., (2004). Relationships between operational practices and performance among early adopters of green supply chain management practices in Chinese manufacturing enterprises. *Journal of Operations Management, 22*(3), 25–65.

419. Sarzynski, A., Marilyn, B., & Frank, S., (2008). *Shrinking the Carbon Footprint of Metropolitan America Brookings Institution*. 29-63.

420. Savin-Baden, M., & Howell, M. C., (2013). *Qualitative Research: The Essential Guide to Theory and Practice* (3rd edn.). London: Taylor & Francis Ltd.

421. Scarbrough, H., Swan, J., Preston, J., & Institute of Personnel and Development, (1999). *Knowledge Management: A Literature Review*. Issues in People Management. Institute of Personnel and Development.

422. Schaltegger, S., Markus, B., & Erik, G. H., (2013). Trans disciplinarity in corporate sustainability: Mapping the field. *Business Strategy and the Environment, 22*(4), 219–229.

423. Schrettle, S., Andreas, H., Scherrer-Rathje, M., & Thomas, F., (2014). Turning sustainability into action: Explaining firms' sustainability efforts and their impact on firm performance. *International Journal of Production Economics, 147*(Part A), 73–84.

424. Schwartz, M., & Carroll, A. B., (2003). Corporate social responsibility three-domain approach. *Business Ethics Quarterly, 13*(4), 503–530. (View Article Google Scholar).

425. Schwartz, S. H., & Bilsky, W., (1990). Toward a theory of the universal content and structure of values: Extensions and cross-cultural replications. *Journal of Personality and Social Psychology, 58*(1990), 550–562.

426. Scott, L., (2009). *Chandler Company to Help McDonald's Cut Energy Use, Cost*. The Arizona Republic. Retrieved from: http://www.azcentral.com/community/chandler/articles/2008/12/31/20081231cr-engenuity0102.html?&wired (accessed on 14 June 2021).

427. SDSN, (2015). *Indicators and a Monitoring Framework for Sustainable Development Goals: Launching a Data Revolution for the SDGs*. New York and Paris: Sustainable Development Solutions Network.
428. Searcy, C., McCartney, D., & Karapetrovic, S., (2007). Sustainable development indicators for the transmission system of an electric utility. *Corporate Social Responsibility and Environmental Management, 14*(3), 135–151.
429. Seawright, K. K., & Sampson, S. E., (2007). A video method for empirically studying wait-perception bias. *Journal of Operations Management, 25*(5), 1055–1066.
430. Sen, S., & Battacharya, C., (2001). Does doing good always lead to doing better? Consumer reactions to corporate social responsibility. *Journal of Marketing Research, 38*(2), 225–243.
431. Senge, P., (1992). *The Fifth Discipline: The Art and Practice of the Learning Organization, Century Business*.
432. Seuring, S., & Mueller, M., (2008). From a literature review to a conceptual framework for sustainable supply chain management. *Journal of Cleaner Production, 16,* 1699–1710.
433. Shaver, K., (1985). *The Attribution of Blame: Causality, Responsibility, and Blamevalueiness* (pp. 54–78). Springer, New York, NY.
434. Shi, L., Chu, E., Anguelovski, I., Aylett, A., Debats, J., Goh, K., & Roberts, J. T., (2016). Roadmap towards justice in urban climate adaptation research. *Nature Climate Change, 6*(2), 131–137.
435. Shin, M., Tony, H., & Ruth, A. S., (2001). From knowledge theory to management practice: Towards an integrated approach. *Information Processing and Management, 37*, 335–355.
436. Shreve, C. M., & Kelman, I., (2014). Does mitigation save? *Reviewing Cost-Benefit Analyses of Disaster Risk Reduction.*
437. Shu-Mei, T., (2008). Knowledge management system performance measure index. *Expert Systems with Applications, 34*(1), 734–745.
438. Shu-Mei, T., (2008). The effects of information technology on knowledge management systems. *Expert Systems with Applications, 35*(1,2), 150–160.
439. Skarmeas, D., & Leonidou, C. N., (2013). When consumers doubt, watch out! The role of CSR skepticism. *Journal of Business Research, 66*(10), 1831–1838.

440. Smith, A., & Stirling, A., (2010). *The Politics of Social-Environment Resilience and Sustainable Socio-Technical Transitions. 210-460.*

441. Smith, N. C., (2003). Corporate social responsibility: Whether or how? *California Management Review, 45*(4), 52–76.

442. Smith, W. J., Wokutch, R. E., Harrington, K. V., & Dennis, B. S., (2001). An examination of the influence of diversity and stakeholder role on corporate social orientation. *Business and Society, 40*(3), 266–294. (View Article Google Scholar).

443. Social Accountability International, (2009). *SAI Training Programs.* 34-98.

444. Social Investment Forum, (2007). *Report on Socially Responsible Investing Trends in the United States*. 21-90.

445. Sodexo, (2008). *Sustainable Food Procurement*. Dublin. Retrieved from: http://uk.sodexo.com/uken/Images/SustainableProcurementbrochure_tcm15–160012.pdf (accessed on 14 June 2021).

446. Sodhi, M. S., Son, B. G., & Tang, C. S., (2012). Researchers' perspectives on supply chain risk management. *Production and Operations Management, 21*(1), 1–13.

447. Solomon, J., (2010). *Corporate Governance and Accountability* (pp. 68–108). Wiley, West Sussex.

448. Spangler, W., Matthew, M., & Robert, S., (2014). *Sustainability-Focused Knowledge Management in a Global Enterprise*. 36-95.

449. Spence, L., (2016). Small business social responsibility: Expanding core CSR theory. *Business and Society, 55*(1), 23–55. (View Article Google Scholar).

450. Staples, (2006). *Energy and Climate*. Staples.com. Retrieved from: http://www.staples.com/sbd/content/about/soul/energyclimate.html (accessed on 14 June 2021).

451. Stead, J. G., & Stead, W. E., (2000). Eco-enterprise strategy: Standing for sustainability. *J. Bus. Ethics, 24*, 313–329.

452. Steffen, W., Åsa, P., Lisa, D., Jan, Z., Mark, W., Katherine, R., Carole, C., et al., (2011). The Anthropocene: From global change to planetary stewardship. *Ambio, 40*(7), 739–761.

453. Steiger, J. H., (2007). Understanding the limitations of global fit assessment in structural equation modeling. *Personality and Individual Differences, 42*(5), 893–898.

454. Steurer, R., Langer, M. E., Konrad, A., & Martinuzzi, A., (2005). Corporations, stakeholders, and sustainable development I: A theoretical business-society relations. *Journal of Business Ethics, 61*(3), 263–281.

455. Stiglitz, J. E., Jonathan, M. O., & Peter, R. O., (2006). *The Impact of Asbestos Liabilities on Workers in Bankrupt Firms*. Sebago Associates, commissioned by the American Insurance Company. Washington, DC, 2002.

456. Strunz, S., (2012). Is conceptual vagueness an asset? Arguments from philosophy of science applied to the concept of resilience. *Environment Economics, 76*, 112–118.

457. Struthers, C. W., Eaton, J., Ratajczak, A., & Perunovic, M., (2004). *Social Conduct toward Sumer Attributions of Blame: Defense Attributions in Product-Harm Crises in*, 1–17.

458. Sudmeier, K., & Jaboyedoff, M., (2013). *Operationalizing Resilience for Disaster Risk Reduction in Mountainous Nepal*. 112-160.

459. Surminski, S., & Tanner, T. M., (2016). *Realizing the Triple Dividend of Resilience: A New Business Case for Disaster Risk Management*. Dordrecht: Springer International Publishing.

460. Surroca, J., Tribó, J. A., & Waddock, S., (2010). Corporate responsibility and financial performance: The role of intangible resources. *Strategic Management Journal, 31*(5), 17–46.

461. Sustainable Resources Defense Council, (2009). *Green Business: Green Business Guides*. Retrieved from: http://www.nrdc.org/enterprise/greeningadvisor/ta-idling.asp (accessed on 14 June 2021).

462. Swanson, D. L., (1995). Addressing a theoretical problem by reorienting the corporate social performance model. *Academy of Management Review, 20*, 43–64. (Google Scholar).

463. Swanstrom, T., (2008). *Regional Resilience: A Critical Examination of the Environment Framework*. Working Paper 2008-07. Baltimore MD: Institute of Urban and Regional Development.

464. Tanner, T., & Allouche, J., (2011). Towards a new political economy of climate change. *IDS Bulletin, 43*(3), 1–14.

465. Tennen, H., & Affleck, G., (1990). Blaming others for threatening events. *Psychological Bulletin, 108*(2), 209–232.

466. The Hackett Group, (2006). *The Hackett Group: Supplier Diversity Does Not Drive Increased Costs*. Retrieved from: http://www.

thehackettgroup.com/about/alerts/alerts_2006/alert_08172006.jsp (accessed on 14 June 2021).

467. The International Council on Clean Transportation, (2006). *Air Pollution and Greenhouse Gas Emissions from Ocean-Going Ships: Impacts, Mitigation, Options and Opportunities for Managing Growth.* Retrieved from: http://www.theicct.org/ (accessed on 14 June 2021).

468. The Triple Bottom Line, (2006). *Does It All Add Up?* (pp. 1–16). Earthscan, London, UK.

469. Thomas, J. B., Stephanie, W. S., John, C. H., James, B., Thomas, S., & Watts, S., (2001). Understanding 'strategic learning': Linking organizational learning, knowledge management, and sensemaking. *Organization Science, 12*(3), 331–345.

470. Transparency International, (2015). *Corruption Perception Index 2014 Results*. Berlin: Transparency International.

471. Turner, B., (2010). Vulnerability and resilience: Coalescing or paralleling approaches for sustainability science? *Global Environmental Change, 20*(4), 570–576.

472. Twigg, J., (2007). *Characteristics of a Disaster-Resilient Community: A Guidance Note*. London: Benfield UCL Hazard Research Center and Interagency Coordination Group.

473. U.S. Environmental Protection Agency (EPA), (2006). Executive summary: Inventory of U.S. *Greenhouse Gas Emissions and Sinks: 1990–2007*. http://www.epa.gov/climatechange/emissions/downloads09/ExecutiveSummary.pdf (accessed on 14 June 2021).

474. U.S. Environmental Protection Agency, (2006). *Design for the Environment Partnership Highlights*. Retrieved from: http://www.epa.gov/dfe/pubs/index.htm (accessed on 14 June 2021).

475. U.S. Environmental Protection Agency, (2006). *Essential Principles for Reform of Chemicals Management Legislation*. EPA.gov. 45-91.

476. U.S. Environmental Protection Agency, (2006). *Green Chemistry*. Summary of 2007 award entries and recipients. Presidential green chemistry awards. Washington, DC, 2007. 19-50.

477. U.S. Environmental Protection Agency, (2006). *Green Suppliers Network*. Retrieved from: http://www.epa.gov/oppt/ar/2007–2009/workig/gsn.htm (accessed on 14 June 2021).

478. U.S. Green Building Council, (2006). *Genzyme Project Overview*. 38-98.

479. UN, (2015). *Transforming Our World: The 2030 Agenda for Sustainable Development*. New York: United Nations.
480. UNDP, (2015). *Human Development Statistical Tables*. Human development report 2015. New York: United Nations Development Program.
481. UNEP, (2009). Finance initiative asset management working group. *Fiduciary Responsibility: Legal and Practical Aspects of Integrating Environmental, Social and Governance Issues into Institutional Investment*. Retrieved from: http://www.unepfi.org/fileadmin/documents/fiduciaryII.pdf (accessed on 14 June 2021).
482. UNEP, (2016). *UNEP Live Sustainable Resources: Resource-Efficient Indicators*. Nairobi: United Nations Environment Program.
483. UNESCO, (2015). *UIS Database*. Paris: United Nations Educational, Scientific and Cultural Organization.
484. Unilever, (2009). *Environmental Responsibility: Water*. Unilever.com. Retrieved from: https://www.unilever.com/Images/sd_unilever_and_sustainable_agriculture-water_tcm244-409786_en.pdf (accessed on 14 June 2021).
485. Unilever, (2010). *India: Lifebuoy Promotes Hand Washing with Soap to Improve Health*. Retrieved from: https://www.unilever.com/Images/slp-lifebuoy-way-of-life-2010-12-oct12_tcm244-409816_en.pdf (accessed on 14 June 2021).
486. United Nations Office for Disaster Risk Reduction (UNISDR), (2015). *Making Development Sustainable: The Future of Disaster Risk Management*. Global Assessment Report on Disaster Risk Reduction. Geneva: UNISDR.
487. United States, Department of Energy, Industrial Technologies Program, (2004). *Best Practices: Corporate Energy Management Case Study*. Washington, DC.
488. United States, National Bureau of Economic Research, (2007). *Transparency and Corporate Governance*. Massachusetts: NBER (Working Paper 12875).
489. United States, National Bureau of Economic Research, (2008). *The Role of Boards of Directors in Corporate Governance: A Conceptual Framework and Survey*. Massachusetts: NBER (Working Paper 14486).

490. United States, National Bureau of Economic Research, (2009). *The State of Corporate Governance Research*. Massachusetts: NBER (Working Paper 15537).

491. UN-Water, (2006). *Coping With Water Scarcity: Challenge of the Twenty-First Century*. Retrieved from: http://www.fao.org/nr/water/docs/escarcity.pdf (accessed on 14 June 2021).

492. Urda, J., & Loch, C. H., (2013). Social preferences and emotions as regulators of behavior utility functions, and competitive advantage. *Strategic Management Journal, 31*, 56–74.

493. USAID, (2016). *Knowledge Management Support*. https://usaidlearninglab.org/working-group/usaid-knowledge-management-reference-group (accessed on 14 June 2021).

494. Vachon, S., & Klassen, R. D., (2006). Green project partnership in the supply chain: The case of the package printing industry. *Journal of Cleaner Production, 14*(6, 7), 49–120.

495. Vachon, S., & Klassen, R. D., (2008). Environmental management and manufacturing performance: The role of collaboration in the supply chain. *International Journal of Production Economics, 111*, 299–315.

496. Van, B. E., & Van, O. K. E., (2013). Cooperating to commercialize technology: A dynamic model of fairness perceptions, experience, and cooperation. *Production and Operations Management, 22*, 114–128.

497. Van, D. H. A., Driessen, P. P. J., & Cramer, J. M., (2010). Making sense of corporate social responsibility: Exploring organizational processes and strategies. *Journal of Cleaner Production, 18*(18), 1787–1796.

498. Visser, W., (2006). Revisiting Carroll's CSR pyramid: An African perspective. In: Huniche, M., & Rahbek, E. P., (eds.), *Corporate Citizenship in Developing Countries: New Partnership Perspectives* (pp. 29–56). Copenhagen: Copenhagen Business School Press. Google Scholar.

499. Visser, W., (2011). *The Age of Responsibility: CSR 2.0 and the New DNA of Business*. West Sussex: John Wiley and Sons. Google Scholar.

500. Wahlström, M., (2015). New Sendai frameworks strengthens focus on reducing disaster risk. *International Journal of Disaster Risk Science, 6*(2), 200, 201.

501. Walker, B. H., Holling, C. S., Carpenter, S. R., & Kinzig, A., (2004). Resilience, adaptability, and transformability in social-environment systems. *Ecology and Society, 9*(2), 5.

502. Walker, B., & Salt, D., (2012). *Resilience Thinking: Sustaining Ecosystems and People in a Changing World*. Washington DC: Island Press.

503. Wartick, S. L., & Cochran, P. L., (1985). The evolution of the corporate social performance model. *Academy of Management Review, 10*, 758–769. Google Scholar.

504. Watkiss, P., & Hunt, A., (2016). Assessing climate-resilient development options. In: Fankhauser, S., & McDermott, T. K., (eds.), *The Economics of Climate-Resilient Development*. Cheltenham: Edward Elgar Publishing Ltd.

505. WBCSD, (2000). *Corporate Social Responsibility: Making Good Business Sense*. World Business Council for Sustainable Development, Geneva.

506. Weber, M., (2008). The business case for corporate socially responsible company-level measurement approach for CSR. *European Management Journal, 26*(4), 247–261.

507. WEF, (2015). *The Global Competitiveness Report 2015–2016*. Colony, Switzerland: World Economic Forum.

508. Weichselgartner, J., & Kelman, I., (2015). Geographies of resilience: Challenges and opportunities of a descriptive concept. *Progress in Human Geography, 39*(3), 249–267.

509. Weiner, B., (1986). An attributional theory of achievement motivation and emotion. *Psychological Review, 92*(4), 548–573.

510. Weiner, B., (1995). *Judgments of Responsibility: A Foundation for a Theory of Social Conduct* (pp. 26–90). New York: Guilford.

511. Welford, R., & Gouldson, A., (1993). *Environmental Management and Business Strategy*. Pitman, Boston: MA.

512. Welsh, M., (2014). Resilience and responsibility: governing uncertainty in a complex world. *The Geographical Journal, 92*(4), 548–573.

513. White, I., & O'Hare, P., (2014). From rhetoric to reality: Which resilience, why resilience, and whose resilience in spatial planning? *Environment and Planning C: Politics and Space, 32*(5), 934–950.

514. Williams, P., (2009). *Written Testimony of IBM to the US Senate Committee on Energy and Sustainable Resources, in Support of a Hearing on the Energy-Water Nexus* (pp. 137–142). Email to Brooke Barton.

515. Wood, D. J., (1991). Corporate social responsibility revisited. *Academy of Management Review, 16*, 691–718. Google Scholar.

516. Wood, D., & Jones, R., (1996). Research in corporate social performance: What have we learned. In: Dwight, B., & Dennis, Y., (eds.), *Corporate Philanthropy at the Crossroads*. Bloomington: Indiana University Press. Google Scholar.

517. Woods, D. D., (2015). Four concepts for resilience and the implications for the future of resilience engineering. *Reliability Engineering & System Safety, 141*, 5–9.

518. World Business Council for Sustainable Development (WBSCD), (2009). *Transforming the Market: Energy Efficiency in Buildings*. Retrieved from: http://www.wbcsd.org/Plugins/DocSearch/details.asp?DocTypeId=25&ObjectId=MzQyMDQ (accessed on 14 June 2021).

519. Wright, T., (2000). IMS three into one: The advantages of a single integrated quality, health and safety, and environmental management system. *The Quality Assurance Journal, 4*(3), 137–142.

520. Wu, Z., & Pagell, M., (2011). *Balancing Priorities: Decision-Making in Sustainable Supply*, 120–160.

521. Xerox, (2006). *Xerox's Emulsion Aggregation Toner-An Environmentally Friendly Technology*. 290-380.

522. Yong, J., Seokwoo, S., Sambamurthy, V., & Young, L. L., (2012). Entrepreneurship, knowledge Integration capability, and firm performance: An empirical study. *Information Systems Frontiers, 14*(5), 1047–1060.

523. Yoon, Y., Gürhan-Canli, Z., & Schwarz, N., (2006). The effect of corporate social responsibility (CSR) activities on companies with bad reputations. *Journal of Consumer York, NY* (pp. 140–220).

524. Young, T., (2009). *US Energy Firms Commit to Electric Vehicle Fleets*. BusinessGreen.com. Retrieved from: http://www.businessgreen.com/business-green/news/2250177/energy-firmscommit-electric (accessed on 14 June 2021).

525. Zebrowski, C., (2008). Governing the network society: A biopolitical critique of resilience. *Political Perspectives, 3*(1), 1–41.

526. Zhu, Q., & Sarkis, J., (2004). Relationships between operational practices and performance among early adopters of green supply chain management practices in Chinese manufacturing enterprises. *Journal of Operations Management, 22*, 265–289.

527. Ziek, P., (2009). Making sense of CSR communication. *Corporate Social Responsibility and Environmental Management, 16*(3), 137–145.

528. Zutshi, A., & Sohal, A. S., (2005). Integrated management system: The experiences of three Australian organizations. *Journal of Manufacturing Technology Management, 16*(2), 211–232.

529. Zwillinger, D., & Kokoska, S., (2000). *CRC Standard Probability and Statistics Tables and Formulae* (pp. 38–92). Chapman and Hall: New York. Section 14.7.

530. Zyglidopoulos, S. C., (2001). The impact of accidents on a firm's reputation for social performance. *Business and Society, 40*(4), 416–441.

INDEX

P

S

T

U

W